Praise for *Beef, Bible and bullets*

'So often there is a lack of context brought to news reporting of today's Brazil. Lapper masterfully brings us that necessary context, weaving first-hand accounts from primary sources together with a rigorous chronicle of the country's recent history and politics. One of the clearest pictures of Brazil in 2021 and how it got there. A must-read for anyone covering Latin America.'

Lucinda Elliott, journalist,
The Times

'Finally, a book that looks beyond easy narratives to explain the real reasons for Jair Bolsonaro's rise. One of the world's most knowledgeable experts on Brazil, Richard Lapper shows us not just the postcard image of Rio de Janeiro, but the country of evangelical mega-churches, cattle ranches, walled-off mansions and shopping malls that elected this total outsider. *Beef, Bible and bullets* is the best chronicle to date of how the "Trump of the Tropics" came to power.'

Brian Winter, Editor-in-Chief,
Americas Quarterly

'This is the best book in English on the rise to the Brazilian presidency of the volatile and polarising figure of Jair Bolsonaro. It also focuses on the emergence of Bolsonarismo, Brazil's version of national populism, and the base of support for and changing fortunes of the Bolsonaro administration in its first two years in power. Interspersing insightful portraits of Brazilians in different regions of the country with convincing explanations of events, *Beef, Bible and bullets* is an indispensable aid to the understanding of a political phenomenon that sometimes seems to defy logical analysis.'

Anthony W. Pereira, Professor, Brazil Institute and
Department of International Development,
King's College London

BEEF, BIBLE AND BULLETS

MANCHESTER
1824

Manchester University Press

BEEF, BIBLE AND BULLETS

BRAZIL IN THE AGE OF BOLSONARO

RICHARD LAPPER

MANCHESTER UNIVERSITY PRESS

Published by Manchester University Press
Altrincham Street, Manchester M1 7JA
www.manchesteruniversitypress.co.uk

British Library Cataloguing-in-Publication Data
A catalogue record for this book is available from the British Library

ISBN 978 1 5261 4901 5 hardback

First published 2021

The publisher has no responsibility for the persistence or accuracy of URLs for any external or third-party internet websites referred to in this book, and does not guarantee that any content on such websites is, or will remain, accurate or appropriate.

Typeset by
Servis Filmsetting Ltd, Stockport, Cheshire

To Fátima

CONTENTS

INTRODUCTION

It's hard to miss the office of Igino Marcos Oliveira in Prosperidade, a poor neighbourhood of the central Brazilian city of Uberlândia. As a paved urban highway slowly gives way to dusty rutted tracks at the edge of the city, you come across a single-storey building with the sign "Lula Livre" (Free Lula) carefully painted in large white letters on a dark red front wall. Inside a modest office, the 47-year-old bearded and bespectacled labour lawyer cuts a frustrated figure. Luiz Inácio Lula da Silva, or just Lula – the firebrand trade unionist who became a successful but very controversial president in 2003 – was still in jail when I visited Oliveira in the middle of 2019. And support for Lula's Workers' Party (PT) was at a low ebb in Uberlândia, a city of 700,000 people that grew quickly during Brazil's short-lived economic boom of the early 2000s. Not only did 60 per cent of voters cast their ballots in 2018 for Jair Bolsonaro, an iconoclastic extreme right-wing outsider, but the PT lost control of Minas Gerais – the state of which the city is part. Oliveira's own effort to win a state government seat for the PT came to naught and the party's representation in the city was more or less wiped out. Oliveira was still struggling to cope with the way so many of the people he has spent the best part of three decades trying to help had voted the way they did. "I am disappointed with the people", said Oliveira, who, after a four-year spell as an official in the left-wing government led by Lula between 2003 and 2010, returned to Uberlândia to help organisations of poor urban immigrants acquire titles to occupied land. "I'd say four out of ten of our homeless movement voted for Bolsonaro. That's 40 per cent of our public, people who live in shacks, were with Bolsonaro."

The defeat had been particularly bitter because a year before the election, Oliveira and his colleagues had successfully saved 2,200 homes in the nearby poor neighbourhood of Glória, an informal settlement whose planned demolition would – Oliveira claimed – have been one of the largest in Latin America. The legal team had pulled out all the stops to save the homes. Their campaign had drawn in the PT governor of the state, Fernando Pimentel, to help negotiate a deal. Even President Dilma Rousseff and Lula himself had lent a hand. "If it hadn't been for the PT, we would have been out", explained Valdeir Soares, who was active in the campaign. Now 35, Soares runs a restaurant called Tok Céu in the neighbourhood where over a lunch of beans, rice, chicken and farofa (a flour made from cassava that Brazilians use to add extra carbohydrate to their food), he and Oliveira talked about the campaign. "Every day we were up against it. There was one legal ruling after another", said Soares. "There were days when we were so anxious that we couldn't sleep."

The scale of the political upheaval was especially shocking in these poor areas of Uberlândia, but Brazil's 2018 election result was an earthquake for an entire political class. The defeat of the PT was striking, but Brazil's other mainstream political parties, which had been central to Brazil's economic and political stability over the previous quarter of a century, did even worse. Geraldo Alckmin, the governor of Brazil's most populars state of São Paulo and until the summer of 2018 the candidate for the country's financial and business establishment, won only 4 per cent of the vote in the first round of the contest in October. It was a stunning defeat that turned conventional Brazilian politics upside down. As two influential political marketing specialists commented, Bolsonaro's victory represented "the most surprising election result in Brazil's political history".[1]

Brazil's National Congress had gone haywire. The Social Liberal Party (PSL) – the latest in a string of small, right-wing parties adopted by Bolsonaro – had been widely expected to disappear in the run-up to the contest, but was now the second largest force in the lower house, with 52 of the assembly's 513 deputies. Among the elected newcomers for the PSL and a plethora of other right-wing parties were dozens of people who, when their predecessors were sworn in four years earlier, had not the faintest inkling that they would become representatives. Kátia Sastre, a corporal in the military police and a new PSL deputy, had sprung to overnight national fame in May 2018 after she shot and killed a man who attacked a group of parents outside a school in Suzano on the outskirts of São Paulo. Corporal Sastre had been off duty at the time and was taking her own daughter to the school. The shooting was caught on security cameras, broadcast on social media and then picked up by national media. Twenty years earlier, there had been barely any police officers in Brazil's Congress, but in 2018 more than three dozen won seats. Oliveira's Workers' Party clung on to governorships and congressional seats in the poor north-east of the country, where its social programmes – and especially its financial handouts – had been highly popular. But Bolsonaro swept the board in the more developed south and south-east and in the agricultural heartlands of the centre-west. And in the rural settlements, the smaller towns and cities that make up what Brazilians call the *interiorzão* (the big interior), the former army captain had done especially well. Why had this happened? And what did the future hold for Bolsonaro's administration?

I was close to the subject for several reasons. As a journalist since my mid-20s, I'd had a long-standing interest in Latin America. In the mid-1970s as a radical sociology student, I'd met Chilean refugees from the Pinochet dictatorship and become interested in their stories. From the early 1980s I travelled regularly to the region. I learned Spanish in Guatemala, lived for a couple of years in Central America, and wrote for a publication called the *Latin American Newsletter* about the bloody guerrilla wars sweeping through that part of the world. Unquestioningly, I blamed United States policy for Central America's problems. In fact, I sided with the Sandinistas and the left-wing guerrillas of El Salvador and Guatemala in much the same way as an earlier generation might have identified with the Spanish Republicans in the 1930s.

My political views have shifted quite a bit since then. As a young journalist, I soon learned that rigid Marxist categories were more a hindrance than an aid to understanding and explaining the complexities of history, politics, culture and economic development, whether in Latin America, back at home in Britain or anywhere else in the world. The closer I got to the reality of Latin America, the more critical I became of dependency theory, the semi-Marxist framework through which in my sociology classes I'd first been introduced to the region. Even in the 1970s, countries such as South Korea and other East Asian Tigers had shown that a dependent relationship on the "metropolitan powers" of North American and Europe was not necessarily a barrier to economic development. By the 1980s it was becoming increasingly evident to me that sometimes a country's problems were due not to capitalism per se, but to a particular form of capitalist economy. It wasn't too much competition that allowed inefficient monopolies and oligopolies to flourish, but too little. If it took state-owned telecommunications companies years to provide their customers with telephones, maybe it made sense to look to the private sector for quicker and better service. Bloated and inefficient public sectors may have served the interests of public-sector workers, but they were hardly in the interests of consumers or society as a whole. By the time I started writing for the *Financial Times* in 1990, I was sympathetic to the liberal reforms beginning to sweep through the region.

But then came another twist. Having embraced the market in the 1990s, Latin America shifted sharply to the left in the new century. As Latin America editor of the *Financial Times*, I covered the failures of those same free market reforms and the financial crises of the late 1990s and early 2000s and closely watched the rise of the region's so-called pink tide: the emergence of left-wing governments and the development of a burgeoning trade and investment relationship with China. During that period, I met many of the key figures: Brazil's Luiz Inácio Lula da Silva, Evo Morales from Bolivia, Rafael Correa of Ecuador, Andrés Manuel López Obrador, the current Mexican president, and Hugo Chávez, the rumbustious, larger-than-life character who, until his death in 2013, led Venezuela's disastrous experiment with 'twenty-first-century socialism'. For five years I headed up the Brazilian end of a project at the *Financial Times* to better understand the development of Brazil, Russia, India, China and South Africa (BRICS), the large developing economies whose emergence was, we all thought at the time, reshaping the prospects of the global economy.

Brazil is a country with which I have a personal and emotional – as well as an intellectual and professional – relationship. In 1998, at the beginning of my time as the *Financial Times* Latin America editor, I met and eventually married my Portuguese teacher. Since then we've spent a good deal of time with her friends and family in Salvador, Uberlândia and a string of other Brazilian cities. From this vantage point, I've been particularly conscious of the growing polarisation of Brazilian politics in recent years. The rise and fall of the PT, the deep recession of the mid-2010s, the Lava Jato ('Car Wash') corruption scandal, the growth in concern about violent crime, the triumph of Bolsonaro and the devastation wreaked by the COVID-19 pandemic have all coincided with the increasing popularity of social media. My family's WhatsApp groups – like those of thousands of other Brazilian families – have shown the depth of divisions. Older family members revere Brazil's leader, extolling his virtues. Younger members are in despair. My wife, for example, cannot bear to look at Bolsonaro's picture and didn't even want him on the cover of this book.

None of these political fashions has brought complete success. None has brought complete disaster. Latin America has changed dramatically since I first visited. The region is more stable economically. Living standards are higher. Government is less authoritarian. The oscillation between free market liberal reform and left-wing state-centred populism has continued. But the election of Bolsonaro has opened up a very different prospect in the continent's largest country. So what do Bolsonaro and 'Bolsonarismo' represent?

In this account, I characterise Bolsonaro as part of a broader populist phenomenon. I label him a populist – rather than a fascist – because it seems to me, at least so far, that Bolsonaro has yet to develop the kind of political machine or introduce the institutional capacity that he would need to bring fascism into being. But it would not be inconceivable for Brazilian politics to take some steps along that path. There are certainly some possible components of a fascist party, the violent militias of Rio de Janeiro and Pará states being the most obvious examples. However, nearly two years into the Bolsonaro administration, Brazil's institutions – an independent Congress and judiciary – not only remain intact, but have limited to a significant degree the reach of some of the president's intended reforms. Efforts to form a loyalist party – the Alliance for Brazil – have stumbled quite surprisingly. Instead, I see Bolsonaro in this book as an extreme right-wing populist, as someone similar to leaders such as Donald Trump, Viktor Orbán, the Hungarian president, or Rodrigo Duterte, the Philippine leader.

But first, some background. What do I mean by populism? Essentially, I see it as a political philosophy that seeks to reduce complex problems to simple choices. Almost invariably, populism scapegoats either the elite or a particular social group – bankers, immigrants or corrupt politicians – for the problems of society.

6

Compared to the corruption or venality of these groups, populism suggests that the people as a whole are pure. In the language of political scientists, populism is a "thin-centred ideology" that has a restricted "morphology" and has to combine with a "full-centred ideology" such as fascism, liberalism or nationalism.[2] Populism can take a left-wing or right-wing shape depending on the histories and circumstances of particular countries, although "broadly speaking left-wing populism combines with socialism, right-wing populism with nationalism".[3]

Brazil's latest episode of populism draws on two distinct trends. First, it represents the latest iteration of what has been an extraordinary powerful political tradition in Latin America. During the 1930s and 1940s, left-wing populist regimes took over in Brazil, Argentina, Mexico and Ecuador. Getúlio Vargas, Juan Domingo Peron, Lázaro Cardenas and José María Velasco Ibarra all pursued policies designed to benefit urban workers and small farmers at the expense of financial elites linked to international capital. In the 1990s, by contrast, Carlos Menem in Argentina, Alberto Fujimori in Peru and Fernando Collor de Mello in Brazil all came to office claiming to represent popular interests not against the financial elite, which had been targeted in the founding populist wave, but in alliance with it and against the state. All three presidents were radical privatisers. Finally, came the pink tide populists of the 2000s. In Venezuela, extensive corruption discredited the country's two mainstream moderate Social and Christian Democrat parties and opened the way for the election in 1998 of Hugo Chávez, a firebrand left-wing former army officer. The country's economic troubles also contributed to this shift, although the difficulties of the 1980s and 1990s pale alongside the disastrous decline over which Chávez and his incompetent successor, Nicolás Maduro, have presided. Under Maduro, Venezuela's economy has collapsed and the populist government, which still enjoys the backing of the armed forces, has resorted to all-out repression in order to maintain power.

Left-wing populists close to Chávez have run four other countries – Argentina, Bolivia, Ecuador, Nicaragua – for extended periods.[4] The electoral successes of Mexico's Andres Manuel López Obrador, Alberto Fernández in Argentina and Bolivia's Luis Arce Catacora in 2018, 2019 and 2020 respectively suggest that this brand of politics remains attractive, in spite of the disasters of Venezuela. But the new strain of Brazilian populism is really best understood by looking elsewhere. Bolsonaro has plenty in common with controversial politicians such as France's Marine Le Pen, Matteo Salvini of Italy and Nigel Farage, the British maverick nationalist and conservative politician who formed the UK Independence Party and perhaps did more than anyone else to stoke popular enthusiasm for the eventually successful campaign for the United Kingdom to leave the European Union. Like Marine Le Pen's now estranged father, Jean-Marie Le Pen, the founder of the Front (now the Rassemblement) National, it could be said of Bolsonaro that he says "out loud what the people are thinking inside".[5] Bolsonaro's similarities with Donald Trump are also notable, particularly because the Brazilian leader has openly expressed his admiration for the former US president. Both are anti-establishment figures who depended a great deal on their use of social media to be elected. Both men are always happy to attack the mainstream political consensus, around issues such as crime, immigration and global warming. Trump and Bolsonaro voters like the fact that their leaders are not intimidated by political correctness. In his recent book on identity, the American political scientist Francis Fukuyama describes Trump as "the perfect practitioner of the politics of authenticity […] [He] may be mendacious, malicious, bigoted and un-presidential but at least he says what he thinks."[6] Much the same could be said of the Brazilian leader.

Their elections and their presidencies have been surrounded by accusations and counter-accusations of fake news and conspiracy. Trump's constant allegations labelling critical media coverage as

fake news were designed to keep him aligned with his core con-
stituency and show, as David Runciman argues, that "conspiracy
theories are no longer just for losers. The winners believe in them,
too."[7] Again, the same could be said of Bolsonaro, who shamelessly
accused environmentalists of setting off the wave of Amazon forest
fires during August 2019. International protests were motivated by
the fact that Bolsonaro claimed that the governments involved –
notably France, whose president was the most vocal critic – were
looking to control the natural resources to be found there.

The connection between Trump and Bolsonaro even assumed
an organisational dimension when Steve Bannon, the ideo-
logue closely associated with Trump's 2016 election campaign,
invited Bolsonaro to form part of The Movement, a club of like-
minded political leaders and parties based in Brussels. Perhaps
more significant in this assessment of Bolsonaro is the popularity of a number of right-wing populist figures in middle-income
countries similar to Brazil. Russia's Vladimir Putin and Turkey's
Recep Tayyip Erdoğan are often cited as examples of authoritarian right-wing leaders like Bolsonaro, but parallels can also be
seen with three lesser-known but very popular democratic leaders:
Rodrigo Duterte, president of the Philippines since 2016; Jaroslaw
Kaczyński, leader of the Law and Justice Party in Poland, which
has controlled the legislature and presidency since 2015; and Viktor
Orbán, the prime minister of Hungary since 2010.

Like Bolsonaro, Duterte comes from outside his country's political
establishment, relies on a loyal group of family members and friends
for support, and has made much use of social media to convey his
ideas. Just as Bolsonaro's three oldest sons – Flávio, Carlos and
Eduardo – are central to his political project, so Duterte's daughter Sara, who took over from him as mayor of the city of Davao,
is a possible successor. He has known some of his most influential
cabinet members since childhood. A creative social media campaign played a big part in his 2016 election victory. Like Bolsonaro,
Duterte is something of a provincial – more at home in the city

of Davao than in Manila – and in the same way as the Brazilian president, Duterte continues to dismiss concerns about the rights of drug traffickers and other criminals. Duterte has showed no compunction about sanctioning police violence. In his first two and a half years in office, 5,000 people were killed by the police (although opposition groups claim there were more than 20,000 killings in 2018 alone). "Duterte cast aside any pretensions of respect for democratic norms, mocked human rights advocates, and encouraged violence against drug users and criminals", writes Sheila Coronel, a well-known Philippine journalist.[8] Duterte's approval ratings have rarely dipped much below 80 per cent.

There are strong parallels too with the eastern European strongmen Orbán of Hungary and Kaczyński, the leader of Poland's Law and Justice Party. Andrzej Duda, the Law and Justice Party's candidate in the 2020 presidential election, rode to office by weaponising the issue of LGBTQ rights. During the campaign, Duda labelled LGBTQ activism a "dangerous ideology" and compared it to communism. The state-owned TV station TVP, over which the government has strengthened editorial control since it came to office in 2015, continued to broadcast stories about the "rainbow plague", which it described as "an invasion designed to tear down traditional families". Concerns over the country's economic downturn, the high rate of COVID-19 infection and corruption allegations were all overshadowed. Unwittingly, Duda's opponent in the campaign, Rafal Trzaskowski, the mayor of Warsaw, had himself triggered the controversy by launching a school education programme to tackle homophobia. For Brazilians who followed Bolsonaro's campaign, the whole affair was resonant of the way the so-called 'gay kit' – an education package on gender rights that was commissioned by the PT government – inflamed passions among evangelical Christians. The programme was eventually scrapped but fuelled support for Bolsonaro, who was quick to exploit the issue. And in another echo, Poland recently became the first country in the world to make chemical castration compulsory for certain classes of sex offender. Chemical castration was one of the few legal initiatives that Bolsonaro launched when he was a deputy.

Perhaps more than any other European politician, Viktor Orbán is a theorist of what political scientists call 'illiberal democracy', that is, rule by a majority but without liberal protections for individuals or minorities, whether they be defined by ethnicity, religion or gender. In a speech in 2018, Orbán defined Christian democracy as a system that "protects the ways of life springing from Christian culture. It means defending human dignity, the family and the nation."[9] It is a recipe that seems tailor-made for Bolsonaro, a man whose campaign slogan was "Brazil above everything, God above all".

There are, of course, some big differences between Trump and the European right-wing populists on the one hand, and Bolsonaro on the other. For one thing, Bolsonaro's military background – which we will look at in more detail in the next chapter – makes him distinctive. And then there is the issue of immigration. Opinion polls suggest that concern about steep rises in immigration, especially Muslim immigration, drove support for Brexit in the UK.[10] It has helped underpin the rise of the far right in Europe and transformed Orbán from a minor player, quietly chipping away at liberal freedoms in Hungary, to a figure of European relevance. Immigration largely from Venezuela is something of a concern in Brazil but recently has never been as disruptive or as culturally controversial as Muslim immigration to Europe or the very large inflows of Mexicans and Central Americans to the United States.

What have been the trigger issues for Bolsonaro's brand of populism? I argue that three factors came together to activate the dormant genes of Brazilian populism. First, the country's recession between 2014 and 2016 was the worst in its modern history (although the current COVID-related downturn may well turn out to be more severe). Following a period of increasing prosperity and rising expectations, the psychological impact of the financial contraction was harsh. Second, the economic deterioration coincided with a highly publicised scandal that exposed the corrupt relationship between state-owned companies, politicians and private construction companies. Corruption in Brazil was not new, but never before had it become so visible to the public. Politicians and Congress saw their popularity plummet. The governing Workers' Party that had come to office in 2003 promising to introduce a new, cleaner style of politics suffered disproportionately. The third issue that triggered Bolsonaro's brand of populism was the increase in violent crime, which became the subject of obsessive interest in the press and on social media. Homicides had fallen in Brazil during the 2000s, but in 2016 Brazil's two biggest gangs, the São Paulo-based First Command of the Capital and the Rio de Janeiro-based Red Command, started a war to take control of lucrative new drugs routes in the north and north-east of the country. Murder rates in hitherto relatively peaceful regions started to rise. The gangs took their war to Brazil's poorly policed prisons and the gruesome massacres that resulted served to highlight a sense of almost apocalyptic crisis.

But this is not the whole story. Bolsonaro also brought together a broad conservative alliance, uniting people who had been unhappy about Brazil's drift towards the socially liberal left. The title of this book – beef (or more accurately ox, from the Portuguese word *boi*), Bible and bullets – provides a broad sense of the nature of that coalition. I use this title partly as a way to express the individualist, socially conservative and militaristic values of Bolsonaro's supporters. But the combination was originally used in Brazil to describe three conservative congressional lobbies that since Brazil's return to democracy in 1985 have become important in shaping the country's political life. The beef lobby – better known as the *ruralistas* – has sought to allow Brazil's powerful farmers more freedom to exploit the country's plentiful land and water and to produce more food. They have sometimes railed against the environmental controls that have constrained their activities. Brazil's biggest farmers – in particular its powerful soya sector – have become more environmentally conscious in recent years, not least because they know green credentials are necessary if they are to retain their share of important markets. But there are plenty of smaller operators on the fringes of the Amazon who want to be free to cut down or burn rainforest as and when they need land.

The bullet lobby describes politicians who espoused the values of Brazil's gun owners and who in some cases had been financed by the country's arms industry.[11] When the lobby first emerged, it sought to oppose the gun controls introduced by the first Lula government. Subsequently, the security lobby has become closely associated with the interests of Brazil's police forces, who want to be less constrained in the way they tackle violent crime. Thirty-seven former policemen were elected to Brazil's Congress in 2018, more than twice as many as in 2014 and five times as many as in 2002.

The Bible lobby, which is closely associated with the rapidly growing and financially powerful evangelical church, has opposed moves to liberalise education and family relations. The group is stronger than ever in the current Congress. Opposition to abortion has united them with the country's dwindling Catholic majority, but evangelicals from both mainstream churches, like Baptists and Methodists as well as Pentecostalists, oppose gay marriage and gender education and were particularly enraged by proposed legislation to criminalise homophobia.

In the first two chapters of this book, I consider the rise of Bolsonaro and explore the relationship between his army and political careers. While Brazil's democratic politicians kept their distance from the military dictatorship that had run Brazil between 1964 and 1985, Bolsonaro had served as a captain in the 1970s and 1980s and extolled the virtues of military life. The army, particularly his relationships with lower ranks, had shaped Bolsonaro's personality and as a politician he lobbied for military interests. But whereas politicians and the media tended to dismiss Bolsonaro as an eccentric irrelevance, his pro-military views were not so unpopular among ordinary Brazilians who were overall less opposed to the armed forces than their elected representatives. In Chapter 2, I describe the way in which the extraordinary growth of social media and the increasing competitive pressures faced by traditional newspapers, radio and TV helped Bolsonaro overcome the disadvantages that Brazil's political establishment believed would keep him from office. Several factors helped propel his successful social media campaign. Bolsonaro's second son, Carlos, designed an effective strategy. The popularity on the internet of Olavo de Carvalho, a Brazilian philosopher notable for his unconventional extreme right-wing views, was significant, while the knife attack that left Bolsonaro hospitalised for much of the electoral campaign also turned out to be to the candidate's advantage. Above all, it was Bolsonaro's anti-political style that proved attractive to more conservative Brazilians. Bolsonaro's homophobia and sexism, and his repressive ideas about crime and punishment shocked international opinion, but like Donald Trump and Rodrigo Duterte, Bolsonaro benefited by openly opposing political correctness.

Chapters 3 and 4 take the story back to Brazil's 'magic moment'. By 2010 fifteen years of economic stability and a China-generated export boom seemed to have transformed the country's economic prospects. New approaches to social policy, a wave of job creation and the expansion of credit had lifted millions of Brazilians out of poverty, creating a new consumer class. Brazil, however, failed to capitalise. Deteriorating economic performance led to a big increase in unemployment and put consumer spending under strain. Having borrowed heavily to finance their spending, many families became over-indebted. In many ways, the successes of the early years generated a crisis of expectations.

Chapters 5 and 6 explore the demonstrations of June 2013, the Lava Jato corruption scandal and the impeachment of President Dilma Rousseff. In the run-up to the Confederations Cup of 2013 – the football competition that serves as a dry run for the World Cup – frustrations combined with growing disquiet about the quality of public spending, culminating in an explosion of discontent. With the Workers' Party government on the ropes, the sensational Lava Jato investigations delivered a knockout blow. Lava Jato represented a political earthquake in Brazil. It exposed the entire political and economic establishment to unprecedented scrutiny, although the Workers' Party was worst hit, ironically since the probe had been facilitated by reforms introduced by Rousseff herself.

Chapter 7 looks at the way in which growing fears about violence helped fuel demands for the kind of hardline security policies championed by Bolsonaro. It starts in Fortaleza, in the northeastern state of Ceará, where poor neighbourhoods have been devastated by fierce gang wars. Organised crime linked to the sale and trans-shipment of cocaine and other illegal narcotics had become a growing problem during the 1980s and 1990s, with homicide rates in the cities of Rio de Janeiro and São Paulo among the highest in the world. During the 2000s Brazil was able to improve security significantly in the south of the country, but from 2012 the number of violent deaths started to increase, especially in hitherto relatively peaceful parts of the country such as Fortaleza.

In Chapter 8, I focus on the growing importance of paramilitary militias, particularly in the state of Rio de Janeiro. Over the past twenty years these militias have controlled a growing number of poor neighbourhoods, and for many poorer Cariocas (residents of Rio de Janeiro) they are a cause of greater concern than the drug traffickers they were set up to combat. Their links with the police and local politicians make reform a complex challenge. Rio also highlights a broader national problem: the rise in the number of killings by police officers and growing support among police officers for the repressive public security strategies advocated by Bolsonaro. In 2018 more than twice as many police officers were elected to the Brazilian Congress as in 2014, increasing the political weight of the so-called bullet lobby in Brazilian politics. At the grass roots, substantial numbers of military police provide firm support for Bolsonaro, constituting in the words of one writer the president's "shock troops".[12]

In Chapter 9 I return to Uberlândia to examine the role of the rapidly growing neo-Pentecostal churches. An estimated 30 per cent of Brazilians were evangelical Protestants in 2020, up from only about 6 per cent in 1980. The socially conservative churches, particularly the large and financially powerful neo-Pentecostal churches, are increasingly influential at all levels of Brazilian society and have established close links with Bolsonaro and his family.

Chapter 10 explores the social and economic conflicts in the Amazon region. The small farmers and miners who have settled in states such as Pará and Amazonas over the past half-century are Brazil's equivalent of US 'rednecks': strongly independent, fiercely conservative and big supporters of right-wing politics. This section of the book starts in Roraima, a state with a large indigenous population, where the settler population voted heavily in favour of Bolsonaro in 2018.

Chapter 11 looks at the breakdown of Brazil's efforts to control deforestation and the growing international concern about the destruction of the Amazon rainforest. This chapter considers some of the issues that have divided Bolsonaro's supporters. The increase in deforestation and a number of dramatic forest fires in 2019–20 brought to the fore international concerns about global warming. Bolsonaro's administration has weakened the institutions whose monitoring and policing work reduced the rate of tree loss in the period between 2004 and 2012. Bolsonaro also provided encouragement for his wilder supporters – the small farmers, informal miners and loggers and property speculators who have colonised parts of the Amazon. The town of Novo Progresso in Pará celebrated Bolsonaro's first six months in government by coordinating a series of fires in neighbouring tracts of rainforest. Yet many powerful commercial interests are alarmed by the impact of environmental damage on Brazil's reputation abroad and the potential loss of markets and investment. A painstakingly negotiated and valuable trade deal with the European Union completed in 2019 may well come unstuck, for example.

Chapter 12 takes a look at another divisive issue: China. Over the last twenty years, Brazil has become increasingly dependent on the Chinese market. Bolsonaro's more radical supporters want to reduce or even break links with China, arguing that Brazil's national sovereignty is at risk. But China is comfortably Brazil's biggest trading partner, and the agribusiness and mining interests worry that they could lose markets. At the same time, China's investments in energy and telecommunications are strategically important for Brazil. Unwinding these connections would carry a heavy economic cost and would be politically controversial. During the coronavirus pandemic, tensions with China have grown. Bolsonaro's supporters have blamed China for the virus and opposed the use of the vaccines developed by Chinese companies, but during 2020 China's rapid recovery means that it has become an even more important market for Brazil's commodity exports.

Chapter 13 looks at the divisions within the Bolsonaro administration during its first year and a half in office. Tensions between ideological extreme right-wing activists and the movement's socially conservative base, and more pragmatic conservatives from the private sector and within the armed forces, were a constant feature of Brazilian politics throughout 2019, and became even more serious as a result of the pandemic. Bolsonaro underplayed the seriousness of the disease and opposed local leaders who sought to impose quarantines in order to diminish its impact. Conservative politicians such as João Doria, the governor of São Paulo, Wilson Witzel, the suspended governor of Rio de Janeiro, Luiz Henrique Mandetta, the government's first health minister, and Sérgio Moro, the justice minister, all supported Bolsonaro in 2018 but will almost certainly oppose him in 2022. Bolsonaro's idiosyncratic approach to the pandemic also brought him and his supporters into acute conflict with the Supreme Court. In May 2020 these battles threatened to lead to an institutional crisis.

Chapter 14 examines the sudden and unexpected rise in Bolsonaro's popularity during the second half of 2020 and assesses his prospects for the rest of his four-year term and beyond. The temporary emergency grant paid to 67 million Brazilians dramatically increased the spending power of the poorest Brazilians. Opinion polls suggest that Bolsonaro's popularity in the north, north-east and centre-west of the country has increased, even though his COVID-19 denialism and shoddy management of the pandemic has alarmed many private-sector and middle-class supporters. A new political alliance with a group of conservative parties known as the big centre or the *Centrão* has helped shore up the president's support in the legislature and headed off the risk of impeachment. These advances, however, were not based on solid ground. As this book went to press – in late March 2021 – the rapid rise in coronavirus cases and deaths brought the conflicts between Bolsonaro's radical right-wing base and more mainstream conservatives out into the open. Bolsonaro came under fierce pressure from Brazil's powerful business elite and his new congressional allies to change his stance on the country's health crisis. Impeachment was yet again in the air. Bolsonaro's political future seemed far from assured.

1

THE OUTSIDER

In April 1970 a rebel army captain got wind of military plans to encircle his guerrilla training camps in the densely wooded landscape of the Ribeira Valley, 150 miles south-west of São Paulo, Brazil's biggest city. Thirty-three-year-old Carlos Lamarca had been radicalised by his experiences as a captain in a United Nations peace mission in the Middle East. He had deserted the army the previous year, stolen a lorry full of rifles and sub-machine guns and joined a left-wing group that called itself the Popular Revolutionary Vanguard (VPR). From a base in the remnants of Brazil's Atlantic rainforest, Lamarca was now teaching a small group of young activists to handle weapons, spring ambushes and launch sabotage raids. Lamarca wanted to create what Régis Debray, a French intellectual inspired by Che Guevara, had called a guerrilla foco: a nucleus of committed militants who would attack police and army posts and supposedly inspire a subdued population to resist their oppression, eventually, as had happened in Cuba in 1959, overthrowing the government.

All this was at a time when the armed forces were consolidating their hold over Brazil, establishing in the process one of the longest military dictatorships in recent Latin American history. The 1964 coup against President João Goulart had been motivated in large part by the left-wing president's planned social reforms and friendly policy towards Cuba, during a period in which Washington was concerned about Cuban and Soviet influence in the region. From the late 1960s onwards, the military had become increasingly repressive, closing down Congress and opposition parties and imposing censorship in the press, broadcast media and the arts.

Lamarca's group of young far-leftists had successfully executed bank robberies and kidnappings, notoriously that of the Swiss ambassador Giovanni Enrico Bucher, who had been released earlier in the year in exchange for seventy political prisoners. But now in the dense jungle of Ribeira, things were going wrong. A VPR militant had been captured by the security services in Rio de Janeiro and had given away details of Lamarca's plan, and for weeks nearly 3,000 troops of the Second Army had been laying siege to the camps. Lamarca was public enemy number one and this was the unit's biggest ever operation. As they sought to escape, Lamarca and a few of his comrades managed to get hold of a truck, but on the evening of 8 May 1970 they were stopped at a police roadblock close to the main square of Eldorado Paulista, a small town in an area of orange groves and banana plantations on the edge of the forest. The unit blasted its way out, wounding three policemen, and fled into the jungle. For Lamarca, it proved to be a Pyrrhic victory. He was arrested and shot by soldiers a year later.

But the affair left a mark on the town. Many of Eldorado Paulista's 15,000 inhabitants have vivid memories of the firefight. "My dad said, 'get down, get down'", remembers Nizilene de Oliveira, the deputy director of the local school, who was 10 years old. "There was a lot of shooting."[1] For one person living in Eldorado at the time, the battle left an even deeper impression. Jair Bolsonaro, then a 15-year-old schoolboy, lived a couple of hundred yards from the main square. After the shootout, dozens of soldiers took over the town, searched houses and interviewed locals. It caused some tensions, but Bolsonaro and his teenage friends sympathised with the wounded policemen, got to know the troops, and used their local knowledge of the area to try to help them find Lamarca. Bolsonaro's help was not crucial, but he had often tramped about the nearby forest, having spent a good deal of his adolescence looking for heart of palm and passion fruit or fishing in the Ribeira river, and then selling the products to raise extra money for his family. "He told them where the guerrillas might have gone", said Antonio Avelino, a school colleague of Bolsonaro at the time.[2]

In the weeks that followed, Bolsonaro made friends with the soldiers. "After this he always used to say that he wanted to join the army. He thought what they did was great", said Avelino. Another Eldorado contemporary adds that Bolsonaro's interest in the military became obsessive. "He never shut up about it", one told a reporter. Gilmar Alves, a close friend from the period, said that Bolsonaro had tried to persuade him to join the army too. "He used to say all the presidents were soldiers and he was going to be president."[3] Certainly, in his subsequent political career the future president never lost an opportunity to remind people about his collaboration. He has mentioned it more than thirty times in speeches. "I took part in a quiet way in tracking down Lamarca", he told Congress in a speech in March 2012, for example.[4]

Bolsonaro's infatuation with the army was, in a way, surprising. Born in 1955, he was the second child of Percy Geraldo 'Gerardo' and Olinda Bolsonaro, Brazilians of largely Italian descent, and had grown up in modest circumstances. Gerardo made a living repairing and extracting teeth and making dentures, although he had never obtained the professional qualifications of a dentist. The couple had lived modestly in a number of small towns in the rural interior of São Paulo state in the south-east of Brazil before settling on Eldorado, precisely because there was no dentist in the town. Gerardo was by all accounts a gregarious character, who chain smoked, drank heavily and loved football. He named his son Jair in homage to Jair Rosa Pinto, a midfielder who had starred in Brazil's 1954 World Cup team and was coming to the end of a prolific spell at Palmeiras, the São Paulo club traditionally favoured by the country's sizeable Italian community. But Gerardo was no fan of the dictatorship. In fact, he competed unsuccessfully for a seat on the local council for the Brazilian Democratic Movement (MDB), the opposition party to the military government. Gerardo was investigated by the security forces for his political activities and then arrested for practising dentistry without professional qualifications, although he was subsequently acquitted. But there was little money for Jair and his two brothers and three sisters. And maybe Brazil's armed forces represented – as they did for many less well-off families – a potentially important source of economic security and social mobility.

Early in 1973 Bolsonaro started cadet school in the city of Campinas and passed the tough exams necessary for entry to the much more exclusive Agulhas Negras military academy in Resende, in the state of Rio de Janeiro. Three years later he graduated as an artillery captain. The experience was a formative one. The armed forces had indeed offered Bolsonaro a route to social advancement, and it had done so at a critically important time. Bolsonaro had stumbled across the possibility of joining the army during the first phases of its counter-insurgency operations. As he started his officer training, the military was engaged in another big battle against the left, this time in the form of a small guerrilla force launched by the Maoist-oriented Communist Party of Brazil (PCdoB). A few dozen fighters had tried to establish a rural stronghold in the Araguaia river basin on the edge of the Amazon. Just like Lamarca, the PCdoB made little progress. By the time Bolsonaro was finishing his second year at Agulhas Negras, the military had crushed the operation, killing sixty of the eighty guerrillas. Many of Bolsonaro's instructors had been involved in the Araguaia action. They were "adored by the students", according to one retired colonel.[5] The government justified its repression as a necessary response to terrorism, a version of events that Bolsonaro seemed happy enough to accept and which he has continued to repeat even though most democratic politicians argue that the repression entailed unacceptable abuses of human rights. In any case, Bolsonaro was doing well. He learned to parachute and became a jump instructor. By all accounts, he was a more than competent soldier and he won something of a reputation as an athlete, representing military teams in the pentathlon.

. But soon another issue started to influence Bolsonaro's military career. Lacking personal means, he always seemed to be interested in earning extra money. Perhaps this was due to growing family responsibilities. After marrying Rogéria Nantes Nunes Braga in 1978, Bolsonaro was soon father to three children. His sons, Flávio, Carlos and Eduardo, were all born in the first half of the 1980s. Internal reports suggest that an otherwise extremely well-regarded officer came into conflict with the top brass as a result of material frustrations. In 1979 Bolsonaro requested a move to a garrison based in Nioaque, in the western state of Mato Grosso do Sul, where in his spare time he farmed rice and then, more successfully, watermelons. A 1983 holiday expedition with fellow officers to a garimpo (an informal gold mine) in Bahia led to criticism from his superiors, who claimed they were concerned by his "excessive economic and financial ambition". It was a sign of "immaturity [that he was] attracted to the business of garimpo. He should be placed in a job that demands energy and commitment so he can get his career back on track", read one senior officer's report.[6]

From then on Bolsonaro seems to have been an active campaigner for higher wages and more generous benefits. In 1986 he controversially broke military discipline by writing an article for the widely read weekly news magazine *Veja* in order to publicise his arguments. Under the headline "Wages are Low", the article explained the financial problems confronting army officers. "In the end someone who dedicates the best years of their life to a military career, working no less than 48 hours a week, with commitments on Saturdays and Sundays and holidays, working at night, cannot just think of patriotism, as many want to do, when they can't even dream of bringing up a family", he wrote. "I am a Brazilian who does his duty, a patriot with a great record but I can't dream of the minimum that a person of my cultural and social level aims at."[7]

The piece won him plaudits from colleagues and brought him to national prominence for the first time. There were even demonstrations by military wives in his favour. But the article enraged senior officers, who believed that he was out to cause trouble. A military court judgment earned him a fourteen-day prison sentence. A year later, he found himself in even hotter water. In a piece published in October 1987, *Veja* named him as one of the ringleaders in a plot to bomb military installations: armed action designed to lend force to his group's 'trade' union-style demands. The attacks never took place and a military court found him not guilty, although the affair effectively marked the end of his military career. In December 1988 Bolsonaro quietly transferred to the army reserve.

Into politics

The incident may have effectively finished Bolsonaro's military career, but Bolsonaro the politician would be a dependable military ally. As a city councillor in Rio de Janeiro, where he was elected in 1988, and as a federal deputy, Bolsonaro was initially a member of the Christian Democrats, a small centre-right party largely confined to the fringes of Brazilian politics. But party association was always less important than his connections to the military lobby. When he was a councillor in Rio, Bolsonaro spent his time "reading the papers and looking for news of soldiers who had died. When he found some he would send a note of condolence to the widow."[8] Elected to the lower house of Congress in 1990, Bolsonaro continued to press for wage improvements, retirement benefits for former officers, bus passes and other benefits for ordinary troops, frequently clashing with senior officers who had banned him from entering military barracks. "Soldiers, corporals and sergeants are not treated as if they are human beings", Bolsonaro insisted.[9]

At a time when few other politicians would dare praise the record of Brazil's military rulers, Bolsonaro was always upfront in his support for the military view of the dictatorship's record. He was openly, unapologetically contemptuous of democracy. "Elections won't change anything in this country", an angry Bolsonaro told an interviewer on the programme *Câmara Aberta*, broadcast by TV Band in 1999. "It will only change on the day that we break out in civil war here and do the job that the military regime didn't do, killing 30,000 people. If we kill some innocent people that's fine [because] in every war innocent people die." Shouting at the interviewer, an intemperate Bolsonaro said that if he became president he would dissolve Congress on his first day in office, and he defended the use of torture. "I'm in favour of torture. You know that and the people are in favour as well."

Bolsonaro's views were deeply unfashionable in political circles, as newly elected politicians sought to distance themselves from the tired military regimes of the 1970s and the early 1980s. Brazil's political climate had been influenced by the very large mass demonstrations that led the military to allow the president to be elected by direct popular vote rather than, as they had wanted, by the indirect votes of Congress. Virtually every Brazilian political party – irrespective of its actual policy stance – called itself progressive, democratic, popular, social or socialist. One of Bolsonaro's own parties first labelled itself Progressive Reform, then Progressive. The biggest right-wing party, which had supported the military, called itself the Liberal Front and then rebranded as the Democrats. Right-wing ideas were out of favour.

A new Constitution approved by a constituent assembly in 1988 guaranteed individual rights, breaking with the authoritarian logic of its predecessor, approved in 1967. But ironically, the particular kind of party and election arrangements chosen by Brazilian politicians in the document opened up a space for politicians such as Bolsonaro. Under the military government, except for a brief period in the late 1960s and early 1970s, moderate and right-wing parties had been allowed to operate. However, there were tight restrictions on the formation of new parties and representatives had not been allowed to change their allegiances. By contrast, the new democratic regime was much more permissive and gave "maximum latitude to politicians at the expense of parties".[10]

Since the early 1930s voting in Brazil has been by proportional representation, and voting districts have had a relatively large number of representatives. The open list of a party's candidates means that voters decide which candidates they want to vote for, reducing the ability of party managers to order which representatives are elected.[11] A closed list, by contrast, ensures that those candidates favoured by headquarters are placed towards the top of the list and secure the lion's share of votes. With the restrictions of the military period lifted, candidates such as Bolsonaro who had strong links with particular causes or lobbies (or who could access their own independent sources of political finance) were able to do relatively well, while those who were simply party loyalists playing a more low-profile role inside the party machine found the going harder. Arguably the system represents a kind of post-authoritarian over-reaction to "the institutional framework of military rule"[12] or "democratic libertarianism".[13]

Bolsonaro did well in elections because he counted on solid backing from his own lobby and increasingly and more generally from voters who liked his hardline stance in relation to crime. By 2014 he was the most voted-for deputy in the state of Rio de Janeiro. Nevertheless, in spite of this advantage inside Congress itself, Bolsonaro was a deputy with little influence. He was rarely responsible for legislative initiatives. "His career was always very modest and consisted mainly in making amendments to projects of interest to the military."[14] His political ideas were regarded as anachronistic and out of tune with the liberal democratic mood of the 1990s and 2000s, and perhaps even as a bit of joke by his professional colleagues. And Bolsonaro did show a penchant for the bizarre. He proposed, for example, to make it compulsory for civilians to raise their right arm and hold it across their left breast when they were singing the national anthem. Another proposal was to add a new entry in Brazil's *Book of National Heroes*: Enéas Carneiro, a cardiologist well known for his long black beard, who was the last of the far-right politicians to have any serious following in Brazil, finishing third in the 1994 presidential contest.

Bolsonaro was a politician not taken seriously by his congressional colleagues. When, in February 2017, he put himself forward as a candidate for president of the lower house – an important position from which he would have had real influence over the government's agenda – he won the votes of only four of the assembly's 513 deputies, one of which was his own. His office was in the unpopular annex number three of the Congress building, reserved for the least influential legislators and nicknamed after the notorious Carandiru prison on account of its poor facilities. His small, poorly furnished room, without private bathroom, was well known for the framed portraits of all five of Brazil's most recent military presidents.

In the 1990s Bolsonaro's explicit pro-military views also put him at odds with many pro-business and pro-market conservatives. Loyal to the military regime's nationalist economic policy, Bolsonaro had opposed the privatisations of state companies piloted through in the late 1990s by President Fernando Henrique Cardoso, and had even suggested that Cardoso should be shot for having sold off the publicly owned telecoms company, as well as stakes in the state-owned mining and oil companies. During the 2000s, as Brazil's political culture was increasingly influenced by the tide of social liberalism and a broader human rights agenda, Bolsonaro acquired new enemies. He began to rail against issues such as gay marriage or plans to improve sex education in schools or conditions in prisons. In fact, on any issue of liberal concern Bolsonaro could be relied upon to provoke outspoken opposition not only from radical left-wingers or pro-market privatisers but from liberal moderates, middle-of-the-road sorts who were simply in favour of a kinder and more humane world.

His pronouncements on sexuality and violence were so inflammatory and outrageous that they seemed designed to tweak liberal sensibilities. "I've got five kids but on the fifth I had a moment of weakness and it came out as a girl", he told an audience at the Clube Hebraica in São Paulo in April 2017. Three years earlier, in an angry exchange with PT congresswoman Maria de Rosário, he told her that "she was too ugly to rape", prompting Rosário to press criminal charges, and the left-wing publication *The Intercept* to describe Bolsonaro as "the most misogynistic, hateful elected official in the democratic world".[15] Bolsonaro also became well known for his homophobic views. In an interview delivered in 2011, he told *Playboy* that he would be "incapable of loving a homosexual son" and would "prefer him to die in an accident than show up with a guy with a moustache".[16]

The hellish conditions in Brazilian prisons brought to international attention by the film *Carandiru* (2003), based on the 1992 prison riots, shocked many; however, for Bolsonaro prisons were "wonderful places [where] people pay for their sins, not live the life of Reilly, in a spa. Those who rape, kidnap and kill are going there to suffer, not attend a holiday camp."[17] The organisation of the landless, the Landless Workers' Movement (MST), might win plaudits outside Brazil from human rights activists, but Bolsonaro was solidly behind landowners and supported their efforts to defend their properties. "Our calling card for the criminals of the MST is a 7.62 rifle cartridge", he said.

As the governments of Lula and Rousseff introduced policies to improve opportunities for black Brazilians such as university quotas, Bolsonaro was steadfastly opposed. Rather than protect quilombos, the rural villages set up by escaped black slaves, Bolsonaro sought only to undermine them. "I visited a quilombo and the least heavy afro-descendant weighed 230lbs", he said in 2017. "They do nothing and they are not even good for procreation." He also decried moves to protect Brazil's indigenous minorities, comparing indigenous reserves dotted across the Amazon to

the disease of chicken pox. "We need to put a stop to the demarcation of indigenous land", he said.[18]

These illiberal and anti-democratic views shocked middle-class
progressives, but at the grass roots of Brazilian society, especially
in socially conservative smaller towns and rural areas that constitute the *interiorzão* (the big interior), they struck a chord. Away from
the giant coastal cities of Rio de Janeiro and São Paulo, Brazil is
much more socially conservative than people outside the country
generally appreciate. The images from Brazil's annual Carnival,
where for nights on end semi-naked people dance and cavort to
the sound of samba, lead many foreigners see Brazil as something
of a libertarian paradise. But the reality is very different. Brazil is
a country where, according to a *Veja*/FSB poll taken in February
2020, 61 per cent of people support Bolsonaro's idea to open new
schools run by the armed forces, 60 per cent favour mandatory
religious instruction in schools, and majorities oppose gay marriage and abortion.[19] The majorities are bigger among the less
well-off and less educated.

Indeed, according to one extensive survey of social attitudes
published in 2007 on issues ranging from crime to sexuality, many
poorer Brazilians tended to have reactionary views.[20] No fewer
than 40 per cent of those interviewed thought that a rapist should
himself be raped in prison as a punishment. A third of the sample
believed that police were within their rights to beat up prisoners
so that they confess their crimes. Attitudes towards sexuality were
equally retrograde. The same survey showed that the majority of
Brazilians were extraordinarily narrow-minded in their attitudes
even towards heterosexual relationships, and that's even before
we come to what in Brazil is a particularly delicate question of
same-sex relationships. Nearly three-quarters of survey respond-
ents thought anal sex was wrong, half of the sample was against
oral sex and roughly the same number against masturbation. Of
those who had not gone to university, 90 per cent were opposed
to homosexuality.

Research for the survey was conducted in 2002, and it is possible that attitudes have become more liberal in recent years as a younger generation of Brazilians have been more exposed to modern attitudes, not least through their greater exposure to international media on the internet. By the same token, however, the rapidly growing Protestant churches hold notoriously old-fashioned attitudes towards sex, especially homosexuality. Evangelical pastors have courted popularity by promoting therapies designed to 'cure' gay people. The decision by the education ministry to commission a set of educational materials designed to tackle homophobia in schools was hugely controversial.

In many ways, the liberal consensus over rights for prisoners or for LGBTQ people is out of sync with the instincts of those less well-off who did not attend university. This is the case in the US, the Philippines, Hungary or any of the other countries where right-wing populists have scored recent successes. But in Brazil, an additional factor helped Bolsonaro. Many Brazilians believed that their elected representatives – their congresspeople and councillors – inhabited a different world from them. The huge Lava Jato corruption case increased the sense of distance Brazilians felt from the world of representative politics, but Brazil's political system had in a way always been unique. The decision in the 1950s to relocate Brazil's capital to the modernist city of Brasília was designed to help develop the interior of the country. It was a laudable aim, but it succeeded in making federal politics seem even more remote from everyday life. This was contradictory in a way because Brazil had become dramatically more democratic since the end of the Second World War, with the percentage of its citizens eligible to vote rising from 16 per cent in 1945 to 70 per cent in 1994, as people who couldn't read or write and those over the age of 16 were added to the electoral roll.

But generally, Brazilians did not feel close to the people who they voted for. Politicians paid themselves exceptionally well, even by international standards, which meant that they were seen by many Brazilians as an entrenched and highly privileged elite. Consistently during the 2000s, the annual polls conducted by the Chile-based research organisation Latinbarómetro showed that Brazilians had less faith in their representative democracy than their Latin American neighbours.[21] In 2018 only 6 per cent of those interviewed had any confidence in parties, and only 12 per cent in the legislature, among the lowest in the hemisphere. By contrast, the armed forces were more popular in Brazil than in countries such as Argentina, Chile or Uruguay, where military dictatorships had also ruled the roost in the 1970s.

One of the reasons for this was that the Brazilian military governments had been less repressive and more economically successful than those of their neighbours. As the reports of a 2012–14 National Truth Commission made clear, the Brazilian military had been guilty of shocking human rights abuses, but even so, the scale of killing and torture paled alongside that inflicted on the left-wing oppositions of Argentina, Chile and Uruguay.[22] In Chile, at least 3,200 people were killed by General Augusto Pinochet's military dictatorship. Argentina's repression was more savage; between 9,000 and 30,000 people were killed between 1976 and 1982. In Brazil, tens of thousands of people were detained and several thousand exiled. But the National Truth Commission set up in 2012 by President Dilma Rousseff, a former member of the VPR who was captured and tortured in prison, found evidence for only 191 assassinations and 243 disappearances. However, we now know that many hundreds of indigenous people died from disease and other causes when the military governments accelerated the development of the Amazon.

Nonetheless, Brazil's military was much more successful than its peers in the region. As Timothy Power writes, "paradoxically under military rule, the minimum wage was always higher than it was for the first two decades of the post-1985 democracy".[23] "It is alarming to recognise and even more painful to say so in print," Power continues, "but the military dictatorship vastly improved the material condition of most Brazilians even while depriving them of the right to change their government."[24] Many people had fond memories of day-to-day life under the military, which contrasted with the chaos and instability of the first few years of democratic rule. Growth slowed and inflation eventually ran out of control in the first decade of civilian rule. The new democratic regime was "slow to be loved".[25] That sense of unease had dissipated in the 2000s, but it returned with a vengeance as Brazil stumbled through the 2010s. As the recession deepened in 2016, and anger about corruption and anxiety about violent crime mounted, strong populist winds started to blow. Bolsonaro was far better placed to advance than many people realised. He might have been isolated in Congress, but there was always going to be a market in Brazil for a political outsider.

2

COMING IN FROM THE COLD

A group of marching figures in paramilitary fatigues surround a white-suited politician in a downtown area of a Brazilian city. To the strident trumpet of a military band, the figure is led by a uniformed dwarf on to an improvised open-air stage and invites questions from the crowd. The man is Márvio Lúcio, a popular Rio de Janeiro-based comedian and mimic, and the politician is 'Bolsonabo', a satirical representation of the presidential candidate. The format is simple. Someone from the audience might ask whether a woman needs a driving licence and Bolsonabo replies that there is no need to drive from the sitting room to the kitchen. As the spectators yell their appreciation, Bolsonabo's team starts to chant "Mito, Mito" (Legend, Legend) and bubbles containing the same word slowly rise up the screen behind the performers. Then a woman in the crowd approaches the microphone, tells Bolsonabo how ugly he is and asks why he doesn't have plastic surgery to improve his self-esteem. Bolsonabo says she looks like ET, but at least people were interested in ET. Again, there is uproar and chants of "Mito" from the uniformed goons on stage, and the word rises up the screen. Arguably, this is tame, cringe-worthy stuff, but in Brazil there was clearly an audience who appreciated it.

The 'Legends of Bolsonabo' sketch was part of a weekly comedy show called *Panic on the TV* (*Pânico na TV*) broadcast by Band TV,

one of Brazil's smaller terrestrial stations. Lúcio, who had mim-
icked Dilma Rousseff and Michel Temer to acclaim, started his
Bolsonabo impression early in 2017. Its aim was clear enough: to
mock Bolsonaro's militarism, poke fun at his sexism and deride his
sons. But according to researchers, the mockery backfired amid the
corruption scandals that damaged the popularity of establishment
figures. Just as candidates were jockeying for position ahead of the
election campaign, the show highlighted Bolsonaro's authenticity. According to Maurício Moura and Juliano Corbellini, the
show played a "critical part" in building Bolsonaro's image and
establishing him as one of the favourites ahead of the election
campaign.[1] By 2018 as many as 20 per cent of those interviewed
said they would vote for Bolsonaro – nearly twice as many as the
previous year. Even so, in early 2018 – and indeed towards the
middle of the year – very few Brazilians thought Bolsonaro could
win. During a brief visit to Brazil in January 2018, I had lunch with
an old contact in São Paulo, a former diplomat who now worked
as an adviser for a number of private companies. He told me
that everything favoured Geraldo Alckmin, the governor of São
Paulo state and the candidate of the Brazilian Social Democratic
Party (PSDB), the pro-business moderate force that had dominated Brazilian politics alongside the left-wing PT for the previous
quarter of a century.

We were in Piselli Sud, a fashionable Italian restaurant in a
luxury shopping mall in the Faria Lima financial district, the near-
est that Brazil has to a Wall Street. Under high hardwood ceilings
and over pasta we chatted about Brazil's slow recovery from recession, the Lava Jato corruption scandal, and how they would affect
Brazilian politics. My friend, a long-time member of the PSDB,
told me that the fears about Bolsonaro were overblown. "Don't
worry. As soon as the campaign gets under way, TV time will
work in our favour." Alckmin might be a bit colourless, my friend
agreed, but he had just negotiated a deal with a number of small
centrist parties and this block would now command the majority

of TV time. And links to powerful state governors would enable the PSDB to exercise considerable influence on voters at a local level. The boss of a big Brazilian bank had told me much the same thing when I'd met him in London a few months earlier. He'd shrugged off my concern about Bolsonaro's buoyant ratings and the possibility that the vote in Brazil might spring a surprise, as had happened in the US with the election of Donald Trump and in the UK with the Brexit vote. And these establishment voices were not alone.

As Jairo Nicolau wrote in the immediate aftermath of Bolsonaro's triumph, "the dominant vision about the election was that it would repeat the pattern of earlier contests".[2] That optimism was partly informed by the fact that the considerable political and economic tumult of 2013–14 had had a limited impact on the country's last presidential contest four years previously, when the PT's Dilma Rousseff secured a narrow victory over her moderate PSDB rival, Aécio Neves. Analysts thought there was a limit to Bolsonaro's potential support because his illiberal views would be anathema to Brazil's middle class and business elite. "I was more sceptical [about the limitations of Bolsonaro's appeal] than my colleagues", wrote Nicolau.

> I thought the political system would be affected by all that had happened and I was well aware of Bolsonaro's popularity. But I thought he'd win no more than 15 to 20 per cent of the vote. It would be like France where support for Bolsonaro – like Marine Le Pen and the Rassemblement National – would be limited to a particular segment of the electorate.[3]

Some fairly solid trends underpinned the consensual view. Since the mid-1990s, Brazil had benefited from remarkable political stability, with the PSDB on the right and the PT on the left forming the core of two sprawling centre-right and centre-left alliances. Both parties had emerged at the end of the 1980s, as Brazil moved back to democratic rule after two decades of military government.

But this stable political landscape was also a very fragmented one, partly because of the 'democratic libertarian' nature of the electoral system. The number of parties competing for Congress had risen from five in 1982, to twelve in 1986, nineteen in 1994, and twenty-eight in 2014. But between the PSDB and the PT, together with the centrist MDB, an axis had formed, around which the parties all turned. The MDB backed the PSDB government of Fernando Henrique Cardoso (1994–2002), and the left-wing administrations of Luiz Inácio Lula da Silva (2002–10) and Dilma Rousseff (2010–16). Indeed, the fact that the three presidents elected in this period had all won second terms in office lent an air of "seeming stability to party politics".[4] Rousseff's impeachment in 2016 had led to a two-year period in which the MDB itself had been in charge, but most observers thought Brazil was sufficiently stable and predictable for the established pattern to resume in 2018.

This stability was beginning to break down, however, at a quicker rate than many people realised. Bolsonaro was isolated and ineffective in Congress, but as controversies continued to swirl through Brazilian society this proved to be an advantage. He was untouched by the wave of financial scandals. The disapproval of fellow legislators and his fleeting relationships with political parties were strengths rather than weaknesses. As Moura and Corbelli argue: "Voters thought he operated on a different plane, simple and more elementary. The fact that Bolsonaro had lived in this corrupt environment for so long – he had been elected for seven separate mandates – was perceived as comprehensive proof of his honesty."[5] While opinion polls showed that Brazil's Congress and political parties were generally disliked, many Brazilians thought favourably of the armed forces. The military's prestige was enhanced during the 2000s as a result of its participation in the Haiti peacekeeping mission and interventions in Brazilian cities, where the armed forces were invited by state governments to support police crackdowns on organised crime.

Style was a pivotal factor. Traditional politicians and analysts might write off Bolsonaro for his lack of sophistication and inconsistencies, but for many socially conservative voters alienated by the marketing spin of the mainstream, the former army captain was a breath of fresh air. Bolsonaro spoke "on another frequency". "His simplicity, grammatical errors and clumsy way of expressing himself were all signs of authenticity. If political discourse is associated with lies and manipulation of the truth Bolsonaro's talk is outstanding for its boorishness, for going straight to the point."[6] Bolsonaro lost his temper in interviews at the drop of a hat and was quick to insult journalists whose outlets he didn't like. "Bolsonaro speaks without filters", wrote one Brazilian commentator. "He's never worried about where the cameras are placed, whether he should be standing up or seated, whether he should button up his shirtsleeves or mention humanitarian groups, whether he should smile or look seriously at other candidates. Authenticity is his biggest and best marketing tool."[7]

Bolsonaro's trademark was the way he shaped his body as if firing a rifle. The stance neatly expressed his radical approach to crime and corruption and reflected his military past, but it was as if he was aiming at the whole of the liberal establishment. It was a visual framing of his position, what marketing specialists would call a meme, which was widely imitated and shared among his supporters and helped give them the sense that that they belonged to an in-group.[8]

The decline in the influence of traditional media

All this was happening at a time of enormous change in Brazil's media industry. Just as elsewhere in the world, the crisis of commercial media in Brazil opened up a space for Bolsonaro's unconventional messages and ideas. Old-fashioned terrestrial television – as my friend in the Italian restaurant had insisted – had traditionally been pivotal to success in Brazilian elections.

But that was changing. Since the 1970s the Globo media empire had established a huge influence over Brazilian minds. Military governments had invested heavily in transmitters and other infrastructure. Millions of people had bought TV sets for the first time, and Globo's mix of melodramatic soap operas known as *telenovelas*, live football matches and an hour-long news bulletin, the *Jornal Nacional*, were widely watched. Everybody, it seemed, structured their evenings around the novela and talked about the latest development the next day. TV shaped social life for millions. At election times, ten-minute election slots funded by the government in proportion to parties' and candidates' presence in Congress were hugely influential.

But during the 2000s audience numbers on the old-fashioned channels began to dip, as the better-off started to pay for cable TV services that offered a wider variety of programming, often from international providers. In addition, younger Brazilians spent more and more time on their phones, increasingly participating in embryonic social media. Between 2000 and 2013 terrestrial television lost 28 per cent of its audience, with the pressure especially acute for Globo, which saw well-funded rivals like Record – owned by the neo-Pentecostal Universal Church of the Kingdom of God – win market share.[9] Television in Brazil remains widely viewed. Recent surveys suggest that Brazilians spend several hours a day watching TV. But commercial pressures were prompting producers to take an increasingly tabloid approach to news coverage. News stories about political swindles and gang killings became more and more prominent, reflecting a growing national preoccupation with violent crime and corruption. Back in 2009 the cut-throat battle for viewers had been highlighted by an extraordinary scandal in the Amazonian city of Manaus, later popularised by the Netflix series, *Killer Ratings* (2019).

The series was a documentary based on the journalist and presenter Wallace Souza. Souza won a loyal and enthusiastic following for his Canal Livre news programme, which featured a combination of dancing girls, puppets and gory real-life crime scenes. Canal Livre's crack reporters were always first on the scene after murders had been committed, bringing live studio audiences graphic pictures of victims. The ratings went through the roof, but after taking testimony from a former policeman who had worked with the channel, police and prosecutors came to believe that Souza himself was ordering many of the murders. The presenter, who had by this time capitalised on his media profile to win a seat in the Amazonas state legislature, was arrested, impeached and imprisoned. He suffered a heart attack and died in 2010, still protesting his innocence.

It was possible that the events at Canal Livre might have been a one-off. But during the 2010s I noticed that corruption and crime stories dominated TV output to an even greater extent than when I had lived in São Paulo between 2002 and 2008. Go into a bar or restaurant or someone's front room and there was a decent chance you would catch an earnest-looking young reporter running through the gory details of some favela killing. Efforts to democratise TV output only seemed to further narrow the editorial focus. For example, a recent Globo series, *O Brasil Que Eu Quero* (*The Brazil That I Want*) offered viewers the chance to make their own 15-second videos about a local issue of their choosing. These invariably reflected the same preoccupations as mainstream news coverage, raising the profile of corruption and violence even further.[10]

Two other factors were in Bolsonaro's favour. In 2018 new rules introduced in the wake of the Lava Jato corruption scandal were imposed to reduce both the amount of spending on political broadcasting and the length of the campaign. Dilma Rousseff and Aécio Neves had spent R$350.25m and R$227m respectively on their 2014 election campaigns, which had begun broadcasting in early July. By contrast, spending for the two leading candidates in 2018 was cut to R$100m and campaigning began a month later. All this further reduced the advantage that the established parties enjoyed through their substantial congressional presence and meant that Bolsonaro was, relatively speaking, in a stronger position.

During the 2010s social media such as YouTube, Facebook, Twitter and especially WhatsApp started to play a much more important role in political debate. Growing use of smartphones was partly responsible for this shift. According to the Brazilian Statistics and Geographical Institute (IBGE), 138 million Brazilians owned mobile phones by 2018, and nearly half used their phones to access the internet. Other research suggested that usage was even higher. The Getúlio Vargas Foundation, a business school and think tank, suggested that more than 220 million smartphones – more than one per person – were being used in Brazil. The same research indicated that Brazilians were on average consulting their smartphones thirty times per day.[11] Facebook and WhatsApp were beginning to dominate the market for news and information. I knew from the make-up of my own Facebook and Twitter followers that Brazilians were early adopters of new technologies, so it wasn't surprising to see how widespread the use of Facebook and YouTube had become in Brazil by the mid-2010s. According to surveys by the Santiago-based pollster Latinbarómetro, 58.8 per cent of Brazilian respondents used Facebook in 2018, up from 42.8 per cent five years earlier.[12] Over the same period, the use of YouTube had risen from 22.6 per cent to 37 per cent. WhatsApp was particularly popular, with 65.9 per cent of Latin Barometer's interviewees using the service in 2018.

Bolsonaro was quick to establish his own social media presence. Much of this was down to his sons, Flávio, Carlos and Eduardo. Carlos seems to have been especially important, setting up the family's Twitter account in 2009 and a family blog a year later. He recruited bright young bloggers such as José Matheus Sales, a student from Ceará who had developed a series of humorous videos about Bolsonaro and had come up with the nickname of Mito (Legend). In 2014 Sales was contracted to over-see the family's social media network, while Bolsonaro's sons established a close connection with Olavo de Carvalho, a contro-versial journalist-cum-philosopher, whose own internet success added momentum to the Bolsonaro campaign.

Olavo de Carvalho's influence

The US-based Carvalho is widely regarded as an intellectual guru of Brazil's new right and is well known for his strident attacks on political correctness, global warming and the liberal world order in general. Over the last decade, he has become something of a fulcrum for the Bolsonaros, so much so that Eduardo Bolsonaro – the youngest of the sons – claimed that victory would have been impossible without him. As Moura and Corbellini described, Carvalho was the "urban legend" who served as something of a "dynamo" for the Bolsonaros' social media operations.[13]

Carvalho's background is unusual. Born in 1947, in his late teens he became an opponent of the military regime and by 1966 was a member of the Communist Party. After just two years Carvalho left the Communist Party and went to university to study psychol-ogy. In the early 1980s he wrote *A imagem do homem na astrologia* (*The Image of Man in Astrology*, 1980) and *Astrologia e religião* (*Astrology and Religion*, 1986). Carvalho became a journalist, writing columns for papers ranging from the *Folha de São Paulo*, one of Brazil's most popular dailies, to the erudite (and now defunct) political monthly, *Primeira Leitura*. By now Carvalho was drifting towards the right. Following the election of Luiz Inácio Lula da Silva, he found him-self increasingly ill at ease in a country that had begun to embrace gun control, quotas in the education system and other progres-sive social changes and where Carvalho perceived a growing lib-eral bias in the media. "All of it made him feel claustrophobic", wrote Terrence McCoy, who interviewed Carvalho in 2019 for the *Washington Post*.[14]

Carvalho moved to the United States in 2005 to work as a correspondent for the *Diário de Comercio*, a little-read Rio de Janeiro-based business daily. It was work that he quickly tired of, and had it not been for the growth of social media, Carvalho might well have then sunk into obscurity. But after settling in a country area south of Richmond, Virginia, he started to offer distance courses in philosophy. Carvalho's ideas attracted the interest of far-right activists, including Bolsonaro's sons. In 2012 Flávio Bolsonaro, the oldest son and a member of the Rio de Janeiro legislature, travelled to Virginia to award Carvalho the Tiradentes medal, the state body's highest distinction. By 2013, as the PT government of Dilma Rousseff began to encounter turbulence, Carvalho's writing and YouTube videos were attracting a powerful niche following, and his book, *O mínimo que você precisa saber para não ser um idiota* (*The Least You Need to Know to not be an Idiot*, 2013) sold more than 300,000 copies. Carvalho's YouTube channel launched in 2015 and steadily built up its audience. Eventually Eduardo Bolsonaro travelled to Virginia to meet him and take personal classes with the teacher who he would later describe as the "greatest living Brazilian philosopher".

Carvalho's ideas are so complex, bizarre and casually offensive that critics frequently don't take them seriously enough. His prolific output of videos, blogs and social media posts are spiked with obscenity and vicious homophobia. His interactions with many mainstream journalists are hostile and seem to be deliberately provocative. Letícia Duarte, a Brazilian journalist who interviewed him in 2019, described the encounter: "He greeted me with a deep frown and wide eyes before pointing at a printout of a recent article I had written and bellowing, 'What the fuck is that?'"[15] Duarte noted that the interview was filmed and set up to expose the journalist's liberal prejudices. In Carvalho's office, an audience had assembled – in almost surreal fashion – to watch the show: "His wife, daughter, and a handful of other relatives and friends sat on a couch behind me, eating Burger King and smoking cigarettes."

During the interview, Carvalho called Duarte a "slut" and at the end of the encounter "his tone suddenly turned solemn: 'I wanted you to know that you disgusted my whole family.' Then it rose again as he stood up and snapped, 'Get out!'"

Carvalho's main argument seems to be that a form of extreme liberalism, a phenomenon that he labels "cultural Marxism", has gradually come to dominate intellectual life both in Brazil and more globally. It is a discourse found in far-right thinking elsewhere, especially in the United States. For Carvalho, liberal policies designed to reduce gender and race inequalities, enshrine the rights of LGBTQ people and tackle the climate crisis are part of a much broader extreme liberal or left-wing strategy. The left, Carvalho argues, has been preparing societies for more radical economic policies by sowing left-wing ideas about culture and expanding its influence across universities, schools and the media. Building on an idea coined in the 1930s by the Italian Marxist Antonio Gramsci, the strategy aims to achieve 'cultural hegemony' as a precondition for winning political power.

The idea is highly contentious. Internationally, this perspective puts George Soros, the Rockefellers, the Council on Foreign Relations, the United Nations and the World Health Organization – as well as liberal leaders like Barack Obama and Angela Merkel – in the same camp as traditional labour movement types, the Chinese Communist Party and the more old-fashioned communist dictatorships still in charge in Cuba and North Korea. Carvalho contends that the liberal alliance in Brazil encompasses the country's entire political establishment, linking political opponents like the liberal former presidents Fernando Henrique Cardoso or the conservative José Sarney with their left-wing successors Lula da Silva and Rousseff. Liberalism is so dominant, Carvalho argues, that conservative ideas have been squeezed out of circulation and politicians are obliged to express themselves in the language of the left, which is at odds with the conservative character of the country. As Brazil's crisis deepened,

Carvalho was seen by many as a prophet or an oracle. "At a time when nobody identified as being right-wing, he was a man on his own and this preaching in the desert brought rewards", wrote Pablo Ortellado.[16] For Brian Winter, the editor of New York-based *Americas Quarterly*, Carvalho was "the only person who saw the apocalypse coming".[17]

Throughout this period, the Bolsonaros maintained regular contact with Carvalho. Even prior to the announcement of his presidential candidacy in 2016, Bolsonaro was a guest at least three times on Carvalho's YouTube channel. A student of one of Carvalho's online courses, Filipe Martins, was recruited to join the family's media team. In 2017, as Bolsonaro's campaign got under way, Eduardo Bolsonaro broadcast a video from Carvalho's house, wearing a T-shirt that read *Olavo tem Razão* (Olavo is Right). Bolsonaro's campaign propaganda targeting the idea of a liberal and left-wing conspiracy was influenced in part by Carvalho's writing. "2018 is the last chance to recover Brazil", began a post on the family blog. "Brazil was taken from us in 1985 and from then until now the same corrupt system has been maintained in power." And later, "Sarney, Collor, Cardoso, Lula, Dilma and Temer all belong to the same criminal ideological group [which] has wrecked our education, our culture, our values, our business and our dignity." Indeed, after the successful outcome, Eduardo conceded that his father "couldn't have won the election without Olavo. Without Olavo, there would be no President Bolsonaro."[18] Olavo's *The Least You Need to Know* was one of four books on Bolsonaro's desk (alongside the Bible, the Brazilian Constitution and Winston Churchill's *Memoirs of the Second World War*) when the newly elected president made his first speech to the nation. "What I want most is to follow God's teachings alongside the Brazilian Constitution", he said. "I also want to be inspired by great leaders, giving good advice."[19]

Bolsonaro's social media rise

By the time he was interviewed by Consuelo Dieguez of *Piauí* in September 2016, Bolsonaro was already something of an internet phenomenon. He was recording one or two videos daily, some of which had been watched more than a million times. Like other less controversial Brazilian YouTube stars, he was acquiring a celebrity status that transcended conventional media or politics. "As he walks down the halls of Congress, he seems less like a Congressman and more like a pop star", wrote Dieguez.

> No matter where he's headed, he's interrupted countless times with requests for photos or videos. Men and women, most of them young, hasten over to express their admiration. Bolsonaro smiles and gives them a thumbs-up – or points his fingers as if he were holding a submachine gun, in what has become his signature gesture.[20]

Over the next two years, his followings on Facebook and YouTube rose steadily. By the end of 2017 he had 4.5 million Facebook followers.[21] By August 2018 that number had risen to nearly six million and by October he had more than eight million followers. "The data for Bolsonaro was incredible", wrote Moura and Corbellini. "By the end of campaigning for the first round of the election, 40,000 WhatsApp groups each with 100 members were pushing out the messages of Bolsonaro's team."[22]

Not only was Bolsonaro's internet presence boosting his presence in the mainstream media, but his TV appearances were helping to drive success online. An interview broadcast on *Roda Viva*, an influential political talk show on TV Cultura, was a case in point.[23] The YouTube stream attracted 228,000 viewers – one of the biggest audiences for any Brazilian political show. The audience equalled the size of that which had watched the congressional proceedings that led to the impeachment of Dilma Rousseff in 2015 and exceeded by 100,000 views an interview with Sérgio Moro, the judge in the Lava Jato case, who had also become something of a celebrity figure on the web. Interviewed by journalists from *Veja, Folha de São Paulo, Valor Econômico* and *O Estado de São Paulo,* Bolsonaro touched on all his most provocative themes, including his plans to abolish racial quotas and his praise for Colonel Carlos Alberto Brilhante Ustra, a former army officer who had been responsible for the torture of dozens of political prisoners during the dictatorship. The political scientist Miguel Lago described how Bolsonaro simply outflanked his interviewers.

> They had been looking for coherent arguments. He responded by turning questions back on the interviewers, by slogans and one-word answers, some clever, others barely formulated […] Bolsonaro was incapable of formulating rational arguments with a beginning, a middle and an end. He only communicated in a fragmented way.

And by using a terrestrial TV show on his online channels, Bolsonaro was also breaking new ground. "He used TV as a way to develop free material for multiple promotional videos."[24]

This came to a head at the beginning of the election campaign, when on the afternoon of 6 September 2019, a political activist very nearly killed him. Bolsonaro was meeting and greeting sup-porters in Juiz de Fora, an industrial city of 500,000 people in the state of Minas Gerais. Wearing a yellow T-shirt printed with *My Party is Brazil,* Bolsonaro was being carried shoulder high when a fist reached out and drove a kitchen knife into his stomach. Within half an hour of the attack, Bolsonaro was in hospital and his son Flávio had tweeted details of the incident. By 6 p.m., with Bolsonaro undergoing emergency surgery in intensive care, news of the incident was going viral. Outraged supporters expressed their anger as part of an "unprecedented" online response.[25] The hashtag #ForçaBolsonaro had received two million mentions by early evening.

Physically, Bolsonaro suffered badly. The knife had done so much damage that for many months after the attack he had to wear a colostomy bag. But the attack brought him multiple political benefits. Opponents were obliged to soften their criticism of him and condemn the attacker, Adélio Bispo de Oliveira, a 40-year-old bricklayer, who claimed that his motive was personal. However, Bispo de Oliveira had been a member of the far-left Socialism and Liberty Party (PSOL) until four years previously. The attack made many Brazilians more sympathetic to Bolsonaro than they otherwise would have been. More importantly still, it made him too weak to take part in formal presidential debates – where his inability to present coherent arguments might have left him vulnerable. As Moura and Corbellini argue, "Bolsonaro left the real world to inhabit the digital one. The attacker took him away from formal presentations and debates and put him in the centre of social media. He was in his comfort zone."[26]

A few weeks later, Bolsonaro won the 2018 election, scoring a decisive victory in a run-off against Fernando Haddad, the candidate of the PT. It amounted to a stunning rise for someone who had been at the margins of the political system for so long, and an equally extraordinary fall from grace for the PT. To understand why things went wrong for the PT, we must return to 2010, when an enormously successful President Luiz Inácio Lula da Silva left office and handed over to his hand-picked successor, Dilma Rousseff. Brazil was living – as Lula never failed to remind people – in a 'magic moment'.

3

THE MAGIC MOMENT

A bullet train whizzes passengers from São Paulo to Rio in less than two hours. Formerly harassed air travellers move effortlessly through shiny new terminals. Where once they left squalid favelas to battle for hours through gridlocked traffic, city commuters set out from brand new flats and houses on fast-flowing buses and metros. Soya from the central plateau glides by barge and train to efficient new ports in the North East instead of tumbling down pot-holed roads to overcrowded ones in the south. The country hums to half a million megawatts coursing through its integrated grid and the whole show is paid for by oil gushing up to multi-tentacled production platforms from miles below the surface of the sun-kissed south Atlantic.[1]

This was a utopian vision sketched out in the *Financial Times* in 2010, but at the time it didn't seem too far from reality. At the end of a decade, Brazil seemed to be making incredible progress in overcoming its historic difficulties. The hyperinflation that had dogged the country throughout the 1980s and early 1990s had been vanquished, and supported by a dramatic increase in demand from China, Brazil was flush with dollars and building up a deep cushion of international reserves. Social and economic inequalities had been reduced and millions of Brazilians were starting to buy smartphones, cars and overseas holidays.

Alongside China, Russia, India and South Africa, Brazil was one of the large emerging economies whose dynamism was supposedly changing the shape of the global economy. Foreign companies were queuing up to sign deals, with direct investment inflows rising from $10.1bn in 2003, to $44.5bn in 2007 and $101.1bn in 2011. At the end of April 2008 Brazil had been awarded investment grade status by Standard & Poor's, a credit rating agency whose approval effectively opened up Brazil to a much wider group of pension fund and big insurance companies, increasing potential demand for the country's bonds and significantly reducing its potential borrowing costs.[2] "It means Brazil was declared a serious country with serious policies and that it manages its finances seriously and that therefore we deserve international confidence", said President Luiz Inácio Lula da Silva, who left office with his popularity ratings in the stratosphere. In a poll conducted by the Datafolha agency in December 2010, 83 per cent of interviewees considered he had done "a good or excellent" job.[3]

During the summer of 2008, when the bankruptcy of the giant US investment bank Lehman Brothers triggered a global financial crisis, Brazil's economy – like those of other emerging market countries – stumbled. But buoyed by the resilience of China, by then one of its largest trading partners, Brazil was soon back on track. Lula minimised the impact, claiming at a time when many Europeans and Americans still feared for their savings that the crisis might have been a tsunami in the United States, but in Brazil it was no more than "a little wave". Adding to the sense of potential was the dawning reality that Brazil was about to become an oil power. In 2006 an exploration team from the state-owned Petrobras had struck oil at the Tupi field offshore from Rio de Janeiro. The oil was hard to get at. It lay deep in the sea below a layer of salt and rocks and it would be expensive to exploit. But it was plentiful, and every time a well was drilled, oil was struck. A government official estimated in 2008 that reserves could amount to between 60bn and 100bn barrels. Brazil could have as much oil as Kuwait and more than established players such as

Russia or Nigeria. Ministers were soon talking about joining the Organization of the Petroleum Exporting Countries. The financial markets were euphoric with optimism, neatly symbolised by the *Economist*'s iconic "Brazil Takes Off" cover, which depicted the Christ the Redeemer statue in Rio de Janeiro as a rocket being launched into the sky.[4] The country's left-wing leaders were giddy with their own sense of achievement. In June 2009 Luciano Coutinho, the president of the state-owned Brazilian Development Bank, praised the president's "strategic vision" and referred to Lula as "the great helmsman".

Lula never missed an opportunity to talk about Brazil's 'magic moment'. In October 2010, donning an oil worker's fluorescent jacket over his smart shirt and tie, Lula visited Brazil's stock exchange to celebrate the successful sale of shares in Petrobras.

> Who could have imagined that I would come today to the stock exchange and hear what I have heard. This could only be a gift of God because ten years ago when I came through these doors people would tremble with fear and ask: where is this 'destroyer of capitalism' going? After eight years in the presidency this same 'destroyer of capitalism' has participated in an honourable way in the most auspicious moment of world capitalism.[5]

As Brazil prepared for the 2010 election, Lula was ebullient. The success of the country's bids to host the 2014 World Cup and 2016 Olympic Games were seen as markers of Brazil's status as a global power. Brazilian diplomats were at the helm of the World Trade Organization and the UN's Food and Agriculture Organization. The Brazilian army had led a peacekeeping mission in Haiti.

Lula spent his last months in office talking up Brazil's achievements. He tried to persuade sceptical world leaders that a $20bn bullet train project designed to link the country's two biggest cities would become reality. During a speech to an audience of bankers and policymakers at the Waldorf Astoria in New York, where the Woodrow Wilson Center awarded Lula its prize for public service, the president went out of his way to thank Eike Batista for supporting the government's infrastructure drive. During Lula's time in office, Batista, a former gold trader with a taste for flashy cars and an expensive lifestyle, had raised billions of dollars for a series of mining, oil, port and shipbuilding projects. By 2010 he was one of the richest men in the world, his fortune emblematic of Brazil's new international status. Yet within less than four years, this 'magic moment' had turned sour. Brazil had woken up from its dream of grandeur. By 2013 Batista was bankrupt.[6] Like innumerable other infrastructure schemes, the bullet train was bogged down in a tangle of bureaucratic, regulatory and financial obstacles. And five years later the "great helmsman" himself was in prison.

In retrospect, it seems obvious that the foundations of Brazil's transformation were too fragile for these positive changes to be sustained. At the time, though, it didn't seem so evident. By the time Lula left office in 2010, Brazil was a very different country to the one that had emerged from military dictatorship in 1985. Three fundamental economic changes had occurred that seemed to be well rooted. First, the changes that Fernando Henrique Cardoso forced through in 1994 – as finance minister in the government of Itamar Franco and then as president for two terms for the PSDB – had finally brought inflation in Brazil under control. Second, China's opening up to the international economy from the late 1990s and the breakneck growth of its cities and infrastructure had triggered a huge demand for Brazil's minerals and agricultural commodities and a dramatic rise in its exports. Third, Lula had begun to successfully extend the fruits of this stability and growth. As a result, during the 2000s, millions of Brazilians emerged from poverty and started to spend money in the consumer economy for the first time. By 2010 Henrique Meirelles, a former banker who had managed the central bank during Lula's two terms in office, was able to claim that Brazil was "gradually overcoming our vulnerability to crisis".[7]

Low inflation

It is hard to exaggerate how intractable inflation used to seem in Latin America. When I first started to write about the region in the 1980s, country after country seemed to be forever scrapping their currencies and launching one rescue plan after another in order to change expectations and reduce the rate of price increases to manageable levels. High public-sector and trade deficits were generally part of the problem. Governments frequently spent more money than they raised and made up the gap by borrowing or simply printing money. External deficits were another major bugbear. During the 1980s the prices of most Latin American commodity exports were relatively low. Most countries in the region struggled with persistent trade and current account deficits, and after oil prices and interest rates rose sharply in the early 1980s, almost every large economy defaulted on its external debts, a development that made it either very expensive to borrow or entirely ruled out contracting foreign loans or raising money on international capital markets.

Brazil was forced to reschedule its foreign debts in 1983, lost access to international capital markets for several years, and for nearly two decades struggled with its external accounts. Every time the economy grew, it had to import more. In turn, this increased the trade gap, depressing the local currency, increasing the prices of imported goods and adding to inflationary pressures. As prices increased, the central bank raised interest rates and borrowing costs, which further depressed growth. Fiscal problems were also acute. Between 1981 and 1994 the annual average fiscal deficit amounted to 5.5 per cent of GDP. The central bank covered much of this essentially by printing money, contributing to chronic monetary instability.[8] Brazil seemed to be trapped. The country's economic growth was – as economists used to say at the time – like the flight of a chicken. It would take off and sustain its flight only briefly, before crashing back to earth.

During the 1980s the country had become extremely skilled at living with high inflation. Annual percentage price rises were in two digits and more usually in three digits until 1994, so accountants developed special techniques to help companies adapt to constant increases. Businesses spent an inordinate amount of time recalculating prices. Supermarket checkers changed the stickers on items sometimes more than once a day. The wages of workers with formal jobs with the government or larger companies were linked to rising prices through elaborate systems of indexation. My wife worked as a secondary school teacher in Salvador during the second half of the 1980s. Over a three-year period, her labour card shows that not only was the amount of her salary adjusted every month in line with inflation, but the currency it was paid in changed three times, as one failed counter-inflation plan replaced another.[9]

All this changed in 1994, when Fernando Henrique Cardoso piloted the Real Plan, a complex monetary and fiscal reform that tied a newly created currency to the US dollar. Unlike previous plans, Cardoso's took more serious action to reduce deficits, although it wasn't until after another foreign exchange crisis in 1999 that Brazil was able to finalise this reform, with the approval of a fiscal responsibility law that imposed rigid spending constraints on local as well as national governments, forcing governments to review spending regularly and reduce spending in the event of a shortfall. Lula and his left-wing Workers' Party had opposed the reforms, arguing that trade unions and especially public-sector workers were being made to pay the price for the counter-inflationary adjustment. As late as December 2001 the PT approved a document calling for "a necessary rupture with the neo-liberal model" and the International Monetary Fund, and the nationalisation of the banks. It was hardly surprising that investors initially took fright at the prospect – indicated by opinion polls – that Lula was likely to win the 2002 presidential election.[10]

Having lost three previous elections, however, Lula was beginning to rethink his earlier belief about the need for a radical break
with financial markets. Convinced that the country's poor and
the particularly large informal sector had benefited from the fall
in inflation and the gradual increase in popular consumption,
Lula issued a letter to the Brazilian people, arguing that just as
Brazil had changed, so had he: "Stability and control of the public
accounts and of inflation are today the patrimony of all Brazilians",
explained Lula.[11] Despite this, Brazil lived through some turbulent
months, being forced in August – as the presidential election campaign was starting – to negotiate an IMF bailout package to shore
up its battered currency and financial markets.

Once elected, Lula backed up his commitment to stability
by appointing Henrique Meirelles, a banker who had contested
the election as a candidate for a senatorial seat for Cardoso's
PSDB party, to the central bank. The incoming finance minister,
Antônio Palocci, appointed a series of 'market-friendly' techno-
crats to advise him. Palocci had been a Trotskyist in his youth,
but as a mayor of the city of Ribeirão Preto he had become much
more pragmatic, opting to privatise services. Now in government,
he immediately took steps to limit the generous benefits paid to
public-sector pensioners and pursued generally tight fiscal policies.
These market-friendly policies prompted some left-wing dissidents
to quit the party and form a new organisation of the left, but
investors were delighted. By 2004 the new government's "commitment to economic stability and reform had become clear".[12]

The China dividend

With the threat of economic mismanagement fading, two other
changes boosted business confidence. From the late 1980s onwards
China had grown increasingly quickly, with government investment programmes stimulating rapid growth of the country's
cities. China had already reduced its tariff levels in the 1990s, but

after it was formally admitted to the World Trade Organization in December 2001, trade relations became increasingly open.[13] Chinese manufacturing exports to Latin America surged, placing increased pressure on local manufacturers in countries such as Mexico. But for Brazil, the key trend was the way China's breakneck industrialisation and urbanisation absorbed raw materials. Soya beans were needed to provide the animal feed necessary if local pork and chicken producers were to satisfy the newly urbanised population's demand for meat. Growing local production of steel girders and sheets – needed for the construction and manufacturing industries – led to sharp rises in shipments of iron ore. Chinese industry had a seemingly limitless thirst for oil. By 2011 exports to China, which had generated only $5.2bn when Lula took office, were worth $46.5bn.

The rise in demand for these and other commodities was so great that it helped stoke a boom in commodity prices. Prices had been depressed in the 1980s and 1990s, but from 2000 they started to increase. Between the time Lula took office in 2003 and Dilma Rousseff's succession in 2011, the IMF's commodity price index almost tripled. For all South American commodity-exporting countries, this represented a major shift. Countries such as Argentina (a large exporter of grains and soya beans), copper producers such as Peru and Chile and oil giants such as Venezuela began to benefit from trade surpluses, rather than the deficits that had been typical in the 1980s and 1990s. For Brazil and President Lula, the boom was unparalleled. "It was", as the authors of one of the best books on the country's recent economic history put it, "a dream scenario. Whatever you produced you kept selling more and prices got higher and higher."[14]

Brazil was already the world's second largest producer of soya and a major agricultural power, among the world's top producers of beef, chicken, pork, coffee and sugar. Since the 1970s the Embrapa government research institute had been developing new agricultural techniques that had allowed Brazil to expand the cultivation of many crops away from traditional centres in the south and south-east, to the vast tropical savannah dry lands of the centre-west and north-east, areas known as the Cerrado. Today, varieties of soya bean and coffee have been genetically modified so that they are more resistant to drought. Between 1990 and 2010 the land devoted to agriculture expanded by about a third, while yields also rose, increasing the benefits for farmers.[15] Soya prices by 2011 were more than twice as high as they had been eight years previously.

Sales of iron ore – the other large export to China during this period – rose even more dramatically. After hovering between $10 and $14 per ton for the previous twenty years, prices rose by more than fifteen times in the 2000s. As Chinese steel producers sought to secure the supply of raw materials, this was a golden time for Brazilian iron ore miners such as Vale, the state-owned company that had been privatised in the 1990s. When I visited Carajas in 2007, an endless stream of monster Caterpillar tractors were working round the clock, slowly circling the giant open pit mines that had been carved out of the Amazon jungle thirty years earlier.

Piles and piles of the rusty red ore found their way by mechanical line, hopper and railway wagon to the port of São Luís, where it was shipped in giant bulk carriers to China. As a Vale executive told me at the time, it was as if a giant conveyor belt had been built over the sea. The company was racing to fulfil orders. Demand had increased tenfold between 1997 and 2007, and shortages of parts, equipment and skilled labour were a constant issue. At the plant, messages on an electronic board exhorted workers to greater efforts: "It will be a historic moment. Only 36.8 million tons until our first billion." Vale's encouragements lent an epic quality to the effort, conjuring comparisons with the Soviet industrialisation of the 1930s. The company had hunted high and low to find workers, and many of the new employees were women, unfamiliar with the rigours of the industrial world. Leudiani Vasconcellos, who was 25 at the time and had been working in a shop, now patrolled the machines that separated rough lump ore from finer material called sinter. The seven-foot-high wheels of the giant digger she had learned to drive dwarfed 26-year-old Vanessa Mara. She had been an office receptionist five months before. "My friends say I must really be gutsy to drive this, but it is easier than handling a car. You just have to keep to the procedures. My mum runs a hairdresser and she is very proud of me."[16]

Another trend was helping to strengthen Brazil's trading. Stability and investment had improved the productivity of several manufacturing industries. In the early 2000s, in sectors ranging from transport to aviation, food and fashion, Brazilian executives began to talk enthusiastically about the country's export potential. Marcopolo, a bus manufacturer based in Rio Grande do Sul, was limited to its domestic market until the 1990s, but was now selling specially made vehicles as far afield as Saudi Arabia and Mexico. Meanwhile Embraer, a loss-making state aerospace company privatised in 1994, had by 2004 captured an estimated 40 per cent share of the regional jet market, becoming one of the few emerging market competitors in the high-technology aerospace industry. Embraer anticipated growing international demand for smaller jet airliners that flew shorter distances more efficiently. When I met him in 2004, Jorge Gerdau, the then 67-year-old president of the Gerdau steel company, was, after half a century at the heart of Brazilian industry, more confident than ever. "This is not Brazil's first attempt to become an export power", he told me. "But it is the most promising."[17] The result was several years of growing trade surpluses.[18] Foreign reserves had been more or less exhausted during the 1980s, but they gradually built up after the Real Plan and then – as the trade bonanza continued in the second half of the 2000s – they surged to more than $300bn. Brazil, which had repeatedly looked to the IMF for financial help during the 1980s and 1990s, repaid its obligations to the Fund.

When I interviewed him in 2006, Lula da Silva talked a lot about this combination of economic stability and trade growth. He had grown up on a farm in rural Pernambuco in the northeast, and in the early 1950s made the long trip to São Paulo with his mother and brothers on the back of a lorry. During his teens, Lula had sold oranges and peanuts at the port of Santos, before working in the motor plants and other factories of the southern ABC periphery of São Paulo (Santo André, São Bernardo and São Caetano) as a lathe operator. Lula became a trade unionist and eventually led the giant metalworkers' union, before becoming a founder of the PT in 1980. He was outspoken in his demands for fairer deals for poorer people and poorer countries, and he may have been speaking ironically when he told the *Financial Times* in 2006 that "we can only spend what we have. We don't spend for others to pay. If we need to increase our [budget] surplus, we will do so. I learnt when I was young that when you take on a debt, you pay it. So we have taken on the commitment of honouring our debts." Equally though, his experience as a union leader had taught him the importance of low prices and stability. "Controlling inflation is no small thing in a country like Brazil. [But] we understand that controlling inflation is a real gain for the workers. Controlling inflation means higher salaries for the part of this country that works."[19]

Critics would claim that Lula had been lucky. During the 1990s his party had opposed both the Real Plan and the subsequent rounds of fiscal austerity that had eventually vanquished inflation. The trade boom – from which his government benefited – was mainly a result of China's own growth and opening to world markets, and the neat fit between this and Brazil's agricultural, mineral and oil wealth was pure coincidence. But Lula did make a difference on one issue. Through a series of social and economic policies – including innovative social welfare payments, a major expansion in the availability of credit, and a large increase in jobs and subsidies that helped poorer Brazilians gain access to further education – Lula's government paved the way for a dramatic change in the living standards of the least well-off.

The consumer boom

On the international stage, Lula is best-known for his Bolsa Familia (family grant) social programme. Like his famed economic stabilisation policies, the grant was initiated by his main political opponent, Fernando Henrique Cardoso. Cardoso's wife Ruth, a sociologist like her husband, had come up with the idea of linking a social payment to families who ensured that their children attended school. Lula's first foray into social policy didn't quite work. Under the so-called Zero Hunger Initiative, the government launched "an old-fashioned and inefficient scheme for food stamps".[20] After a few months in office, Lula and his team changed tack, opting to mould the previous government's welfare plans into one single payment to poor families with children, with receipt dependent on school and clinic attendance and payment made directly to mothers. The most important element of Lula's family grant programme was that the payment was made to many more people. Under Cardoso, only three million families had received the payment. Under Lula, there was a fourfold increase in the number of recipients, with thirteen million families benefiting under the scheme. Today, fifteen million families receive a Bolsa Familia payment.

Lula's government also increased the minimum wage much more generously than his predecessor. When Lula took office, the minimum wage was enough to buy 1.3 *cestas básicas*, a basic monthly basket of food for a family of four. Four years later, it bought 2.3 of these baskets. The government expanded the number of jobs in the formal sector, partly by increasing public employment. In addition, it made it harder for large companies to avoid paying tax and social contributions. The labour card, which gave workers access to various social benefits, was becoming something of a defining feature of the PT government, as Brazil formalised its labour force. Between 2003 and 2014 the percentage of the workforce with labour cards rose by 10 per cent to 51 per cent.

It wasn't just about income though. Another crucial change was the way that poorer Brazilians were able to borrow. Late in 2004 legislation was introduced to allow lenders to deduct repayments for loans directly from wages. As the economy began to grow more rapidly, retailers became braver about extending credit. Just as working-class Europeans had bought their first TV sets and refrigerators on hire-purchase during the 1950s and 1960s, Brazilians stretched out payments for expensive items such as flatscreen TVs and mobile phones. While covering the presidential campaign in the north-east, ahead of the 2006 election, I met dozens of Brazilians who had benefited from these changes. "Before, it was much more difficult to get credit", Helenita Santana, who was earning R$350 a month as a domestic servant for a middle-class family in Salvador, told me. In the previous two years Santana had bought a new television, a DVD player and a refrigerator from Insinuante, a local chain of household goods stores.[21]

By the mid-2000s these changes were beginning to affect the pattern of wealth distribution. Brazil has always been an unequal society, with a small number of wealthy people, a larger number of relatively well-off middle-class people, and vast quantities of poor people. Represented visually, the income pyramid resembled an isosceles triangle: squat at the base with its two equal sides. In the 2000s Brazil's income pyramid began to bulge in the middle, as the poor acquired more spending power. Brazil's national statistics agency, which monitors these matters in great detail, divides the population into five income bands: A, B, C, D and E, with A being the wealthiest and E the poorest. By 2010, 35.7 million people had become upwardly mobile, mainly into the so-called class C (families in an income band that in 2019 received between R$1,892.65

and R$8,159.37) and the number of people in the lowest D and E income categories had fallen by 23 million. Throughout this period, Brazil's traditionally very high rates of inequality began to gradually diminish, as the Gini coefficient, which measures the relationship between the richest and the poorest in society, fell from 0.594 in 2001 to 0.497 in 2014, where 1 represents maximum inequality.

By European or North American standards, the growing middle-income group – class C – is not particularly wealthy, but unlike their poorer neighbours, individuals in this economic category started to buy consumer goods, better-quality or branded food from supermarkets or shopping malls, mobile phones, flatscreen TVs and cars on credit. By 2010 the growth in Brazilian demand was attracting international interest, as large companies in sectors ranging from cars to cold cures, and shampoos to sound systems, started to invest. Just ten or fifteen years earlier, international companies such as Procter & Gamble or Unilever had tended to see only about 20 per cent of Brazil's population – around 40 million people – as potential customers. As class C's purchasing power increased, so did the market and potential sales; as many as 140 million Brazilians were now consumers. With sales in mature markets such as the US or the UK already fairly saturated, Brazil (like its fellow BRICS – China, India, Russia and South Africa) became a hugely attractive source of business.

Cultural factors made some sectors especially attractive. By 2011 I had returned from Brazil to London to head up a *Financial Times* research publication called *Brazil Confidential*, which looked in detail at the investment opportunities that Brazil seemed to offer. Frequently, the exaggerated spending of Brazilians surprised us. As part of our research into the local cosmetics market, we found that in 2011, Brazil boasted a beauty salon for every fifty women aged 15 or over, accounting for 11 per cent of the total worldwide spending on cosmetics, up from only 4 per cent in 2004. Our reporters found dozens of examples of Brazilians prepared to spend astounding amounts on cosmetics and beauty treatments: people like Marlene Torreno, a retired nurse, who spent R$130 of her monthly household income of R$1,000 on hair and beauty products, or Eliete Rocha, a 29-year-old car park attendant – earning about the same – who routinely spent R$100 per month on branded sun lotion, lipstick and face creams. Brazilians were spending so much on over-the-counter medicines that retail pharmacies started to crop up on virtually every street corner. Hairdressers, beauty salons and gyms all expanded on the rising tide of retail demand. Clinics offering depilation or plastic surgery were also benefiting from this obsession with the body.[22] In 2011 more than 900,000 plastic surgery operations were carried out in Brazil, a number second only to the United States. New class C customers were a key factor in the increase in procedures, which were up nearly fivefold since 2001.

Poorer Brazilians also started to travel more during the 2000s. Many of the poorest residents of low-income areas of São Paulo or Rio de Janeiro had family connections in the poorer north or north-east, but trips back to visit elderly relatives almost invariably involved an arduous two- or three-day bus journey, since passenger trains are effectively non-existent in Brazil. Routinely until the early 2000s, flights between regional capitals were only 60 per cent full, owing to only wealthy Brazilians being able to afford air travel. From 2005 onwards, however, growing numbers of Brazilians used their greater spending power to take to the skies. Confident that tickets would eventually be paid for, airlines offered customers the chance to pay for flights in instalments, with consumers often spreading the cost of a $300 or $400 ticket over many months. "We saw a new type of consumer", noted an industry survey in 2012.[23] Flying domestically in Brazil during this period, you would often see first-time flyers looking around in puzzlement as they boarded a flight. Between 2002 and 2012 the number of air passengers had risen by 180 per cent. By 2013 aircraft were flying on average at 80 per cent capacity. Package holiday companies started to do a roaring trade and travel agencies could be found in the most unlikely spots. The agency in Rocinha, a favela in the south of Rio de Janeiro, noted that 90 per cent of its customers were taking flights to visit family in Paraíba, Ceará or Bahia.

More Brazilians were travelling abroad as well. The trade and investment boom had strengthened the value of the real so much that it was suddenly possible for many people to visit North America, Europe or neighbouring Latin American countries, very often for the first time, even if they had to pay in instalments to do so. Spending on foreign travel had amounted to $2.2bn in 2003. By 2008 Brazilians were spending $10.9bn on trips abroad, and by 2013, $25bn.

Many Brazilians also chose to spend more money on education. Brazil's education system is well funded and its high-quality federal universities are essentially free; however, demand for places is high and the *vestibular* (entrance exam) is tough. Pass rates are much higher among middle-class children, whose parents can afford private secondary school education. It is hard for those dependent on the deficient public schools to compete, and many end up studying at private universities, for which they have to pay. Lula's government eased the burden by offering a series of subsidies and loans, but education still absorbed a large part of lower-class incomes.[24]

The overall effect of all these changes on the lives of poor Brazilians was becoming evident. I remember interviewing 25-year-old Edilma Silva in the late 2000s. Silva worked as a manicurist near Jardims, a middle-class suburb of São Paulo, and the demands on the R$3,000 that she and her partner Neno brought home each month were considerable: school fees, health insurance, bills for two mobile phones, regular monthly payments for a new Fiat Palio bought the previous year and an occasional evening out sipping a caipirinha cocktail or two at the local dance hall. But Silva was delighted with her lot, which she said had changed beyond all recognition since she left her home in the rural northeast in the mid-1990s. "There are many more options, many more opportunities", she said, "now I am much more independent and have so much more self-esteem."

In 2010 the exuberant consumerist mood was brilliantly captured by two documentary film-makers, Dorrit Harazim and Arthur Fontes, in *Família Braz Dois Tempos* (*The Braz Family: Two Phases*). Back in 2000, Harazim and Fontes had met Toninho and Maria Braz and their four teenage children – Anderson, Denize, Gisele and Eder – and shot a film about their lives in Brasilândia, a low-income suburb in north-west São Paulo. The family had been struggling in 2000. Toninho worked as a plumber and found work on construction sites, while Maria spent most of her days cleaning and cooking for the family. Maria was fearful about leaving the neighbourhood and the older children lacked the money to go to university. Their oldest son, Anderson, then in his early 20s, talked wistfully about travelling to Italy and Greece, but didn't have a passport. Denize was making a living handing out leaflets outside an optician's shop; Eder was an office boy at a pharmacy.

Ten years later, things were quite different. Toninho and Maria had built new rooms on to their house, a tumbledown affair made from bricks and concrete blocks. Toninho was busy at the construction sites springing up all around the city. Maria was more assured than she had been: "Today I see São Paulo differently. I've begun to glimpse [life's possibilities]." Maria explained that her new outlook was largely because her children had begun to thrive on the new opportunities opened up by Brazil's expansion. The two eldest, Anderson and Denize, both had good jobs in the sales departments of expanding local companies. Eder, after a spell as what Brazilians call a motoboy (a motorcycle messenger), had successfully trained as a radiologist and worked in a clinic. Gisele was studying to be a teacher at one of the private universities. Most significantly, perhaps, all the children were car owners. Anderson, who had moved with his wife to an apartment in a leafier suburb nearby, said he had already changed his car twice, but that most of his neighbours switched their vehicles every year.

Work-related bonuses had allowed Anderson and Denize to take flights for the first time and enjoy cruise holidays. Denize had won tickets for a show and taken her parents to see *My Fair Lady* at a theatre in downtown São Paulo, experiencing the "kind of culture that I couldn't have afforded before". Her starry-eyed father still couldn't believe that such an experience had been possible. "When we left the theatre at one in the morning I was grinning from ear to ear", he said.

4

DILMA ROUSSEFF AND THE ROCKY ROAD TO RECESSION

There was torrential rain in Brasília when Dilma Rousseff was inaugurated as president on 1 January 2011. But the mood in Brazil's capital was upbeat, as the country's first ever woman president arrived at the National Congress building in a 1952 Rolls Royce Silver Wraith with her daughter Paula next to her and an all-female security detail jogging alongside. Rousseff had been elected with the blessing of Lula, the man who had left office as Brazil's most popular leader of modern times. On the surface, Rousseff seemed to be exactly the leader that Brazil needed. After the showmanship and panache of the Lula years, Rousseff promised hard work and efficient management. While Lula relied on his advisers, Rousseff liked to be on top of the detail herself.

There was no shortage of challenges ahead for the new leader. In the run-up to the 2010 elections spending had escalated and there were now fears that Brazil's economy, which had grown by 7.4 per cent during the previous year, was overheating. Social provision in many areas remained poor. Brazil's inadequate roads, ports and railways had been exposed by the commodity boom. But Rousseff knew that change was needed, and within weeks she had cut a planned expansion in current spending. Her aim was to restore discipline to government accounts, bring rising deficits under control and enable the central bank to reduce interest rates. Lower rates would mean lower borrowing costs and allow businesses to invest more and grow faster.

I watched all this from London where the *Financial Times* was launching the first editions of *Brazil Confidential*. Many of our sources in the financial markets were reasonably confident about the government's prospects, even though Brazil's stock market had drifted lower in the first few months of the year. The appointment of Antônio Palocci, the market-friendly finance minister of Lula's first term, as Rousseff's chief of staff seemed to be a reassuring move. A report from one of the investment banks had welcomed the cuts in spending, labelling the new Brazilian leader 'Tropical Maggie' in allusion to former British Prime Minister Margaret Thatcher, well known for her privatising governments of the 1980s. The comparison was a stretch. The biographies of the two leaders could not have been more different. Thatcher's father was a grocer and a Conservative mayor of Grantham, a rural market town, and Rousseff was the daughter of a Bulgarian Communist Party member who had arrived in Brazil in the late 1930s. While Thatcher spent her teenage years studying to take a degree in chemistry at Oxford, Rousseff became a Trotskyist activist at 16, later joining a group that eventually became part of Carlos Lamarca's guerrilla organisation, the Popular Revolutionary Vanguard.

At the beginning of 1969 in her early 20s, she had briefly been sent abroad (possibly to Cuba or Algeria) to learn how to use a gun. While Bolsonaro was helping the military track down Lamarca and his comrades near Eldorado, Rousseff ran political education classes and oversaw her group's financial and military logistics. Her status was such that when she was captured early in 1970, military prosecutors described her as the 'Joan of Arc' of the guerrilla movement. While Thatcher was a great fan and personal friend of Chile's President Augusto Pinochet, a man responsible for some of the worst human rights abuses in Latin American history, Rousseff was herself a victim of torture. Early in 1970 she was picked up by security police and held at the notorious Doi-Codi (Department of Information Operations – Center for Internal Defense Operations) detention centre in São Paulo. Like many of Brazil's political detainees, Rousseff was suspended from a device known as the 'parrot's perch', savagely beaten and electrocuted.[1]

Rousseff spent three years in prison, at great expense to her health. After her release she settled in Porto Alegre in the state of Rio Grande do Sul, where her husband and fellow guerrilla leader, Carlos Araújo, was serving the final months of his own jail term. On his release, the couple returned to politics, but this time as part of the democratic left. Araújo successfully stood as a state deputy for the Democratic Labour Party, a reformist party associated with João Goulart (the leader deposed in the 1964 coup) and the populist trade unionist Leonel Brizola. After a series of positions in state-funded economics institutes, Rousseff began to advise the party's legislators. By 2001 she was running energy policy for the state government and had moved to the Workers' Party in order to support the governorship campaign of Tarso Genro, a PT left-winger.

Rousseff was gaining a reputation as a practical realist, a doer rather than a talker, who was happy to work with business. The state of Rio Grande do Sul had escaped unscathed, for example, when Brazil was hit by devastating blackouts in 2001. At meetings called to discuss the PT's energy policy in 2001 and 2002, Lula was impressed by Rousseff's commitment and understanding of technical issues and detail. During the transition, Rousseff won plaudits from outgoing ministers in the Cardoso government. "She was pragmatic, objective and showed she enjoyed good and fluid relations with the private sector", said Pedro Parente, Cardoso's chief of staff, who presided over the team set up to manage the two-month handover period.[2]

With the PT in government, Rousseff's rise was meteoric. Lula was taken by her competence and eye for detail. He ignored the claims of qualified academics and asked her to take over the mines and energy ministry, where she cemented her reputation for prudent planning. Palocci, the finance minister, was impressed that she got on with business. One senior businessman told Maklouf Carvalho that "she liked to learn. Sometimes she even asked me for my notes."[3] During the mid-2000s Rousseff's reputation was advanced by another quality: loyalty. A corruption crisis had rocked the PT in 2005, when it was discovered that it had used state funds to buy votes from deputies of allied parties in the legislature. Lula's chief of staff, José Dirceu, lost his job as a result of the crisis, and Lula himself came under pressure, inviting Rousseff to take over from Dirceu. Palocci, the other heavyweight in Lula's administration, had also been ousted in a corruption scandal, and Rousseff became the heir apparent. Her victory in 2010 was emphatic. She was beginning to leave her own stamp on government, enacting changes that would eventually lead to a radical change in direction for Brazil.

Rousseff changes gear

Economic stability and the defeat of hyperinflation had been pivotal to Brazil's successes since the late 1990s. Underpinning the approach of both Cardoso and Lula had been a trio of policies, known in Brazil as the *tripé* (tripod). First, the exchange rate, which had been tied to the dollar during the early stages of the Real Plan, was allowed to float freely in line with supply and demand. Second, the government would commit to a primary fiscal surplus, allowing it to comfortably make interest payments on its debt without increasing overall indebtedness. Third, it would establish targets for inflation and agree to make adjustments to interest rates in order to meet these commitments. If prices were rising towards the limit of a targeted range, the central bank's monetary council would increase interest rates at its monthly meetings. If prices were lower than expected, policymakers would be free to reduce rates to stimulate economic activity.

The tripod had provided a degree of predictability about government economic policy that had been reassuring for investors. But since the late 2000s stability had been accompanied by trends that were damaging the economy as a whole and undermining its growth potential. Buoyed by the commodity boom and huge inflows of direct investment, the real had strengthened to such a point that it was damaging some sectors. By late 2010 São Paulo had become a very expensive city. In October of that year, as I prepared for the launch of the *Brazil Confidential* publication, I remember meeting a contact and paying the equivalent of £400 for a modest dinner for two at a Portuguese restaurant in São Paulo. Costs were so high that we decided it would be impossible to set up an office in the city, or anywhere else in Brazil for that matter.

More importantly, many manufacturing sectors were struggling to deal with a currency that put them at a disadvantage. Brazilian markets were flooded with cheap Chinese imports and local producers found it hard to compete overseas. Economists were beginning to argue that Brazil was suffering from so-called 'Dutch disease', in which the development of a specific sector – such as oil or natural resources – leads to decline in others. The mechanism through which this happens is the exchange rate. Strong oil exports, for example, can lead to currency appreciation that puts manufacturers at a disadvantage either in export markets or by making them vulnerable to competition from cheap imports. The term was coined in the 1970s to describe the impact of Dutch gas exports on the country's manufacturing sector. The other problem was that the battle to contain inflation had obliged monetary policymakers to push interest rates to very high levels. Rates in Brazil were so high that investors found it attractive to sell other currencies, buy Brazilian reals and leave the proceeds in Brazilian savings accounts. These transactions, which involved switching from currencies in countries with very low rates such as Japan, were known as carry trades, and led to further appreciation of the real. Rousseff and her economic team, led by finance minister

Guido Mantega, now set about trying to address these shortcomings. Notionally the tripod was to stay in position; however, there was to be a new emphasis on reducing interest rates and forcing the currency down. The government would intervene to correct perceived anomalies by protecting or subsidising sectors that were finding it difficult to compete. It was an approach that began to be known as the 'new economic matrix'.[4]

Economic circumstances quickly became more complicated: during 2011, Rousseff's first year in office, the world economy started to slow down. Several governments in the Eurozone were unable to repay or refinance their debts, giving rise to a new phase of the financial crisis that had begun in 2008. The beginning of a period of deceleration in China, which triggered a fall in commodity prices, was especially relevant for Brazil. Chinese growth of 10.6 per cent in 2010 dropped to 9.6 per cent in 2011 and 7.9 per cent in 2012. By the beginning of 2012 the prices of soya beans and iron ore, Brazil's two largest exports, were respectively 13.5 per cent and 22 per cent lower than they had been on the day of Rousseff's inauguration.

Rousseff watched anxiously as Brazil's economy began to slow down. Her government's first move was an unexpected cut in interest rates when inflation was still uncomfortably high, which unsettled many international investors. In March 2012 the president convened a meeting with the leaders of Brazil's largest companies, acting immediately on their grievances. Faced with complaints of high tax burdens, the finance minister introduced a flood of exemptions, temporarily removing payroll taxes from different economic sectors in a bewildering series of announcements. Assailed over energy costs, Rousseff ordered ministers to reduce rates and impose new long-term concessions on utilities. Business had complained about high borrowing rates, so Rousseff's ministers were sent out to encourage banks to reduce their spreads (the difference between the price paid by the banks for the money they borrowed and the price at which they then lent it out to customers). Brazil's big two public banks, the Banco do Brasil and the Caixa Econômica Federal, were told to lead the way by increasing the amounts they loaned and offering lower rates. The Brazilian Development Bank, which had always offered loans to selected customers at privileged rates and had already stepped up its lending under Lula, was told to lend even more.

None of this went to plan. From mid-2012 activity started to pick up, but at a much lower rate than had been hoped.[5] Interviewed in 2013 by *Valor Econômico*, chief of staff Gleisi Hoffmann was perplexed: "Businesses ask for changes, cuts in energy costs, lower interest rates. Everything they ask for the government gives them, but they don't invest."[6] There were all sorts of reasons for this. Critics in the government and the private sector claimed that Rousseff could be a difficult person to work with. She was famously hot-tempered and often overbearing with subordinates. "Dilma is the most democratic leader in the world as long as you agree with her 100 per cent", claimed Luciano Zico, a PT deputy who clashed with Rousseff before she became president.[7] As Lula's chief of staff, Rousseff had occasionally flown off the handle. On a flight aboard the presidential aircraft, Lula had introduced Rousseff to a businessman he was close to. The man had interests in the sugar sector and had tried to talk to Rousseff about his plans to use bagasse as a source of alternative energy. When Rousseff saw the price she simply dismissed the idea out of hand: "This is robbery, you are thieves. Do what you want with this energy because at that price we are not going to buy it. No fucking way, no fucking way."[8]

In the notoriously male-dominated world of Brazilian politics and business, some of the criticisms of Rousseff should be taken with a pinch of salt. After all, she was well known for her hard work and diligence and was never going to accept Lula's more relaxed approach to government. But it's clear that relations with the private sector became more difficult, and that Rousseff – who had been so keen to learn from business in the run-up to the election – became ever more suspicious of private-sector motives.

With some fanfare, Rousseff had invited private companies to bid for valuable contracts to build and operate roads and railways, but the financial terms were so onerous that few businesses bothered to submit bids. Energy companies complained that the government had broken legal contracts, not consulted nor given them sufficient time to prepare. Banks complained that Brazil's banking spreads were high because it was expensive and invariably very difficult to recover loans when borrowers couldn't repay. But Rousseff was deaf to these kinds of complaints.[9] Her problems with the private sector pointed to a deeper and more fundamental disagreement that goes to the heart of the debate about Brazilian development. The controversy – which continues to divide opinion to this day – concerns the Brazilian public sector, which is relatively large compared to those of other developing countries, but according to its critics is very inefficient and organised in such a way that it blocks development. Many in the private sector as well as politicians on the right, centre and moderate left such as former President Cardoso argue that the state has to be reformed and reorganised. On the other hand, the left and the trade union movement have opposed this stance as threatening jobs and living standards. Some left-wingers argue that the state is an essential tool that has to be further strengthened if Brazil is to be able to develop more effectively and hold its own in the global economy. Brazilian nationalists sometimes propose a similar approach. In Lula's first term in office a number of leading figures, in particular the finance minister Antônio Palocci and members of his treasury team, agreed with the reformist view. Lula's government took steps to overhaul the pension system and Palocci had wanted to take even more radical measures. In Lula's second term in office, the increasingly influential Rousseff took a different view, and as president she began to move in the opposition direction. We'll return to these developments, but it is worth pausing for a moment to look in more detail at the Brazilian state.

The dilemma of the Brazilian state

Brazil's public sector is large relative to the size of its economy. Public spending was relatively small at the end of the military dictatorship, but grew substantially over the next few decades, rising from 11.4 per cent of GDP in 1970, to 35.3 per cent in 2000, and to 40.4 per cent at the end of Lula's period in office. It has been cut back a little since then (although it will rise again as a result of COVID-related spending) so that in 2018 the public sector accounted for 38 per cent of economic output. Few other developing economies spend as much. Chinese public spending absorbed only about 34.1 per cent of GDP, Russia's 33.5 per cent, South Africa's 33.4 per cent and India's 26.2 per cent. Brazil's largest South American neighbour, Argentina, spent slightly more in 2018 at 38.9 per cent of GDP, but Mexico and the next three largest regional economies spent significantly less: Mexico spends only 25.7 per cent, Colombia 28.1 per cent, Chile 25.4 per cent, and Peru only 21.4 per cent.

Brazil's state is not only relatively large, but it also spends public money extremely badly. Many developed countries have much larger states. The public sectors of France, Germany and Italy equate to 58 per cent, 48.6 per cent and 44.6 per cent of their GDP, for example. But the money they spend on welfare, which accounts for a significant tranche of overall spending, benefits those who most need it. In Brazil, by comparison, a very large percentage of public spending is channelled towards elite or upper-middle-class groups. For example, welfare payments in the UK make up 92 per cent of the incomes of the poorest 10 per cent of the population, and only 2 per cent of the incomes of the richest 10 per cent. In Brazil, social transfers make up only 31 per cent of the incomes of the poorest 10 per cent, but 23 per cent of the incomes of the richest 10 per cent.

The most egregious example of inequality is furnished by Brazil's lopsided pension system: the state provides a very generous system for public employees, but much more limited benefits for private-sector workers. Groups such as the military, senior judges and top civil servants are particularly privileged. The pension system is a huge burden on state finances, and the government spends more than a third of its tax revenue on pensions, yet a staggering 53 per cent of this goes to the wealthiest 20 per cent of the population. The poorest 20 per cent receive only 2.5 per cent of the total disbursed.[10]

Matters have improved a little of late owing to reforms that were introduced by the Bolsonaro administration during 2019, but Brazil is still full of anomalies. Public-sector workers in general – especially senior civil servants – work relatively few hours, benefit from long holidays and typically retire in their mid-50s on pensions paying the equivalent of their most recent salary. The trade unions that represent civil servants and are often close to the PT are among the most vociferous defenders of these arrangements.

I'd long been aware of these inequalities. A friend who we got to know in the late 1990s had worked as a librarian for the government. She had retired on a full salary in her early 50s and with the real appreciating could afford to decamp to London, where she lived pretty well. Rigid public-sector employment rules mean that many workers receive wage increases based on seniority and academic qualifications, and irrespective of merit. Another family friend, an engineer in his early 50s who worked for a federal university, was studying all the hours he could to obtain a masters' degree that would more or less double his salary just in time for him to retire on the enhanced income. The public was essentially rewarding him to gain skills that he would never use to the public's benefit.

But it's not just spending that benefits the wealthy in Brazil. They also pay less than their fair share of taxes, since a very large proportion of revenue comes from indirect taxes levied on goods and services that disproportionately affect the less well off. By contrast, taxes on incomes and assets are relatively low, a system that

Rozane Siqueria, a professor of economics at the Federal University of Pernambuco, describes as "Robin Hood in reverse".[11] Multiple tax exemptions and subsidies granted to a bewildering range of groups contribute to the bureaucratic complexity that makes it so expensive for businesses to administer their obligations.

How did this bizarre and contorted system develop? Marcos Lisboa, who worked in the finance ministry under Palocci and is now president of the Insper business school in Rio de Janeiro, has argued persuasively that these social policies are part of a pattern of what he calls "institutionalised rent seeking" in which "special interests manage to obtain privileges and benefits from government agencies".[12] In a paper jointly authored with Zeina Latif, another economist, Lisboa describes Brazil's long history of rent seeking, of powerful business and other interests using their political connections to secure tax exemptions, subsidies or control over whole market segments. As early as the 1930s, when Brazil started to industrialise, governments established close connections with large businesses. Brazil's privately owned construction companies, which were badly damaged by the Lava Jato scandal, were beneficiaries. This pattern of privilege was carried over into the way the state raised revenues, distributed welfare benefits, offered tax breaks and subsidised loans. The political debate around the new Constitution (eventually approved in 1988) served as an opportunity for vested interests – such as the trade unions representing public-sector workers – to press their claims for special treatment. Large amounts of spending – especially in health and education – were ringfenced so that elected legislators had less and less control over how money was spent.

Former president Fernando Henrique Cardoso highlighted many of these problems. Cardoso was a sociologist before entering politics and was known as one of the most influential proponents of dependency theory, which rooted the causes of the region's unsatisfactory development in its relations with the rich countries of North America and Europe.[13] Radical advocates of dependency theory, in particular the North American Marxist André Gunder Frank, argued that the region should completely sever its relationships with what they called the 'metropolis' in order to be able to develop its economy. Cardoso took a more nuanced position, arguing that much depended on the specific way in which developing countries were linked to the global economy. Where domestic ownership of industry was substantial, as in Brazil, development was possible and government policies could make a big difference.[14]

Cardoso also argued that inherent aspects of the Brazilian state hindered development. "Our problem isn't the minimum state or the maximum state but the necessary state", he told an interviewer in 1997.[15] Cardoso argued that it was essential to remove ideology from the debate about the state. There were good state companies and bad state companies, good private companies and bad private companies. Governments should look to promote what was good and what worked, irrespective of the nature of ownership. In government from 1994, Cardoso began to make some progress towards his long-term goal of reconstructing the state by launching an important reform to public finances that would prepare the ground for Brazil to spend money less wastefully. At the start of his own tenure, Lula also made some more progress, seeing through an important – though partial – reform of the pension system in 2003. Lula's finance minister, Antônio Palocci, suggested that Brazil needed to restrict the benefits extended to privileged groups. In addition, Palocci argued that Brazil should look to achieve zero nominal fiscal deficits in order to reduce its debt and stabilise its long-term position.

This idea provoked the ire of the left wing of the PT, whose understanding of Brazil's economic problems ran along very different lines. For them, the overriding problem was Brazil's dependency on the large capitalist economies of North America, Europe and Asia. Breaking free of this dependency required a strong state and the promotion of strong national companies. In other words, the PT wanted to re-embrace the national developmentalist model, a perspective that Rousseff very much shared.

When Palocci presented his proposals in 2005 to Rousseff, who was then Lula's chief of staff, she immediately attacked the idea of a nominal deficit as "economic illiteracy". She insisted that "current spending is life. Either you stop the people from being born, from dying or getting ill or you have current spending." Lisboa, who was then working as treasury secretary and had supported the nominal deficit idea, was labelled a "mental defective" and "semi-literate" by Maria da Conceição Tavares, a 91-year-old left-wing economist who enjoyed tremendous prestige on the left of the Workers' Party.[16]

Fiscal stability at risk

By early 2013 Rousseff's views on these matters were becoming clearer as the government pushed to the left. At first, in spite of the modest pace of growth, levels of employment consumer confidence remained relatively high. At the *Financial Times* we'd been monitoring spending patterns in Brazil since the beginning of 2012 by commissioning monthly surveys of 1,500 people. In spite of all the political noise, the high street seemed undaunted. When we broadened our surveys in 2013 to five other Latin American countries (Argentina, Chile, Colombia, Mexico and Peru), it was notable how much more Brazilians were prepared to spend than their fellow Latin Americans.

At the same time, throughout 2012 and well into 2013, Rousseff remained relatively popular. Indeed, during 2012 her ratings improved. With each opinion poll she became more confident and assertive and less tolerant of criticism and counter-arguments. "Now nobody is going to be able to put up with her", said Giles Azevedo, Rousseff's chief of staff and one of her closest collaborators, after she achieved a 59 per cent approval rating in January 2012.[17] The economic team continued to pay lip service to the tripod. But increasingly, ministers and civil servants were told that the priority was to boost economic activity and maintain employment levels.

Rousseff's most loyal lieutenant in this crusade was Arno Augustin, a Trotskyist and long-time member of the most left-wing faction of the PT, Socialist Democracy. He was from Carranza, a small town in Rio Grande do Sul, and, like Rousseff, he had held a number of positions in the state's left-wing government, where the two had met. Augustin, the son of a second-hand car salesman, was an austere, hard-working official, a Marxist economist, well known for his spartan lifestyle. His appointment in 2007 as treasury secretary, a top position in the finance ministry, had been criticised by officials. Augustin had neither activist nor academic credentials, and in the ministry he was to remain an unpopular figure among colleagues. Officials described him as authoritarian and reserved. "It was hard to tolerate more than ten minutes of conversation with him", said one ex-colleague.[18] "He stays quiet most of the time but at the end of every meeting, when everyone was tired, he would present an idea that unravelled everything that seemed to have been agreed", said one of the participants of these meetings. "What he said seemed to make sense for five seconds. But if you thought about it for more than five seconds you could see it was absurd."[19]

Augustin was suspicious of the private sector and critical of the banks and any policy prescription that advocated cuts in spending, which he believed were simply designed to "pay more money to the banks". In his view, the ratings agencies whose positive evaluations had been so welcomed by Lula were simply tools used by rich countries to impede the success of developmental policies. Much of this chimed with the views of Rousseff. "He pressed her buttons", said one official. "They basically had the same political instincts."[20]

Quizzed by construction companies about the need to compensate them for the extra bureaucratic, financial and other costs of investing in Brazil, Augustin said that there was no need, suggesting that high commodity prices and the formidable build-up of foreign reserves had eliminated what businesses typically refer to as 'Brazil risk'. When officials questioned the growth rates on which his calculations for infrastructure concessions were based, Augustin simply accused his interrogators of pessimism.[21]

But it was in his role at the Treasury that Augustin's dogmatism caused the most damage. After the spending cuts that marked her first few weeks in office, Rousseff had changed course. Multiple tax exemptions offered to business had put revenues under pressure at the same time as spending started to increase. It rose by about 1 percentage point of GDP between 2011 and 2014, with the Treasury freeing up money for state governments as never before, on the assumption that it would lead to big increases in investment. After the June demonstrations against Rousseff, which we will look at in more detail in the next chapter, money was spent with even greater abandon. "When [Rousseff] saw people on the streets she got so scared. The response was spend, spend, spend, the numbers all went haywire", one former presidential adviser told me in 2019.

As early as 2012 it was looking increasingly unlikely that the government would be able to meet its fiscal targets. But anxious to maintain the support of international investors and its investment grade credit rating, the finance ministry resorted to subterfuge. "Mantega wanted to achieve a primary surplus by the end of the year. It didn't matter how", said one ex-minister interviewed by Leandra Peres, a reporter for *Valor Econômico*.[22] Creative accounting took various forms: payments due to be made in one accounting period were shifted into another; money that the Treasury should have paid to the Caixa Econômica Federal, a state mortgage bank, was held back throughout 2013 and early 2014. Assets were also shifted into the Treasury from the Brazilian Development Bank and the Sovereign Brazil Fund, in elaborate 'triangulation' operations. By 2014 the Treasury had run up a debt with Banco do Brasil, the other big state bank, of R$9bn.

In order to disguise the extent of these manoeuvres, information flows inside the ministry were restricted. A committee responsible for making fiscal projections never met. In spite of this, senior officials in the Treasury were worried about the extent of the deception. Augustin had been warned about this as early as June 2013, according to internal documents obtained by *Valor Econômico*, but it had made little difference. The treasury secretary had "treated [the warnings] like an act of rebellion" by the "lower ranks". At one tense encounter in November 2013 with more than two dozen officials, Augustin rejected "criticism as an affront to the government's project", wrote Peres, who won one of Brazil's top journalism prizes for her reporting. "It simply gave rise to rows rather than discussions." As one senior official put it, "[this was] a government of a lot of certainties but no doubts".[23]

These operations lost the economic team credibility. "It became evident that the primary surplus was being manufactured in the offices of the finance minister, through tricks and creative accounting."[24] Even people who had been sympathetic were shocked. Delfim Netto, a finance and planning minister in the 1960s, 1970s and 1980s, and an adviser to both the Lula and Rousseff governments, called the operation "a deplorable operation of alchemy". When the federal government's audit body – the Tribunal das Contas da União (TCU) – started to run the rule over the numbers in 2014, they were aghast. "Throughout the audit I couldn't believe what I was finding. I thought I must be doing something wrong", a TCU official told an interviewer.[25]

The fiscal cost of all this was considerable. The government's overall deficit had increased from 2.3 per cent of GDP in 2012 to 3 per cent in 2013, 6.1 per cent in 2014 and 10.2 per cent in 2015. But much of the money had been squandered. The government had started by exempting companies in fifteen labour-intensive sectors from payroll tax, widening that to forty-two sectors by

2014. When finance minister Joaquim Levy, who took over from Mantega after Rousseff's election victory in 2014, started to work on the numbers, he calculated that the fiscal cost of each job created had been three times the amount of wages the job actually paid. "It would have been better to load a helicopter full of money and throw it over [the] Rocinha [favela]", one civil servant said. Even government ministers recognised that the tax exemptions were excessive and had served little purpose. Jacques Wagner, chief of staff in 2013, said the "exemptions had been exaggerated, financing programmes bigger than we could afford. It's for that reason that 2015 was such a tough year."[26]

Few businesses chose to take advantage of the other incentives made available by Rousseff's administration, and Brazil's investment rate proved stubbornly low. Indeed, there is evidence that companies took the cheap loans simply in order to invest in government paper. In such cases, the government was effectively subsidising companies to leave money in the bank: "Paulo Bernardo, the planning minister, was told by a businessman in Paraná that the tactic of borrowing money at subsidised rates to invest in high yielding government bonds was spreading."[27]

But perhaps the biggest and most shocking waste occurred at Petrobras, the state-controlled oil company that back in 2010 was supposed to be Brazil's ticket to the promised land of prosperity. Rather than helping the nation attain a trouble-free and resource-rich future, the mismanagement of the newly discovered resources contributed to the country's growing problems. PT governments were so emboldened by the scale of the new discoveries that they felt free to press ahead with a spendthrift model of development. The company that had made profits of R$35bn in 2010 lost about R$13bn in both 2014 and 2015. As a result, its net debt rose from about R$50bn to nearly R$400bn.[28]

Part of the problem was that new rules designed to secure national control over the assets simply slowed down the pace at which Brazil was able to exploit them. Convinced that foreign investors would be unable to ignore the attractions of the new deposits, the government tightened terms, replacing the old concession model with a partnership structure in which Petrobras would take a 30 per cent stake in each field. New regulations obliging oil producers to source inputs such as pipes and other equipment from local companies were announced. It was a reasonable idea in theory, but Brazilian suppliers were unable to respond quickly enough and foreign companies were soon alleging that the so-called local content requirements were too onerous. As a result, the pace of the exploitation and production of oil was slower than expected, and in 2013–14 Brazil's output actually fell.

Brazil should have been self-sufficient in oil, but given the shortage of refinery capacity, it was continuing with imports at a time when international prices remained strong. Petrobras paid for those imports at world rates, but it was only allowed to sell petrol and diesel at cheaper national prices, bearing the cost of any subsidy on its own accounts. Petrobras's management pressed repeatedly for an increase in domestic prices but they were rebuffed by Rousseff and her ministers. Sergio Gabrielli, an economics professor who had taken over as president of Petrobras in 2005, lobbied unsuccessfully for a change, as did his successor, Graça Foster, a personal friend of the president. Rousseff was always worried that higher petrol and diesel prices would put upward pressure on inflation. In the second half of 2014 the company's internal finance reports showed that losses of about $40bn had been accumulated over the previous four years due to this mismatch in prices.

Urged on by the government, Petrobras had agreed to ambitious plans to build new refineries both in Brazil and overseas. Many of these initiatives were half-baked, designed to serve political rather than business purposes. Petrobras wasted vast amounts of money, either overpaying for existing refineries or exceeding budgets for new projects. In 2006 it paid $360m for a 50 per cent stake in the Pasadena refinery in Texas to a Belgian company called Astra Oil, which, it later emerged, had spent just $42.5m to take over the entire facility one year earlier. Petrobras paid $20bn for a new refinery in Pernambuco that was scheduled to cost just $2bn. Under an agreement signed between Lula and Hugo Chávez, the then president of Venezuela, Pdvsa, the state-owned oil company, was to have been a co-investor. The Venezuelan company did not pay a cent.[29]

The Lava Jato scandal, which essentially involved groups that were part of the government coalition using Petrobras to finance their campaigns and other activities, made a bad situation worse. Petrobras routinely overpaid contractors, and contractors then paid part of these excess profits to the PT and its political allies. The amounts involved were considerable, although the R$6.2bn that was eventually included for corruption losses in the 2014 accounts paled alongside the tens of billions lost through petrol subsidies and wasted investments. Nevertheless, Lava Jato dealt a further blow to the company's credibility. By January 2016 the market value of Petrobras had fallen from over $300bn in 2008 to $17.8bn. But Brazil's financial mismanagement was now beginning to affect much more than Petrobras's accounts. During 2015 and 2016 Brazil's recession evolved into a fully fledged political crisis.

5

THE FOUNDATIONS BEGIN TO SHAKE

I spent Christmas of 2012 in Salvador and stayed on to do some reporting in Belo Horizonte and São Paulo. The country was clearly stumbling. I remember listening to the complaints of top executives at Cemig, the state-owned electricity company of Minas Gerais, about how the government's unilateral decision to reduce power rates had created so many problems for them. But Brazil's numbers were still quite positive. Consumer confidence remained fairly strong, and in spite of all her clashes with the private sector, Dilma Rousseff was polling well. As late as March 2013, 65 per cent of those interviewed by Datafolha rated Rousseff's presidency as good or excellent, up from 62 per cent the previous December. Only 7 per cent of those interviewed thought Rousseff was doing a bad or terrible job.[1]

It was a surprise, then, when sweeping street protests engulfed the entire country in June 2013. What started out at the beginning of the month as a protest against higher bus fares had by the end of the month become a broad-based attack not just on political corruption but on the entire political class itself. Within three weeks Rousseff's popularity fell by 29 percentage points, plunging her government into a crisis that would finish two years later in impeachment and the end of thirteen years of PT rule. It could not have been predicted. As Brian Winter put it, the reaction of

Brazil's chattering classes was one of "utter shock. No-one saw the demonstrations coming."[2]

The June marches were pivotal too in that they were the first sign of much deeper and broader opposition to corruption, which widened as the investigations over the Lava Jato corruption scandal got underway in March 2014. The movement began to reshape the relationship between Brazilian society and the political establishment. The June protests "turned things upside down", wrote André Singer, a political scientist who had served as a senior official in Lula's first administration. "They were a bolt from the blue. The protests assumed such dimensions that something appeared to be happening in the bowels of society, something that could get out of control."[3]

The trigger for these momentous events seemed trivial at the time. After freezing bus fares during 2012 and the first half of 2013, local authorities were finally given permission by the Rousseff administration to increase prices. The proposed rise of 6.7 per cent was small, but transport costs absorb quite a large proportion of the incomes of the poor, and across Latin America increases have often been politically controversial. As long ago as 1879 the residents of Rio de Janeiro had taken to the streets to oppose planned rises to trolley fares.

The left-wing activists who eventually formed the Free Pass Movement – the organisation that gained some notoriety in the June protests – had been campaigning for free public transport since 2003 and had tried to block fare increases in a number of Brazilian cities. On the evening of 6 June a few hundred demonstrators – many of them hooded or masked – met in front of the town hall in the historic centre of São Paulo and started to dump burning rubbish on the nearby 23 May Avenue. By the end of the evening they had blocked three other main thoroughfares, causing São Paulo's worst traffic jams of the year. They were back on the streets again and again over the next three or four days. The demonstrators threw missiles at policemen, daubed public buildings with graffiti, and wrecked a few bars, shops, news kiosks and bus stops.

Gerardo Alckmin, the conservative governor of the state of São Paulo, and Fernando Haddad, the PT mayor of the city, were in Paris, presenting the city's case to host a big international exhibition in 2020. But like the editors of São Paulo's conservative newspaper, the *Folha de São Paulo*, they were outraged. Assuming that the protesters had little popular support, they were initially dismissive of their demands. Alckmin called the demonstrators "vandals" and "thugs". "The police are going to demand that those who destroy public and private assets pay for the damage", he said. "This is absolute violence, it's rioting and it is unacceptable."[4]

The police chief in charge of controlling planned protests also promised a hard line. "We are not going to allow demonstrators the freedom of the city", he said.[5] They were true to their promise, turning, in the words of one foreign correspondent, "a peaceful demonstration into a terrifying rout".[6] Dozens of videos from journalists and participants showed officers with their name badges removed, firing stun grenades and rubber bullets indiscriminately at fleeing protesters and hunting stragglers through the streets. Motorists trapped in the mayhem ended up breathing pepper spray and tear gas. Two journalists were shot in the face with rubber bullets. Demonstrators carrying vinegar, which can ease the effects of tear gas, were arrested.

The repression proved to be a miscalculation. The violence shocked Brazilians. At very close range, a policeman had shot a rubber bullet into the eye of Giuliana Vallone, a journalist for the *Folha de São Paulo*. The image of Vallone's bloodied face became iconic. Within days, some of Brazil's most famous actors were posing with black eyes and the hashtag #ithurtsusall was trending on social media. On the morning of 13 June just over half of those interviewed in a poll by the Datafolha agency said they supported the demonstrations. Four days after the night of violence, 78 per cent were backing the marchers.

Things were changing fast on the streets. On 15 June in Brasília, when Brazil met Japan in the opening game of the 2013 Confederations Cup, many of the 80,000 spectators booed President Rousseff. Slowly the numbers taking to the streets were growing. 65,000 people attended the São Paulo demonstrations of 17 June. By the end of the week, as the unrest spread to other cities, 1.2 million Brazilians were protesting and their list of grievances was growing. The placards on display increasingly mentioned corruption or a dislike of politicians. "Literally overnight, the protests stopped being about solely bus fare hikes – and they became about an unlimited list of causes including freedom of speech, the right to protest, and generalized anger with police and elected officials."[7]

The character of the movement was changing. It was around this time that some of our friends joined the protests. They were middle-class professionals – doctors, dentists, lawyers and journalists in their 40s and 50s – who were vaguely disgruntled with the PT but not the sort of people who usually went on demonstrations. One friend had initially been critical of the so-called black bloc, the anarchist groups who had targeted property, but by mid-June he was among the crowds on Paulista Avenue. Brian Winter, who was writing in São Paulo for the Reuters news agency, attended the 17 June march, recalling an "overwhelmingly peaceful atmosphere [...] Indeed, the protests on that night – and others, over coming weeks – sometimes felt more like a night out at a street party than a tense political act."[8]

"People started to go on to the streets in different cities and for different motives, which were not always clear, often organised through social media", wrote Singer. "It was a surprising crisscross of classes and currents."[9] A similar mood took hold in Rio de Janeiro. Another observer, Luiz Eduardo Soares, a sociologist and also a former member of the Lula government, described how the demonstrations "were not organized, they had no chain of command or fixed agenda, they had no ties to any political party or union, and they were not targeting any clear goals set by general consensus".[10]

And in Rio too, the motives of the marchers were incredibly varied. Soares writes: "For some the movement was right-wing, it was fascist; for others it was left-wing, it was anarchist; still others saw it as entirely depoliticized, against everyone and everything, led by infiltrators serving this or that interest, against the Federal Government, against the conventional media, and so on."[11] "We hadn't been taking these protests too seriously", explained a senior Brazilian journalist, who was covering politics for one of the big São Paulo dailies, "then Giuliana was shot in the eye with the plastic bullet. And it started getting big." On Monday in Brasília, demonstrators broke police cordons, clambered on to the mez-zanine roof of the modernist Congress building and used their mobile phone torches to project their own enormous shadows on to the monumental inverted cupola that sits on top. "Ah fuck, the giant woke up, the people woke up", they chanted.

A crisis of expectations?

What were these movements really about? Some protesters raised the topical question of how much Brazil was spending on its foot-ball stadiums and how little on education, social and health ser-vices. Others carried placards praising the military regime of the 1970s or simply protesting in general terms against a Congress and political class widely regarded as corrupt. Some were simply outraged by police violence or protested issues like the so-called 'gay cure', a phoney medical procedure promoted by a couple of evangelical Christian legislators.

In many ways, there were parallels with the loosely organised social movements that had influenced anti-globalisation politics of the early 2000s, the Occupy protests that followed the finan-cial crisis of 2007–08, and even the grassroots activities that had toppled one Middle Eastern dictatorship after another during the Arab Spring. Like their counterparts in New York or Cairo, Brazilian demonstrators tended to be young. Demonstrators made maximum use of mobile communications and social media like Facebook and Twitter as organising tools. Between 40 and 50 per cent of the demonstrators in Rio and São Paulo were less than 25 years old.[12] In smaller cities, more than 50 per cent were in that age group. Only 12 per cent of those demonstrating in São Paulo were over 36 years old, and in Rio, the number of older demonstrators was only slightly larger. Very few of those demonstrating were from the poor urban periphery. 81 per cent of the demonstrators said they had heard about the 17 June march on Facebook, the use of which was rising quickly among Brazilians.[13]

Alternative media organisations began to appear, and their live streaming of the protests and police violence against demonstrators helped generate wider support. Ninja Media, an outfit from the mid-western state of Mato Grosso that had started live streaming rock festivals, proved especially influential according to some observers.[14] The number of people following Ninja's videos increased from 2,000 to 200,000 during June 2013. As Soares put it:

> It's hard to overstate the role of the live-streamers, especially the so-called Ninja Media group, who had transmitted the whole demonstration live online from the thick of the action, but their participation would become even more important in the aftermath, as they followed the police to record their brutal hounding of the dispersing crowd.[15]

But perhaps there was more to the demonstrations than political fashion. Brazil did not share the repressive characteristics of the Middle Eastern states that had led to the Arab Spring. The impact of the global financial crisis that had triggered the Occupy movement and subsequent widespread popular actions in Spain and elsewhere in Europe was more muted in Brazil. As a bemused *El País* correspondent asked as he watched spectators boo the hitherto popular Dilma Rousseff at the opening game of the Confederations Cup in Brasilia: "Why has a protest movement emerged now when for ten years Brazil seems to have been anaesthetised through its internationally applauded success? [...] The country is going through a kind of schizophrenia."[16]

Maybe this was simply a crisis born of rising expectations. The PT government had in some ways been a victim of its own success. The less well-off were no longer struggling to put food on the table and found it easier to find work, but these successes had simply made them more impatient about the quality of healthcare, education and other services. In a survey conducted in 2013, the quality of healthcare was the biggest concern of 48 per cent of respondents.

The popular focus on corruption had also become sharper during 2013, partly because of the media attention given to the so-called *mensalão* (monthly) affair that shook the Lula government during its first term. Lula had won the presidency in 2002, but the PT had only secured a minority of seats in Congress and needed the support of other parties to be able to govern. In the past, the dominant party would have secured support by offering cabinet seats to coalition parties. The PT, however, chose to buy votes from legislators and kept the lion's share of cabinet seats for itself, partly in order to satisfy the demands of the party's different factions. But in doing so, it broke the law. Certain deputies were paid R$30,000 per month to vote for legislation favoured by the ruling party. The funds allegedly came from the advertising budgets of state-owned companies. By 2013 the case had come to court and the proceedings were attracting big audiences to the live broadcasts. Opinion polls suggested that the number of Brazilians who viewed corruption as the country's most pressing problem tripled in the first six months of the year.

Some achievements were simply creating new problems. Poorer Brazilians may have been buying more cars and travelling to work in greater comfort, but they were also experiencing the misery of São Paulo's traffic jams. Brazil's highway infrastructure was simply not keeping pace with the volume of traffic. Between 2002 and 2012 the numbers of cars on Brazil's roads increased by 80 per cent, with easily available credit making it possible for those on average incomes to acquire a vehicle, even though they might have to pay for it over a period of seven years. Sometimes, efforts to improve roads actually contributed to short-term delays.

The hassle of driving in São Paulo was never for me, but having spent endless hours in taxis I can testify to the frustrations. I remember one Friday evening when a couple who we had invited to dinner eventually arrived at 11 p.m. after a gruelling journey between their own home in Vila Mariana and where we lived in Jardins. It had taken them close to three hours to travel five miles. On 1 June 2012 a staggering 185 miles of the city's roads were gridlocked, establishing an all-time record. By the middle of 2013, when the protests occurred, there were even more cars on the road and the jams had got worse.

The political attitudes of many protesters may have reflected what US political scientist Ronald Inglehart has called "a post-materialist shift", that is, the move away from "physical and economic security" as being the dominant concerns to "self-expression and quality of life".[17] There was a world of difference, of course, between the material security of the US in the 1970s – the context in which Inglehart originally developed his ideas – and the Brazil of 2013. Brazil's social changes were nowhere near so solidly based, but the improvements of the previous twenty years had begun to affect attitudes, particularly among the younger people who made up the majority of demonstrators and had no memory of the hardships endured by their parents.[18]

In addition, there was a particular Brazilian twist to this equation. The state had grown in size but had become unresponsive to the needs of many. It was perhaps this factor more than anything else that explained how the far-left fringe and the traditional right could come together in the June mobilisations. And it was the role of the state that made it so difficult for the PT government, with its ties to public-sector trade unions, to react. As Soares described:

> Pro-government columnists with ties to the PT (Workers' Party) ... couldn't get their heads around it: why are the masses taking to the streets now, if inequality has decreased in Brazil over the last decade, like never before? Why this tidal wave of unrest now? The conservatives had to be behind it, they concluded.[19]

Some on the left began to argue that the establishment and 'mainstream media' had somehow co-opted the protests. The emergence of far-right networks that were every bit as adept at using internet-based social networks as their new left counterparts served to reinforce this perception. Groups like Movimento Brasil Livre and Vem Pra Rua that emerged in 2014 soon became associated with Bolsonaro and the emergent new right.

For the moment, though Rousseff and senior ministers were close to panic, their response to the crisis was to do what they knew best: spend money. "Once the true scope and meaning of the demonstrations became clear, Rousseff's government ... [tried] every possible action to calm things down", wrote Thomas Traumann, who had been Rousseff's head of communications.[20] The old rules went out of the window. Restrictions on spending were ignored, as the government ploughed money into new training schemes and building projects. Rousseff, who had previously opposed the deployment of foreign doctors, negotiated a deal to send thousands of Cuban doctors to remote areas. She announced new subsidies and even more tax breaks, all of which aggravated the country's fiscal difficulties.

And in response to the popular clamour for tough action on corruption, the government launched legislation against organised crime and sleaze. Nestling amid the fine print were new rules that allowed prosecutors to make greater use of plea bargains, offering prisoners the possibility of exchanging information for a reduced sentence. This legislation served to turbocharge a sensational legal investigation that would devastate the political establishment and bring the Rousseff government to its knees.

Corruption protests take to the street

Corruption is far from new in Brazil. It goes back to the sixteenth-century origins of the country, when, lacking either the capital or personnel to develop the colony, the Portuguese crown handed over land grants to private individuals, usually nobles, bureaucrats or military officers, and created so-called captaincies. Subsequently, colonial officials routinely pocketed crown revenues for their personal enrichment. By the nineteenth century, when Brazil became an independent country, corruption was endemic. As a popular satirical verse of the time put it: "Quem furta um pouco é ladrão, quem furta muito é barão, quem mais furta e mais esconde, passa de barão a visconde" (the person who steals a little is a thief, those who steal a lot are barons, but the one who steals the most becomes a viscount).

During the twentieth century, the close relationship between Brazil's political and economic elites changed in character as the country tried to reduce its dependency on agricultural commodities and started to industrialise. But the connections between elected leaders and business remained tight. Businessmen had the capital to finance election campaigns and in return politicians could offer them contracts or map out market privileges. And generally, corrupt politicians and those who paid them bribes got away with it. Until relatively recently in Brazil's history, elected politicians were a breed apart, free from prosecution even for the most flagrant breaches of the law. In one of the most dramatic examples, Arnon de Mello, the father of former president Fernando Collor de Mello, gunned down a colleague on the floor of the Brazilian senate in 1962, in full view of his colleagues. He was arrested, tried, found not guilty and immediately released.

This pattern had been changing, as the *mensalão* had shown. But Lava Jato was more far-reaching in its impact, affecting every corner of the political and business establishment. The case had started almost by accident. In March 2014 police in the southern state of Paraná had been tracking the activities of a black market banker and political fixer Alberto Youssef, when they stumbled across a transaction with Paulo Roberto Costa, a Petrobras director. By May 2016, just two years after the Lava Jato case had begun, Sérgio Moro had passed eighteen judgments and convicted seventy-four people, whose combined sentences exceeded 1,000 years in jail. Brazil had seen nothing remotely like it in its 500-year history. "Never had so many powerful people gone to jail, never had so much been revealed about the functioning of the corruption machine within the Brazilian state and never had so many people decided to tell what they knew, hand back stolen money and cooperate with the judicial authorities", wrote Vladimir Netto, the author of a book that eventually became the basis for a Netflix drama.[21] "Everything about Operation Car Wash was superlative. Between 17 March 2014 and the middle of April 2016, there had been twenty-eight phases of the operation, thirty-eight criminal cases had been started and thirteen cases divided."[22]

Several changes made the sentences possible. First, reforms introduced to the legal system since the return to democracy in 1985 had improved the judicial system. One significant change was to give the public prosecutor's office (what in Brazil is known as the public ministry) a greater degree of independence. Another was to make the selection process for judges more meritocratic, with candidates chosen not for their political connections (as had been the case in the past) but for their knowledge and experience. Today, four out of five judges are chosen in this way. Sérgio Moro, who graduated as a federal judge in 1996, then aged 24, was part of this new generation.

The most important changes to the legal system, however, were those launched by Rousseff in 2013. The new law widened the definition of what constituted a criminal organisation, allowing prosecutors to deploy preventative arrests and "exceptional measures", including exemplary, ultra-long prison sentences. The new plea bargain rules allowed police and prosecutors to offer prisoners the possibility of more lenient sentences in exchange for information. Plea bargains are a common feature of judicial systems based on common law such as the US, but are much rarer in countries such as Brazil, where law is based on a civil code. Brazil started using them in 1990 as a way to tackle organised crime gangs because prosecutors found it difficult to obtain evidence from witnesses (who were frequently intimidated). However, until 2013 only the judge had been able to offer a prisoner the possibility of a plea bargain. Now, prosecutors and the police were able to propose these arrangements. The innovations proved decisive. "Without plea bargains many of the operations would simply not have occurred", wrote one legal commentator.[23]

Prosecutors and judges in the Lava Jato case were heavily influenced by their reading of the experience of *Mani Pulite*, the 'Clean Hands' actions launched by the Italian judiciary against political corruption in the early 1990s. The Paraná task force set up in 2013 by Rodrigo Janot, the chief public prosecutor, was directly modelled on Italy's anti-mafia unit and had the same aim of focusing expertise and resources. Paraná was chosen as a base for the task force because prosecutors there had run an investigation into a huge foreign exchange scandal involving the state's privatised bank, Banestado. Moro had played a big part in that trial and had read a lot about the Italian experience. He recommended a book, *Cose di Cosa Nostra*, written by Giovanni Falcone, an Italian judge and prosecuting magistrate, to friends and colleagues. Both plea bargains and pre-trial detentions had figured in Italy.

Moro felt that Brazil's justice system was simply too slow to deal with the scale of the abuses involved and the speed with which organised crime could act. Brazil's multiple appeals system allowed those condemned in lower courts to evade punishment for years, as Netto writes: "The slowness of Brazil's judicial system, with multiple appeals and up to four different levels of trial, has a knack of indefinitely delaying the application of criminal law, undermining both its effectiveness and society's confidence in the rule of law on many occasions."[24]

Another important lesson that Moro drew from his Italian models was the way in which Italian judges had sought to shape public opinion. They had believed that, however extensive judicial action against corruption might be, in a democracy it would only be effective if it had the support of the public. In an article about the Italian experience published in 2004, Moro wrote: "To the disgust of the Italian Socialist Party leaders [one of the parties badly damaged by *Mani Pulite*] the *Mani Pulite* investigation leaked like a sieve. As soon as someone became a prisoner, details of his confession were sent to *L'Espresso*, *La Repubblica* and other sympathetic newspapers."[25] As Moro himself explained to the *Financial Times* in 2018, "it was important to have public opinion on our side. It could work like a medicine against attempts to obstruct the work of justice."[26]

The popularity of Lava Jato

These legal innovations allowed the Curitíba team to make rapid progress during 2014 and 2015. Testimony offered by Youssef and Costa, entered as part of plea bargains, provided the springboard for the first phase of the investigation. Youssef and Costa provided detailed explanations of the way bribes were paid. Any company working with Petrobras could expect a profit margin of between 10 and 20 per cent. "On top of this amount, the contractor would charge a further 1 to 3 per cent on the final price (thus, given the scale of these projects, inflating the cost by millions), and would then pass this money to the political party that controlled that particular division of Petrobras."[27] As Costa told his interrogators, making this "premium" payment was a condition of doing business with Petrobras. Companies that refused to pay were excluded from any future business. "This is how public resources are channelled. Corruption was institutionalised. Companies took the maximum they could from Petrobras", Costa explained.[28]

These first testimonies took prosecutors directly to the construction companies involved: Camargo Corrêa, Construtora OAS, UTC Engenharia, Mendes Júnior, Engevix, Queiroz Galvão, IESA Óleo e Gás, Galvão Engenharia, and subsequently Andrade Gutierrez and Odebrecht. By contrast, politicians were harder to get at because elected representatives still enjoyed a substantial degree of legal protection. Senators, deputies, government ministers, presidents and their deputies enjoyed what is known in Portuguese as *foro privilegiado*.

When specialist units of armed police started to arrive at the homes of senior executives and take away suspects in handcuffs, it sent shockwaves through Brazil. Indeed, it is hard to exaggerate the impact of these dawn raids on the homes of the wealthy and powerful. Before Lava Jato, only the poor or the badly defended went to prison. The case appealed to the popular desire for fair play. A day after the spectacular arrest of the construction company executives in November 2014, many Brazilians took to the streets in celebration.

The case was hugely popular. Leading judges and prosecutors, most notably investigating judge Sérgio Moro, became hero figures. Celebrity was not necessarily a positive thing though. The desire to speed things up and get public opinion onside was all very well, but there were signs that the Curitíba investigation was becoming increasingly partial. And as it did so, it would start to have an impact on the political landscape in a contentious way.

6

A POLITICAL IMPLOSION

Emerging from a crucial congressional session that approved her impeachment, a puzzled Dilma Rousseff turned to her lawyer and confessed that she "felt like Joseph K", the character in Franz Kafka's *The Trial* (1925) who is arrested and eventually executed for an unspecified crime.[1] It was easy to understand why Rousseff thought her dismissal from the presidency had been Kafkaesque. After all, it was Rousseff who had introduced one of the legal changes that had made Lava Jato so effective in its early stages. And although investigators had looked at her role in the scandal, they had not been able to pin anything on her. In fact, it had been precisely her commitment to what André Singer calls "ethical cleansing" that had made her so many enemies in Congress and accounted for the speed of her dismissal. She had sacked several ministers for corruption and "after every sweep of the brush [...] there were people seeking revenge". The effort to build transparent and clean government, what Singer calls "Republicanism", destroyed the alliance that Lula had built and "the parliamentary base of the government started to crumble".[2]

This was not the way that many Brazilians saw things at the time, however. For many, Rousseff was at the centre of a corrupt and ineffective administration. As the economy contracted and unemployment increased, anger at the PT government's involvement in the Lava Jato corruption scandal grew. Rousseff saw her popularity ratings slump towards 10 per cent. The atmosphere on 17 April 2016, when the lower house of Congress met to consider the motion to impeach her, was frenzied. No one talked about the formal accusations of creative accounting that had breached the country's fiscal responsibility laws and had given rise to the charges. Instead, groups of deputies – mainly men in dark suits and ties – paraded through the modernist corridors of Congress like gangs of football supporters, carrying flags and placards and chanting slogans. "Tchau, Querida" ("Goodbye, love") chanted the right, "Democracia" ("Democracy") responded left-wingers. In the country at large, the mood was electric. Whole families gathered in front of their television sets to watch the decision. "The atmosphere felt almost like a football cup final", wrote one commentator.[3]

During the debate, each legislator made a short speech, many right-wingers dedicating their vote to their families and children or to God. Ever provocative, an elated Jair Bolsonaro – at this time serving his seventh term as an elected deputy for Rio de Janeiro – shockingly offered up his vote to the memory of Colonel Carlos Alberto Brilhante Ustra, the head of the unit that had tortured Rousseff when she had been in prison. The vote – 367 votes in favour and 137 against – simply confirmed what most people already knew: the government's support had evaporated. Less than a month later, the senate vote of 55 to 22 put another nail in Rousseff's political coffin.

Enemies on all sides

Rousseff's political honeymoon ended abruptly, when thousands of people took to the streets in June 2013. The government had bent the rules in order to spend heavily in a bid to recover support, and for a while this effort was successful. In the south and south-east the PT was losing ground among better-off voters, including the increasingly financially stretched Class C. But in the north and north-east it was as strong as ever. Additional spending had paid dividends. Under the terms of a popular housing programme – Minha Casa Minha Vida (My House, My Life) – thousands of people were moving into modest new homes, whose pastel colours and smart lines marked them out from the disorder of poor neighbourhoods. Rousseff's decision to send Cuban doctors to remote areas in the north-east and north of the country had also gone down well.

Rousseff's vote held up enough for her to win re-election in 2014. But the PT's candidate won the elections of October 2014 by a narrower margin than in any of its three previous triumphs. Lula had beaten his PSDB challenger by 21 percentage points in 2002 and 2006. Rousseff herself had been elected with 8 per cent more votes than the PSDB's José Serra in 2010. In 2014 the margin was much closer, with the president only 4 percentage points ahead of the PSDB's Aécio Neves, the grandson of Tancredo Neves, who had been elected president after the end of the military dictatorship.[4]

The PT lost ground in the legislature too, winning eighteen fewer seats in 2014 than it had in 2010, with its MDB allies losing five seats. In the south and south-eastern states Neves won by a significant margin. Only among the poorest section of voters who earned less than two minimum salaries had Rousseff done well. Thus she started her second term as president of an increasingly polarised Brazil. Both social and geographical divisions were becoming more marked.

The reactions of the losing candidate immediately inflamed political tensions. Neves told his supporters that the PSDB's campaign had been defeated by a "criminal organisation", echoing language that was soon to feature in the investigations of the Lava Jato task force. The claims served to stoke a fervid atmosphere.

A number of things now served to intensify the political crisis. First, having failed to stimulate the economy through spending and state intervention, Rousseff changed course completely, inviting a private-sector banker to take over as finance minister. It was an odd appointment. Joaquim Levy could not have been more different to Guido Mantega or Arno Augustin, the big players in Rousseff's first term. Levy was an orthodox liberal economist who had little time for the heterodox approach favoured in the earlier mandate. Having gained his PhD at the University of Chicago, Levy had served at the IMF during a formative part of his career, before working alongside Palocci in Lula's first, more financially conservative administration. He had worked for a long period as president of the asset management arm of Bradesco, one of Brazil's largest privately owned banks, and was regarded as a fiscal hawk. "The differences [between Levy and his predecessor] were profound", wrote Malu Gaspar in *Piauí* magazine.[5] One of Levy's friends, Armínio Fraga, a former hedge fund manager who had served successfully as central bank chief between 1999 and 2002, told Gaspar that it was like "a member of the CIA directing the KGB [...] Levy has nothing in common with this government." Both Fraga and Marcos Lisboa, who had worked at the Treasury during the first Lula administration, advised Levy not to accept the job.

Asked to re-establish Brazil's credibility among investors, Levy started to unpick the economic tangle left by Mantega and Augustín. He aimed to restore a primary fiscal surplus. The expensive and ineffective tax breaks introduced by the previous team were abandoned. This orthodoxy was necessary, but it pushed Brazil deeper into recession. The rise in unemployment and spending cuts made enemies of the urban poor, the social group which had previously been the president's most loyal supporters.

At the same time Rousseff did not do enough to win back support from right-wing allies in Congress, whom she had badly alienated during her first term. She had never been elected a deputy or senator prior to her presidential victory in 2010 and disliked the give and take of political negotiations, meeting relatively infrequently with deputies and senators. Even Singer, who staunchly defends Rousseff's performance between 2011 and 2014, said that her "lack of professionalism in politics which her detractors had always accused her of [...] became very clear now".[6]

Fatally for her chances of survival, Rousseff refused to turn to the one man who could have helped. The president had been expected to invite Lula back into the government following her election victory. Had her predecessor been able to deploy his formidable negotiation skills, it is possible that an agreement could have been forged with the MDB and other parties of the right on which Rousseff depended for legislative support. But she put the decision off until late the following year, and by then it was too late. Rousseff's PT colleagues had backed Lava Jato investigations into Eduardo Cunha, the MDB leader who was also leader of the lower house of Congress, a powerful office whose holder shaped the legislative agenda and could determine which measures came up for voting. In response, Cunha had allowed impeachment proceedings against Rousseff to go forward. By then, increasingly factional Lava Jato investigators in Curitiba had begun to target Rousseff as part of an investigation into Lula and the party leadership.

The president, wrote one sympathetic supporter, had "made the elementary mistake of fighting with the right and the left at the same time". Her popularity now began to nosedive. By August 2015 only 8 per cent of Brazilians interviewed in a Datafolha poll rated her government good or excellent, compared to 42 per cent in December 2014, just after she had won the election. In March 2016, a month before her impeachment, another incident further weakened Rousseff. With the Curitiba task force in hot pursuit, Rousseff finally decided to bring Lula into her government, inviting him to take over as her chief of staff. But the offer had been extended in a telephone call that – unbeknown to her – was being bugged by Lava Jato investigators.

The tape released by Moro to the press suggested that the proposal had been made to protect Lula from legal proceedings. As a minister, his case would be handled by other prosecutors and would need to be approved by the Supreme Court, affording the former leader a valuable layer of legal protection. The telephone tap was illegal, as was the decision to leak the details of the call. But the scale of the revelation overshadowed these finer considerations. Popular opinion was so incensed that the president was forced to withdraw the offer to Lula, at huge cost to her credibility. "It was a crucial complicating moment that changed everything", said a Brazilian journalist friend who had been covering the affair at the time for one of the São Paulo newspapers. Rousseff's departure was now inevitable. As André Singer puts it: "Like a car accelerating and braking at the same time, the car [of government] started to skid."[7]

An activist judiciary against the PT

Many of the judges associated with Brazil's corruption cases had been popular. Joaquim Barbosa, a former Supreme Court judge who had presided over the trials of those guilty of the *mensalão*, was a front-runner in early polls ahead of the 2014 presidential election, but eventually opted to stay clear of politics. Barbosa is one of the few black Brazilians to have made it to senior levels of the judiciary, which gave particular resonance to his calls for equality for all Brazilians before the law. Rodrigo Janot, the chief public prosecutor from 2013 who took the decision to form the Lava Jato task force, was also well liked. As he wrote in his memoir of the period, published in 2019:

> The fact is that for us – prosecutors, judges and policemen – we were experiencing the kind of popularity that – in the legal area – had never been seen before. Everywhere we went whether it was a restaurant, a bookshop, an airport someone would appear and ask for an autograph, take photos or show support.[8]

Sérgio Moro, the investigating judge[9] in the Lava Jato case, became a phenomenon. Within months of the first judgments, Moro's image was everywhere. Demonstrators at a huge anti-government rally in March 2015 wore Moro masks or T-shirts bearing the slogan "We are all Moro". Some even brandished novelty passports for the "Republic of Curitiba". In Olinda, a north-eastern town known for its giant Carnival puppets, a larger-than-life figure of Moro was carried through the streets. After successfully pursuing the construction companies, Moro became nationally known and something of a celebrity.

> Stopping to buy some groceries in the supermarket on his way home, he heard his presence being announced by loudspeaker as he stood at the checkout. The other customers applauded. On arriving at a book launch in São Paulo, the judge was not only recognised but followed around the shopping centre by more than a dozen people shouting things like 'This guy's the pride of Brazil!', 'My children thank you!', 'Ohhh Sergioo Moroooo!' and 'Justice, justice!'[10]

Did all this adulation turn Moro's head? After the ceremony in Rio de Janeiro in 2015 to recognise him as the personality of the year, the columnist Zuenir Ventura raised the possibility that it might have done. After all, Moro, a Catholic from a conservative provincial background, had a reputation for shy seriousness. He had little time for small talk with colleagues, cycled to work, lived in a modest flat and spent his weekends quietly at home with his wife and two children.[11] But in its first few months, the Lava Jato investigation was seen as an unprecedented success. As a result, the judge was in the national and international limelight.

Ventura concluded that Moro was not seduced by his fame. "There is no arrogance in his gestures. He says what he says without boasting or pretending to be omnipotent. He seems normal." A Brazilian journalist friend who covered Lava Jato for one of São Paulo's top dailies was less convinced: "In 2015, when people were on the streets against Lula and Dilma and calling Moro a superhero, I saw him thanking the demonstrators. There really was no need to do that. He really didn't know how to deal with success."[12]

As Moro became more prominent, the investigation began to embody a political position in its own right. To some extent, this was inevitable. Never before had so many wealthy businessmen or distant politicians been taken away to prison in handcuffs. For many Brazilians, Moro was on the side of the people. He was leading a crusade against privilege and corruption on behalf of fairness. But then prosecutors actively embraced the idea of moving the political agenda. The 1988 Constitution had given Brazilians the right to introduce their own legal initiatives on condition that they amassed 1.5 million signatures. In July 2015 a group of prosecutors outlined ten measures that could form the basis of a new and stronger anti-corruption law and started persuading Brazilians to sign up. Deltan Dallagnol, the then 35-year-old leader of the Curitiba task force, was particularly active in the campaign. By February 2016 the prosecutors had collected enough signatures, and later that year were able to submit their proposals to Congress.

In a sense, the activism of the Curitiba prosecutors constituted a political intervention. André Singer refers to them as "robed lieutenants", an allusion to the young military officers whose intervention in Brazilian politics had led in 1930 to the collapse of the country's first liberal republic. "This [the Lava Jato team] was a group of young, technically skilled professionals mobilising in favour of ethical standards in politics."[13] It was soon clear that the Curitiba group identified the PT and Lula in particular as "the core of the problem", even if in its early days the Lava Jato investigation had seemed to be fairly even-handed. To a greater or lesser extent, all Brazilian parties had practised the corruption now being targeted since at least the 1940s. It was by no means just the PT that used public money to bind political allies into a coalition or fight an election. Testimony from the Lava Jato plea bargains had highlighted the involvement of centre and right-wing parties, as well as Lula's left-wing party. Costa, the former Petrobras director whose plea bargain testimony was so pivotal in the early stages, was passing on money to the Progressive Party, which, as we have already noted, is well to the right of the political spectrum. Janot, the chief prosecutor, whose Brasília-based office was responsible for handling cases against congressmen and ministers, issued a list of fifty-four politicians who were under investigation in 2015. They were from a variety of parties. Janot's office later successfully pursued Eduardo Cunha, the MDB congressional leader whose reputation for corruption was notorious. In 2017 he was sentenced to a prison term of fifteen years and four months.

But the Brasília-based prosecutors failed to make much progress against other MDB leaders. They had a strong case against Renan Calheiros, Romero Jucá and José Sarney – all senior figures who it was alleged had received bribes from Transpetro, a Petrobras subsidiary that runs fuel transportation operations. But in Janot's words, it "hit a wall". "We had touched various niches of power in the first two years, but we had arrived at the real bosses of power. Why did this trio escape investigation? They always have good lawyers but in truth this doesn't explain everything. I still don't know."[14]

In contrast, the Curitiba group's pursuit of Lula da Silva and the PT was determinedly single-minded. Lula faced several charges, and his name cropped up in several inquiries by police and public prosecutors. There were allegations that he had used political influence in order to win construction companies business in Angola and Equatorial Guinea. In Angola, Lula's nephew had also won contracts as part of the same deal. The Instituto Lula, a PT research body, had allegedly received land for its São Paulo headquarters in return for favours. Lula was accused of securing a lucrative contract to buy Grippen fighter aircraft from the Swedish company Saab, again in exchange for payment. And in another case, Lula was said to have intervened to make it more attractive for car companies to set up plants in north-eastern states. Many of the cases were weak and were subsequently dropped. Nevertheless, the Curitiba task force persisted with three. They alleged that a ranch at Atibaia in São Paulo state that Lula, his friends and family used as a weekend retreat had been upgraded in return for contracts won from Petrobras. In another case, a seaside apartment in Guarujá on the São Paulo coast was being modernised by OAS, another construction company, again in exchange for the guarantee of business from Petrobras. In the most ambitious case, Lula, Rousseff, Mantega, Palocci and the PT treasurer, João Vaccari Neto, were all accused of being members of a Mafia-like gang that had orchestrated the Petrobras corruption scheme.

The cases proved difficult to put together, however. In September 2016 the task force launched formal charges against the former president in connection to the Guarujá apartment. At the press conference, the lead prosecutor, Dallagnol, made much of an alleged broader conspiracy but provided little evidence or substantiation. A PowerPoint presentation described Lula as the "big boss of the scheme" but was crudely done and met with a fair bit of media derision. "The slides contained a curious jumble of incongruous bubbles and arrows", wrote one left-wing critic. "In the centre was a big bubble marked 'LULA' but among the smaller bubbles pointing toward the centre were words and phrases that failed to elaborate a legal argument."[15]

After two years of investigations, the strongest case that the prosecutors could bring concerned the apartment. But it was complicated and contentious. Back in 2005 Lula's wife, Marisa Letícia, had bought an apartment in the same Guarujá building where the three-storey unit identified by prosecutors was located. For four years, while the development was still under construction, she had paid for it in monthly instalments. Then the credit union responsible for financing the project went out of business, and OAS, one of the construction companies targeted by Lava Jato, took over ownership.

Lula said that his wife once considered exchanging the apartment she owned for the three-storey one, but the couple had never signed a contract nor received a key. They had visited the property once, back in 2013. Leo Pinheiro, the owner of OAS and a co-defendant in the case, provided the only evidence, but even this was somewhat inconsistent.

> Throughout the discovery process, Pinheiro had made numerous statements, always denying that a condo had been given to Lula. Days before the trial, he made another deposition explaining that he had been "told that that the apartment belonged to Lula and his family and that [he] should not sell it, that [he] should treat it as the president's apartment."[16]

It was on the strength of this testimony that Lula was imprisoned for more than nine years.

It was not perhaps surprising to learn, when the left-wing *Intercept* published details of supposedly confidential messages between Moro and Dallagnol, that the prosecutor doubted the strength of his case.[17] The messages were part of a substantial cache of communications between the task force's prosecutors and judges carried on the protected social media site Telegram that had been leaked to the publication. Moro, for example, suggested that the prosecuting team change the sequence of its investigations and offered constructive criticism of the prosecutorial filing.

These concerns about the partiality of the Lava Jato process were heard more and more following Lula's imprisonment. In part, politicians were more prepared to work together to block further cases against them. The corruption initiative that Dallagnol campaigned so hard for is languishing – in watered down form – in Congress, and new clauses have been introduced to prevent abuses of power by judges and prosecutors. More importantly, in 2018 and 2019 the Supreme Court rolled back many of the legal changes that had made Lava Jato so successful between 2014 and 2017. For example, it ruled that crimes involving a breach of electoral law must be handled by Brazil's electoral court. This will take all cases involving illegal party financing away from Lava Jato investigators. Changes to sentencing rules that allow prisoners to go to prison after the failure of their first appeal have also been reversed. Prison sentences can now only be imposed following the completion of the appeals process, which in Brazil is extremely circuitous and can take many years. Lula, who was imprisoned following the failure of his first appeal, would not have served his sentence if the present rules had applied in 2018. In November 2019 he was released from jail as a result. And finally, quite a lot of the evidence against the former president has been discredited. On 23 March 2021 – as this book was going to press – the Supreme Court ruled (by three votes to two) that Lula had not been treated impartially by the Curitiba court.

Michel Temer and the collapse of the centre

When Lula da Silva orchestrated a coalition with the MDB ahead of the election of 2010, he was criticised by the left for accepting Michel Temer as vice-presidential candidate. But Lula was familiar with the realities of Brazilian politics and knew all about the MDB's appetite for the spoils of office. He also knew that in order to govern effectively the PT would have to compromise. In Brazil, Lula said, Jesus Christ would be obliged to make an alliance with Judas Iscariot if he wanted to run things.

Temer, who took over from Rousseff after her impeachment, could not have been more different from his predecessor. Whereas she rarely met with legislators, he was a vastly experienced deal maker. Temer was constantly talking to deputies, senators and governors. His government succeeded in restoring stability. Inflation was brought under control and new constraints introduced that made it impossible for governments to increase annual spending by more than the rate of inflation. A reform of Brazil's extraordinarily rigid labour laws allowed employers much greater flexibility to increase working hours, introduce part-time working arrangements, and left the agreement of terms and conditions to the companies and unions involved. A reform introduced by Temer allowed Uber and other ride-hailing services to operate without restrictions, dramatically reducing the cost of getting around big cities such as

São Paulo. All this was manna to the private sector and the middle class, but Temer was not popular. Far from it in fact. His cabinet – composed for the first time since 1979 entirely of white men – lost a number of its members to corruption charges. During his two and a half years in office Temer himself was constantly under investigation and survived two impeachment votes. His government was the least popular in recent Brazilian history, with good and excellent ratings hovering around 7 per cent by the time he left office. All this led to the further weakening of the political centre, sowing the ground for the extremely polarised election of 2018 and the emergence of political outsiders.

The big traditional parties of the centre and right – the MDB, the PSDB and the Democrats – saw an extraordinary loss of support in 2018.[18] Back in 2010 the PSDB and MDB had 132 deputies and 31 senators between them. By 2018 they were down to 69 and 19. Local elections had also gone badly for these parties. Only three of the PSDB's seven governors had survived, and the MDB had lost half of its six governorships.

The allegations of corruption against Temer had simply confirmed the party's reputation for graft. As well as Cunha's long term, the former governor of Rio de Janeiro, Sérgio Cabral Filho, was sentenced to fourteen years and two months in prison for corruption and money laundering, much of it in relation to the work contracted in the build-up to the 2014 World Cup and 2016 Olympic Games. The PSDB's slump was perhaps more surprising. In the 1990s the party had headed the government that had conquered the beast of hyperinflation and had become – alongside the PT – an anchor of the political system. But some of its leaders had been implicated in Lava Jato, and the party's decision to support the Temer government had been a political disaster. Suddenly, as Bello wryly commented in *The Economist*, "the PSDB looks far closer to extinction than its symbol, the toucan".[19]

The PT was hit even harder. Its candidate, Fernando Haddad, managed to attract a lot of moderate anti-Bolsonaro voters in the second round run-off, but the distance between the two candidates was still a comfortable 10 percentage points. The party's congressional showing was much weaker, with 54 deputies and 6 senators, down from a high point of 88 and 14 in 2010 and 69 and 12 in 2014, having attracted 38.91 million votes, compared with 55.7 million in 2010. It won four governorships, all of them in the north-east, where it controlled the states of Rio Grande do Norte, Piauí, Ceará and Bahia.

When Lula was convicted in March 2018, he was still ahead in the opinion polls. The verdict and prison sentence, however, ruled him out of the race under the terms of Brazil's clean hands law (which prevents candidates who have been impeached or convicted of corruption from running). As in 2014 the PT's vote held up among the poor in the north-east and the north of the country. But – with the party waiting for the result of a legal challenge that might keep Lula in the race – its campaign started too late. So the legal offensive by the Lava Jato team in Curitiba – what some Brazilians were calling the party of justice – had had a major effect. Lula might not have won the election had he been allowed to run. Polls showed that his rejection rates were very high. But his conviction had strengthened Bolsonaro's chances.

Moro's decision to accept the job of justice minister in the new Bolsonaro government badly damaged his credibility. But it was perhaps not a surprising one. Certainly not to Janot, the chief federal prosecutor and the man who had set up the Curitiba task force in the first place. In his memoir, Janot said that he had been sceptical of the Curitiba team's efforts and suggested that the prosecutors had made up their minds about the results of their investigation before it had taken place. "Dallagnol talked about horizontalising", he wrote. "It became clear that this language implied investigation with a focus on a certain result. The term came into my mind when I saw Sérgio Moro travelling to accept the invitation from Bolsonaro to become justice minister."[20]

7

DRUG GANGS AT WAR

When Renato Roseno first visited Pirambu, a favela in the north-eastern city of Fortaleza, it consisted mostly of wooden shacks and dusty roads. "Life was pretty precarious" in the early 1990s, recalled the left-wing politician. "People were battling for access to electricity and basic healthcare. The really big challenge was the high rate of infant mortality." Even in May 2018 when I visited Pirambu the whole area still had a provisional look to it. Houses on one or two levels and shops made from roughly rendered bricks or concrete breezeblocks had sprung up everywhere. Most looked half-finished, as if the money for fresh cement, bricks, paint or tiles had run out. The pavements were uneven and had often crumbled away. There were piles of uncollected rubbish. At street corners washing was hung out, precariously suspended between electricity pylons. Virtually nothing was planned. But there had been improvements. The roads were paved and the power supply was regular. There were dozens of small supermarkets, fast food outlets selling pizza and hamburgers, pharmacies and bars, where men wearing the red and blue hooped football shirts of the local team Fortaleza or the thick red and black hoops of Flamengo, the Rio de Janeiro team that draws support from across the country, sat out on white plastic chairs drinking beer and cachaça (a sugar cane alcohol). Some residents had cars, and motorcycles buzzed by constantly. Infants were no longer dying in such terrible numbers.

Since the early 1990s the mortality rate for under-fives had plummeted by more than two-thirds.

Yet this improvement in living standards had exposed a new dilemma. As prosperity increased, so had violence: the barrio was on the front lines of a bloody gang war sweeping the northern and north-eastern states of the country. "This morning we found this guy's body in a dozen pieces dumped in a wheelbarrow outside a supermarket", said Roseno, who headed up a state committee and a team of community workers that is trying to reduce the bloodshed. "It's not enough to inflict violence, you have to film it as well", he added, as he showed me the grisly image on his mobile phone.[1]

Since the 1990s the homicide rate had quadrupled in the state of Ceará, the state in which Fortaleza is the biggest city. When I visited, the annual murder rate stood at 50 in every 100,000 of Ceará's inhabitants – or one in every 2,000 people – one of the highest rates in the country. In the most violent neighbourhoods, where factions allied to Brazil's two largest drug gangs – the São Paulo-based First Command of the Capital (Primeiro Comando do Capital, PCC) and the Rio de Janeiro-centred Red Command (Comando Vermelho) – were vying for control, the death rate was double that. And among the black youths who are most likely to become foot soldiers for the gangs it was higher still. Across the state two teenagers per day were dying. The pattern was not unique to Ceará. Rather – as Brazil prepared for the 2018 elections – it was repeated all across these northern states. Hitherto quiet, mainly rural states such as Alagoas and Sergipe were wracked with terrible violence.

Prisons across the north of the country were the sites of bloody massacres, where rival gangs of convicts took advantage of weak systems of control and tried to annihilate each other. As usual, the excruciating violence was filmed. Eighteen months before, PCC prisoners at Itapajé, a penitentiary in a southern suburb of Fortaleza, had turned on their peers from rival gangs with extraordinary viciousness, beheading their opponents with makeshift knives. On 16 October 2016 regular viewers of the morning show on Jovem Pan, a popular television and radio channel, were treated to images of a group of prisoners playing football with a human head. "These are degrading scenes we can't show too much", said the programme's presenter. "They are kicking a human head. Can you imagine human beings getting to this point?"[2]

I'd chosen to come to Fortaleza to look in greater detail at why all this was happening. I spent a few days with Roseno and his young colleagues who were trying to keep kids in school and develop community programmes that could give teenagers an alternative to crime. Over a week we drove around the city's periphery, visiting schools, cultural centres and sports grounds that had been the battlegrounds for a gang war and the sites of tit-for-tat murders.

Plenty of people wanted to do something about this disaster. There was Evandro Rocha, a 40-year-old a former prisoner who had served a long sentence for murder but was now working as a mediator in Pirambu, trying to calm the tensions between rival gangs and persuade youngsters not to follow in his footsteps. "When they threaten me I say you are not going to do that here", said Rocha. "The kid doesn't say anything because I've known him since they were little."

At Bom Jardim, on the other side of the city, young colleagues of Roseno were organising theatre groups and musicians were running workshops in a recently built leisure centre. In Palmeiras, a sprawling settlement nearby, Paulino, a former professional foot-baller, had teamed up with World Vision, an evangelical Christian charity, to run an after-school club called Children of God, where a couple of hundred young children – many of them from gang families – were taught basic Christian values alongside dribbling and heading skills. The kids on the pitch played happily together. Around the perimeter their parents appeared to have temporarily agreed to put aside their differences. Paulo Uchôa, the coordina-tor, told me that the parents of three-quarters were involved in one way or another with the gangs, and roughly half had lost a relative in the bloodletting. "Their parents are mortal enemies but they agree that prevention is the solution."

But I sensed it was an uphill struggle. Many of the kids who joined the gangs had quit school and Roseno told me that not enough was being done to stop this. "60 per cent of the kids that die have abandoned school. A serious country would not allow this to happen", he said. At a secondary school in the poor neighbour-hood of Canindezinho, the 55-year-old head teacher, Francidélia Conceição Chaves de Moura, confessed that it was getting harder to persuade students to continue studying, mainly because the gangs were having an increasing say over who children could associate with. With the periphery carved up into little fiefdoms, those living in areas controlled by the Red Command were not allowed to talk to those from areas controlled by the Guardians of the State – a local gang allied with the PCC – and vice versa. "Things have changed a great deal over the last four or five years", said Chaves de Moura. In the past the teacher said they would have talked to students to try to persuade them not to get involved. "Not nowadays", she said. "We don't know who is who. Back then we could talk to them and tell them that the students wanted to study. There was great respect for the school. Now there is talk of them invading it."

Part of the problem was that rapid population growth in these areas had outpaced the provision of services. Since 2000 the north-eastern states such as Ceará have grown faster than the rest of the country. Jobs have been created at a faster rate in urban areas, sucking in migrants from the poorer countryside. Fortaleza's pop-ulation has risen by 40.4 per cent in the last twenty years, with many newcomers concentrated in poor peripheral areas such as Palmeiras, Pirambu and Canindezinho. "These places have been absolutely forgotten by the state. 40 per cent of Fortaleza doesn't have sewage. It is a nineteenth-century issue and we still haven't resolved it", Roseno told me. "It has grown so much and the more people come the more problems there are", said Valônia Cruz, a

36-year-old estate agent, who I met at the Meninos de Deus project in Palmeiras where she was a volunteer. "The big problem is
that there is nothing for the kids here."

For many young people, with educational opportunities and
jobs scarce, the offer from the powerful and wealthy gangs was
seductive. Membership offered access to sought-after consumer
goods – such as the latest pair of trainers – and status in the community. Family bonds were often weak, so the gangs provided
an alternative sense of belonging. "Money, power and emotional
affection are all very important for a kid of 16 years old", said
Roseno. "You might be a little cog in a big machine but when
you have no money and live in a society where people are valued
by the power they have crime offers answers to all three of these
needs."

One of the few alternatives was the omnipresent evangelical church. In Chapter 9 we will look in detail at the way the
Protestant churches – and especially the home-grown neo-
Pentecostal churches – have expanded in Brazil, sinking deep roots
into peripheral areas of cities and the edgy settlement frontiers of
the Amazon. In Fortaleza, the churches were everywhere, offering emotional connection and social support. But it didn't always
work. Cruz told me she and her husband had been active members of Brazil's Central Baptist Church for the last twenty years,
but had not been able to stop their own teenage son's involvement
with the gangs. He was now in a youth detention centre and she
was desperately worried about his safety. "Incredible as it seems
I was the last to know he'd got involved. It's the influence of
friends, that rebellious instinct. He started to behave strangely. We
don't smoke or drink but then he began to use marijuana."

The intensity of gang warfare and the increasing nihilism of
hyper-violent gang culture had steepened the downward spiral.
"It's got worse with this war of the gangs. It is even difficult to walk
from one community to another", said Regis, who worked with
World Vision. "In the past there were gangs but everything was

resolved with knives", said Roseno. Now violence was celebrated in funk song lyrics and bloody deeds were filmed and circulated on social media. Hyper-violence had become the norm. During 2017 there were 100 beheadings in the city. "For the smallest offence a guy can be killed", said Roseno. "The codes are so subtle. We came across this guy who wanted to join the Red Command. But something went wrong with his initiation, and so they tortured and killed him. We found his body on a football pitch."

But gratuitous hyper-violence was also trying the broader public's patience. "For the rest of society these kids are delinquents and vagabonds and society wants results", Roseno told me. "There is a demand for force. Zero tolerance is what they say here." Even though Ceará was one of a handful of northern states run by PT governors, the authorities were under pressure to train and equip the police force to take a hard line against the gangs. The creation of an expensive elite unit, well-armed and specially trained to deal with the gangs, had won the state government plaudits.[3] Dotted around the edge of the city were brand new police stations that looked like little forts. "People think an elite troop will resolve their problems", said Roseno, alluding to the 2007 film *Tropa de Elite* based on the police's response in Rio de Janeiro. "The sentiment is very cinematographic."

The community activists I spoke to were sceptical, criticising the police's lack of engagement. "The police stay in set positions and they are also very violent. There is no dialogue with the community", one of the staff at World Vision told me. In any event, the rising crime figures in Ceará and other north-eastern states were pushing up overall national crime levels, creating the perception that the national government was losing control. Local and national TV news was dominated by stories of robbery, rape and murder. Brazilians were increasingly worried by the prospect that they could fall victim to violence. As the crime rate ticked up in the mid-2010s, surveys suggested that many Brazilians were on the edge of despair. In mid-2016 Latinbarómetro, a Latin American

polling agency, found that 68.2 per cent of its Brazilian interviewees feared becoming the victim of violent crime "almost all the
time". That was nearly twice as high as in 2007 when the question
had first been asked in an annual survey. Even though similar
wars between gangs and with the police were raging in Mexico,
Brazilians – according to this survey – were more than twice as
worried about violence as Mexicans.

In March 2017, just as the national homicide rate started to
rise, the Brazilian Forum of Public Security, an NGO that brings
together academics, policymakers and police officers, found
alarming evidence that the fear of falling victim to crime explained
a surprisingly high degree of support for authoritarian right-wing
politics. A survey commissioned by the Forum and conducted
by Datafolha, one of Brazil's largest pollsters, showed that large
numbers of Brazilians displayed attitudes typically associated with
what the German sociologist Theodor Adorno called an authoritarian personality. In the late 1940s Adorno, a refugee from Nazi
Germany, had devised an index – the so-called F-scale – to cal-
culate the propensity of populations to adopt fascist attitudes at a
time when the world was still reeling from the devastation of the
Second World War and the atrocities of the Holocaust.

The Forum poll found that Brazilians were very likely to submit
uncritically to authority and to display authoritarian aggression
themselves. Those groups who most feared violence were more
likely to display such authoritarian characteristics. "When the
results came out we were shocked", Daniel Cerqueira, an economist and adviser to the forum, told me when we met in July 2019.
"We didn't even publish it. The Forum met Amnesty International,
the Open Society and other organisations to figure out what to do.
I remember we met one afternoon and came out depressed. This
could clearly influence the election. And there was Bolsonaro waiting in the wings."[4]

What's more, the polling evidence suggested that many voters
associated the rise in violent crime with precisely the kind of softer

law enforcement tactics favoured by Roseno. In March 2018, 50 per cent of Brazilians told the pollster Ibope that they agreed with the statement, "A good thief is a dead thief."[5] This seemed to represent high levels of explicit support for the kind of hardline repression favoured by Bolsonaro. So how had Brazil got to this point? The answer lies in the relationship between poor communities, the drug traffic, the growth of armed gangs, the policing response, and the country's chaotic prison system.

The growth of organised crime

Brazil drug gangs have unusual origins in the sense that there is an overlap between both the First Command and the Red Command and the left-wing guerrilla groups that fought the military dictatorship from the late 1960s. The Red Command was formed in 1971 by prisoners at the Cândido Mendes gaol on Ilha Grande, across the water from the seaside resort of Angra dos Reis in the state of Rio de Janeiro. Most were serving sentences for armed robbery and kidnapping and were protesting against overcrowding at the unit. Built to accommodate 540 prisoners, the cells already housed 1,200. Once released, this group started to run marijuana, cocaine and other illegal drugs in the chaotic and impoverished neighbourhoods that had grown up in the mid-twentieth century in the hills above the fashionable middle-class seaside suburbs of Leme, Copacabana, Ipanema and Leblon.

In São Paulo there was a similar connection between former guerrillas and crime, although here the story was slightly different. During the 1980s, as the economy stagnated in the wake of the debt crisis of the early part of the decade, crime soared, with a number of locally based gangs vying for control of the drugs rackets. The result was a rapid expansion of the prison population, up from about 30,000 in the 1960s and 1970s to 90,000 by the end of the decade. New legislation approved in 1990 triggered further increases (the number of prisoners nearly doubled between 1990 and 1995).[6] One day in October 1992 groups of prisoners started fighting and set fire to their cells in block 9 of Carandiru prison. "Some say it started because of a debt for five packs of cigarettes", said the narrator of a successful 2003 film, based on a best-selling book by a doctor who had voluntarily worked at the prison in his spare time.[7] "Others that it was a fight over a soccer game. One or two say it was about a pair of underpants." There was no doubt about what happened next though. To restore order, the state government sent in squads of well-armed military police who proceeded to massacre the inmates, killing 111 prisoners.

In response eight survivors – now housed at the Taubaté high security unit – said they would "organise to avoid another massacre". In the 13th article of its founding statute, the Primeiro Comando do Capital threatened to "shake the system and make the authorities change their inhuman prison system".[8] The group, which sometimes called itself the Party of Crime, promised to fight against the police and "bandits of bad blood" and for "the world of crime and illegality in general. Crime strengthens crime." The PCC's founders were influenced by the *Mini-Manual of Urban Guerrillas* written by Carlos Marighella, the Marxist-Leninist who founded the National Action for Liberation guerrilla group in the late 1960s. During the 1990s and early 2000s the PCC started to dominate drugs distribution and sank deep roots in prisons and poor communities. Members were attracted by a social support mechanism that offered cash benefits for the families of imprisoned members. In return members paid monthly dues, and the organisation's rule book was rigidly enforced, with draconian punishments for transgressors. Anyone found betraying their comrades or helping themselves to the organisation's money was routinely executed. Collaboration with a member of a rival gang could earn a death sentence not just for the member but for his family as well. Lesser offenders were beaten to the point of hospitalisation.

All the groups had their rituals, but the PCC's elaborate bureaucracy, processes and even its language marked it out as perhaps the most institutionally sophisticated of the organised crime gangs. New members were inducted into the PCC in a ceremony described as a baptism, which resembled the rites of one of the new neo-Pentecostal churches.

> A leader plays the role of the pastor and reads the statutes of the group. Two men – one on the right and one on the left place their hands on the shoulders of the new member. The leader asks the member his name, asks whether he has sympathy for any other organisation and requests him to pledge to obey the statute.[9]

The PCC developed separate departments, called *sinfonias* or symphonies, that managed or 'fine tuned' activities such as membership, social support for members' families or relations with lawyers. Its terminology reinforced the sense of exclusivity and apartness. The regular monthly fee was known as a *cebola* (onion), lawyers were called *gravatas* (ties), and marijuana was known as Bob.

Over time the PCC's business operations became increasingly sophisticated. Rather than being active in every corner of the drugs business like the Rio groups such as the Red Command and a dissident faction known as Third Command, the PCC moved to control the wholesale market and offered – for a price – to provide protection for smaller operators in the retail market. But perhaps the most innovative – and to the outsider the most surprising – aspect of organised crime operations was the way the gangs were able to dominate the Brazilian prison system. In a very real sense, the prisons – run by federal or state governments – served as the strategic and operational headquarters of the gangs.

Brazil's prisons: the "universities of crime"

After the Carandiru massacre in 1992 prison numbers continued to grow. During the first twenty years of this century Brazil's overall population has grown from 175.9 million to 212.6 million, a rise of 20.9 per cent. Over the same period, the number of prisoners more than trebled. In December 2019 a system designed to accommodate 461,026 prisoners held 755,274 prisoners, up from 232,755 in 2000.

The system – traditionally run by the Brazilian states – was a mess. Conditions were frequently appalling.[10] Overcrowding was so bad that prisoners sometimes had no floor space on which to sleep. The control of prison administrations was so ineffective that criminal gangs continued to operate inside the gaols and were able to run operations from there. Prisoners – often held in collective cells – managed their own affairs, with chosen leaders holding keys and able to offer protection to other inmates.

Poorly paid prison wardens had little appetite for bloody confrontations with prisoners, and most states were cash strapped and had few funds available either for extra staff or for hardware that might make vigilance more effective. Technology had made gang control much easier. Since mobile phones first became widely used in the late 1990s, they had been ubiquitous among the prison population. Whether formally banned or not, phones were routinely smuggled in by lawyers, thrown over walls, hidden in food parcels or even inside the bodies of wives and girlfriends allowed access on family visits. Efforts by state and federal authorities to limit the phone signal led to extended legal wrangling with phone companies. Thus, rather than being a sanction that limited the ability of criminal gangs to operate, these circumstances meant that imprisonment in Brazil often facilitated the growth of organisations. The PCC, for example, continued to expand, even though a growing number of its members were behind bars.[11]

Some of the measures taken by the authorities in order to contain violence also backfired. Between 1990 and 1997 the number of prison rebellions increased from ten to a hundred. In response ringleaders were transferred to prisons elsewhere. The tactic simply allowed the PCC to extend its organisation. "It stopped the rebellions but instead of demobilising the PCC it ended up allowing the faction to spread its ideology."[12] Since 2006 Brazil has

established five more tightly controlled prisons under the management of the federal government rather than the states. Many of the
more dangerous prisoners have been moved to these new facilities.
Rather than reducing the power of organised crime, however,
these arrangements have sometimes allowed gang leaders to make
contact with their counterparts from different parts of the country,
often facilitating new criminal alliances that have taken violence
to new levels.

Senior state officials have sometimes refused to recognise the
strategic importance of these headquarters for the gangs. In their
book Paes Manso and Dias interviewed Lourival Gomes, an
administrator who had spent five decades of his working life in the
prison system. Gomes had refused to confront the PCC, arguing
that its importance had been blown up out of all proportion by
the media. "He appeared not to understand what was happening.
For the secretary [and his assistants] it was a problem that didn't
exist."[13]

The gangs' domination of prisons stretches belief at times.
Different gangs often control their own entire prison blocks. At
the Itapajé prison in Ceará, rival gangs even controlled the informal settlements that had grown up around the facility's edge and
become home to prisoners' families.[14] The PCC's grip was so great
that its leaders were routinely able to organise teleconferences
linking members imprisoned in various facilities in different parts
of the country. At times it seemed as if the gangs possessed greater
ingenuity than the state itself. One writer describes, for example,
how the PCC organised an elaborate online trial of a member
accused of murdering a sympathiser. PCC prisoners from different jails served as judge and jury. "What's concerning in the case
is the ease with which they from within the prison system are able
to communicate by teleconference, something that even the police
are not able to do", read the police report.[15]

Surprisingly, Brazilian homicide rates declined in the first
decade of the twenty-first century. Rates had been increasing

steadily during the 1980s and 1990s, rising to 25.7 per 100,000 population in 2003. But under the Lula government there was some improvement, with numbers dropping back to a low of 22 per 100,000 by 2010. Several trends explain this. In 2004 the PT government introduced new controls on weapons purchases that made it more difficult to acquire arms. In some states, police units started to make better use of data and began to collaborate more effectively. The most high-profile improvement in policing came in Rio de Janeiro, where in 2008 the state government introduced a pacification programme, training a new cadre of officers in community policing. Police task forces were sent into the favelas and gang members were given time to flee or give up their weapons. Policemen began to patrol communities on foot and supported local activities, helping residents sort out disputes and even coaching football teams. The state planned to follow up by improving social care, building new health clinics and day care centres, and improving power connections and waste collection services. The fall in violence was immediate. Only seven Pacifying Police Units (UPPs) had been set up by 2010, but in that year the overall number of homicides in the city dropped to 1,409, from 3,615 in 2009, a decline of well over 50 per cent. "People looked at the statistics and it was like we were the messiahs", said Robson Rodrigues, a retired police colonel who commanded the UPP programme between 2010 and 2013.[16] In the run-up to the World Cup of 2014, which Brazil had been preparing for since 2007, the government steadily expanded the programme, introducing it to gang strongholds such as the Complexo do Alemão, twenty-two favelas on the low hills to the north-west of the city that are home to between 200,000 and 300,000 people.

Another trend – less comfortable from the authorities' point of view – was also emerging and having an increasing influence. Just as they had done in the prisons, gangs were increasingly beginning to take control of their neighbourhoods, dissuading their members from engaging in petty crimes or casual violence in order to shield their drug sales and other illegal activities from scrutiny. In his biography of Antônio Francisco Bomfim 'Nem' – a gang leader in the Rio favela of Rocinha – Misha Glenny describes how Nem and his predecessor as leader of the Amigos dos Amigos group, Luciano Barbosa da Silva 'Lulu' Rocinha, established a *modus vivendi* with police patrols and clamped down on gratuitous violence that was seen as being bad for business.[17] Nem forbade the use of crack, banned anyone under the age of 16 from working with his gang and outlawed petty crime and thievery. Gang leaders in Rio also extended financial help and social support to their communities in order to shore up their influence. Lulu ploughed profits from his drug trading business back into the community, for example by lending money to residents who wanted to build or buy their own property. In Complexo, Orlando Jogador, a don for the Red Command, provided medical assistance, food parcels and financial help for funerals to needy residents.

Gabriel Feltran in his study of the PCC describes a similar pattern in São Paulo.

> When I asked why young people in the neighbourhood were not being killed anymore, three explanations were typically offered. The first was: "because everyone has already died"; the second: "because they've already arrested everyone"; and the third, more common, answer was: "because you're not allowed to kill anymore."

As Feltran writes, the PCC had emerged as "an authority dispensing justice. Viewed from the periphery, other causes seem, at most, to be ancillary factors in explaining the dramatic shift in the statistics."[18]

Some of these improvements have persisted to this day. When I started to live in São Paulo back in 2002, everyone I met seemed to have stories of how they or their friends had been stopped late at night at gunpoint and forced to abandon their vehicles to groups of youths. You rarely hear about such car jackings these days. But on the other hand, national crime statistics show a sharp rise in the murder rate. Having edged downwards between 2003 and 2010, homicide rates then climbed to reach 30.5 per 100,000 in 2017. In part this rise was a result of the recession and failed policing. In Rio de Janeiro, for example, the military police – which is responsible for day-to-day operations – found it hard to adopt the community policing tactics that the promoters of pacification sought to develop. Brazil's recession has cut into the funding. Rio concentrates a big chunk of Brazil's oil resources, and so is heavily reliant on royalties from oil sales as a source of revenue; the fall of the oil price in 2014 hit the city hard. In 2016 the state's budget was cut by a third and funding for social programmes in the UPP basically dried up. Community halls were built, but without staff they were never opened. Promised water connections failed to materialise.

But the rise in crime nationally masked some very sharp regional differences. While homicide rates in the southern and south-eastern states such as São Paulo and Rio de Janeiro remain lower than they were in the 1990s, violent crime has escalated in the north and north-east, ravaging states – such as Ceará – that were generally much more peaceful twenty years ago. And perhaps the biggest single contributor to this has been the battle to control the lucrative drug trade in the north of the country. The country's two biggest crime gangs, the PCC and the Red Command, together with smaller local allies and rivals, have been at war.

Gangs at war

In its early days the PCC was limited to São Paulo state, and its business operations largely confined to the distribution of cocaine and other drugs. The PCC bought supplies from traders based in Paraguay. The sugar plantations of the interior of São Paulo state provided an excellent operational base, with hundreds of small airstrips used by farmers for crop spraying that could accommodate regular landings by small aircraft carrying cargoes of cocaine.[19]

The PCC's ambitious leaders began to set wider horizons, however. In the early 2000s the PCC members noted how in the late 1990s a Red Command leader known as Fernandinho Beira-Mar had built up activities in neighbouring Uruguay, Paraguay and Bolivia, and had acquired substantial businesses supplying cocaine, marijuana and heavy weapons to the Red Command.[20] Soon the PCC was trying to do the same, looking to establish direct control over supplies of drugs and build up its organisation in the country as a whole.

As the PCC set its sights on expansion, recruitment was stepped up. Membership rates were reduced from R$1,000 a month to R$700 in São Paulo and R$400 elsewhere, and rules were relaxed.[21] Between 2011 and 2018 the PCC increased its numbers from 8,000 to 11,000 in São Paulo, and from 3,000 to 18,000 in the rest of the country. Not only that, but the group also began to stitch together alliances with smaller locally based gangs, such as Ceará's Guardians of the State. At first the PCC maintained an uneasy alliance with the Red Command, its biggest rival. But wary of the PCC's ambitions, the Rio-based Red Command strengthened its links with other local groups.

These commercial battles intensified in the mid-2010s because of a shift in the global trade in drugs. With the European market growing, the north and north-east of Brazil assumed greater importance as centres of distribution and trans-shipment. One of the factors fuelling this shift was the peace agreement in neighbouring Colombia between the government and the left-wing guerrillas of the Revolutionary Armed Forces of Colombia (FARC). The war originated in the 1960s, one of a number of Latin American insurgencies inspired by the Cuban Revolution. But by the 1990s and 2000s FARC and other left-wing armed groups – as well as their right-wing paramilitary opponents – had begun to derive growing amounts of their revenues from Colombia's burgeoning coca and cocaine business. Backed by US aid and economic support, Colombia's government had begun to reduce the amount of land sown to coca plantations during the 2000s, not least through the deployment of crop sprayers loaded with herbicides. When talks between the FARC and the government got underway in 2012, coca was being grown on only 48,000 hectares of land, less than a third of the amount in 2001. The talks were successful and a peace agreement was reached in 2016, a positive outcome that earned Colombia's former president, Juan Manuel Santos, the Nobel Peace Prize. But the end of hostilities in Colombia had an unwanted side effect in Brazil. With aerial spraying suspended, Colombia's coca acreage began to increase, rising year by year to triple by 2017. Although some FARC guerrillas laid down their arms, others turned to crime, with gangs such as Los Caqueteños based in the city of Leticia willingly cooperating with Brazil's Amazonian drug gangs.[22] And there is evidence too that some of the FARC's heavy weaponry found its way to Brazilian groups.[23]

All this brought fresh importance to the Amazonian drug routes, such as the so-called Solimões which runs from the coca plantations, cocaine labs and marijuana plantations of Colombia and Peru through the upriver stretches of the Amazon rainforest down to Manaus, and then on to the coastal cities of north and north-east Brazil. Amazon traffickers – who in 2006 and 2007 had formed their own tightly organised and highly structured organisation known as the Family of the North – knew the Solimões and other Amazon tributaries "like a spider knows its web".[24]

"It is a dispute about the market", a member of a judicial unit set up by Brazil's public prosecutor to combat organised crime told *Época* magazine in October 2016. "These small factions turned to the Red Command because they were worried the PCC was taking over."[25] By then tensions were at breaking point. In June 2016 the PCC's drive to take over Paraguayan wholesale operations had culminated in the murder of Jorge Rafaat Toumani. Known as the 'King of the Frontier', Toumani had controlled the prices of both the cocaine passing through the zone and the marijuana grown in eastern Paraguay, and acted as a wholesaler to both the

PCC and the Red Command. After his death, the PCC gradually took over the region stretching from Ciudad del Este and Foz de Iguaçu in the south to the twin cities of Ponta Porã and Pedro Juan Caballero in the north.

The displacement of the Red Command from the south increased the importance of the Amazon routes, triggering some tit-for-tat killings. In September 2016 the PCC leaders issued a communiqué – a handwritten document known in PCC parlance as a *salve* – which was smuggled out of the Presidente Venceslau prison in São Paulo and which amounted to a declaration of war. "We've been looking for a dialogue for three years", stated the PCC's leadership. "We are always looking for peace and the union of crime. But what did we get in exchange?"[26] A few days later at a penitentiary in Boa Vista, Roraima, a group of PCC prisoners used the remains of a concrete post as a battering ram to knock down the walls of neighbouring cells and attack the occupants – all members of the rival Red Command gang – with screwdrivers and improvised knives. At least two victims were beheaded, their bodies set alight and images of the action immediately broadcast by mobile phone. The next day the Red Command retaliated at another prison in Rondônia, setting the stage for an intermittent pattern of attacks and reprisals that has continued with varying intensity. These were largely ignored by the public, though occasionally – as in January 2017 and again in May 2019 – the scale of the bloodletting attracted international media attention.

Increasingly, these battles were being fought out on the streets, as the two camps – the PCC and its local allies such as Guardians of the State, and the Red Command and the FDN – fought for control of strategically important areas. In popular quarters of Manaus and Belém, street vendors sold videos carrying mobile phone footage of the riots, billing the contest – the FDN versus the PCC – as they would a boxing bout or a football match. Sometimes it was as if the prisons were hosting a sports event, while the battles outside were taking place between rival groups of fans; at other times the event in the street was the main show, and the prisoners were cheering from the sidelines, as they caught film of the event on their phones.

It was these battles whose effect I was witnessing in Fortaleza. But increasingly too, especially in Rio de Janeiro, another factor was having an impact on patterns of violence; the activities of right-wing paramilitary militias that sometimes counted on the implicit or even explicit support of the police. In the next chapter we'll look at how this phenomenon emerged in Rio de Janeiro and how it is starting to complicate the fight against crime both there and elsewhere in Brazil.

8

RIGHT-WING MILITIAS
ON THE MARCH

In 2002 the sociologist Marcelo Baumann Burgos wrote a book called *Utopian Community* about the poor neighbourhood of Rio das Pedras. On the surface Rio das Pedras resembled dozens of other favelas of Rio de Janeiro. But Burgos had found something unusual. The area was remarkably peaceful. Unlike similar settlements, the organised crime gangs such as the Red Command were absent. "In a city marked by an upsurge of urban violence it is quite attractive to live in a favela where you don't have to deal with the shadowy presence of drug traffickers", he wrote. Rio das Pedras was "an oasis amid the barbarism".[1]

The situation in Rio das Pedras was less positive, however, than it seemed. One barbarism had been kept at bay by another. Back in the 1980s community leaders had paid a group of off-duty policemen and other residents to keep out drug traffickers from the nearby City of God (Cidade de Deus), a favela whose gang violence was brought to international cinema screens by the eponymous 2002 film. The vigilantes routinely killed drugs traffickers, often with either the tacit approval or active cooperation of the police. But self-defence and protection soon evolved into extortion. Within a few years the vigilantes – who came to be the first of Rio de Janeiro's militias – had taken control of local minibus and taxi services. They were supplying bottled gas and access to electricity and the internet, and starting to get involved in land deals.

By 2000 similar militias were spreading across the north and west of Rio, competing with the drug gangs for control of territory. In some areas they themselves had taken over the sale of cocaine and other illegal drugs or had established alliances with drug gangs. By 2020 the militias controlled a quarter of Rio de Janeiro's territory and were extending their tentacles into poor communities across the state.[2] In many ways the militias had become as much of a problem as the organised crime gangs they had been set up to combat. One opinion poll conducted in 2019 suggested that Rio's residents were more afraid of the militias than the gangs. And people were right to feel afraid. These paramilitary groups – commonly referred to as militias since the mid-2000s – were economically more powerful than the Red Command and the drug gangs, often enjoyed the protection of the police, and had established connections with many of the city's politicians. Simone Sibilio, a former policewoman and public prosecutor who is now head of an organised crime unit set up in the state prosecutor's office, said the militias acted as a kind of parallel state. "They have public and politicians [working on their behalf]", she said.[3]

Dealing with this problem is a huge challenge, not least because of the involvement of the police. Policing in Rio de Janeiro is particularly conflictive, but in Brazil as a whole relations between the police and poor communities have been antagonistic for decades. As one recent academic study put it, Brazil's police have "gained notoriety for the widespread use of force, especially torture and executions, and corruption".[4] Reform – as we saw in the previous chapter – has been on the agenda, but it has often been stifled, not least because of the hierarchical and defensive culture of the largest of Brazil's five police forces, the 500,000-strong military police.[5] More than a decade ago another specialist noted that although "an antagonistic relationship between the police and the population at large is an almost universal problem in Latin America, the

133

crime and policing situation in Brazil is by far the most extreme" and that a "combination of low levels of professionalism, weak democratic controls, and extremely low salaries perpetuates an extreme politicization of police governance".[6]

This largely remains the case today. In fact, in recent years police violence has appeared to be spinning out of control. Killings by police officers have nearly tripled since 2013 and now rank among the highest in the world. The number of police killings rose from 2,212 in 2013 to 6,220 in 2018. By comparison, police officers in the United States killed 1,146 people in 2019. The number of police killings in 2018 was a small percentage of the total number of killings in Brazil, but proportionately to the size of Brazil's population, police officers in only a small number of countries kill more people. Although police killings stayed at about the same level during the first year of Bolsonaro's administration, during the first six months of 2020 they rose to 3,081, an increase of about 7 per cent compared to the same period of 2019.[7] Moreover, all this has occurred at a time when police officers were playing a growing role in politics and voicing support for policies that would leave them even freer to use their weapons.

Bolsonaro's election in 2018 raised the profile of these issues for several reasons. First, some of Bolsonaro's most fervent supporters are to be found in police ranks. Second, Bolsonaro and his sons – in the past at least – have been defenders of the militias. And finally, the family's links with individuals connected to this shadowy world have – as we will see – become controversial. Relatives of a notable leader of the Rio das Pedras militia were employed in the office of Flávio Bolsonaro, the president's oldest son and a state legislator in Rio de Janeiro, until 2018.

Rio de Janeiro's militia model

Rio de Janeiro is not the only state where militias have been formed. One of the most prominent and best-documented recent episodes of paramilitary violence occurred in Belém, the port city at the mouth of the Amazon. One night in November 2014 a convoy of masked men on motorbikes and in cars gunned down ten boys and young men in the poor neighbourhood of Terra Firme. A highly critical report released at the end of January 2015 by the local state assembly of Pará said police had colluded in the massacre in revenge for the murder of a retired military police corporal and militia leader who lived in an adjacent area. "This militia action in the neighbourhood of Terra Firme happened with the total connivance, protection and backing ... of the military police of the area", said Pará state legislator Carlos Bordalo, who led the inquiry. "The police cars provided logistical support ... [They] stopped the wounded from leaving to receive help outside."

Relying on previous investigations and testimony from witnesses and police officers, the report concluded that at least five militias were operating in Pará and had been behind massacres dating back to 1994 in which police officers were involved, and for which, in some cases, they had been jailed.[8]

Even so, nothing quite compared to what had been going on in Rio de Janeiro. It is hard to say exactly why militias have become so prominent in the city. The causes are complex. For a start, Rio was the centre of a global empire in the nineteenth century and a glamorous, thriving political capital for the first half of the twentieth, but it was badly hit when Brazil's capital was relocated to Brasília in 1960. In the 1970s and 1980s Rio lost thousands of public-sector and financial services jobs to Brasília and São Paulo. It then became the most important centre for drugs distribution, as Colombian cocaine manufacturers started to diversify their markets to South America and Europe. Much of the trade was concentrated in poor neighbourhoods near the centre of the city.

Urban geography has been a factor too. While favelas have developed on the edges of big Brazilian cities such as São Paulo, Salvador and Brasília, in Rio dense concentrations of poor migrants have long lived on the *morros* or rocky outcrops that rise up steeply from the coast. The inhabitants of these settlements – Brazil's original favelas – live cheek by jowl with the glamorous southern beachside suburbs of Leblon and Ipanema. Their terrain makes them easy to defend – unlike the more dispersed settlements of São Paulo – and helps explain why separate drug gangs grew up in each locality. As we saw in Chapter 7, the PCC dominated the drug trade in São Paulo, but in Rio de Janeiro various groups developed, and three of them – the Red Command, Amigos dos Amigos (Friends of Friends) and Tercer Comando Puro (Pure Third Command) – are still active in the state. "Crime in Rio was all about territorial control and it wasn't the same in other states", Bruno Paes Manso, a sociologist who has written extensively on both the gangs and the militias, told me when I interviewed him in December 2020. "Each *morro* had a boss. It was like Game of Thrones."[9]

Rio de Janeiro's growth in the west introduced another element into the equation. At the beginning of the 1970s the completion of big road and tunnel projects suddenly opened up transport routes through and around the mountainous Tijuca National Park, triggering the rapid development of a previously wild rural area inhabited by jaguars and alligators. An extensive beachfront suburb called Barra da Tijuca was the focus, but dozens of new favelas providing homes for the construction workers and service staff grew up alongside.[10] And it was in these communities that Rio's militia phenomenon was born.

In his most recent book, Paes Manso interviewed 'Lobo' (Wolf), a former member of the paramilitaries who started in the early 2000s to work for a militia in Jacarapeguá, which had taken its lead from the group in neighbouring Rio das Pedras. "The work we did was paid for by a security tax paid [by the inhabitants] to the residents' association, which served as an institutional façade for the militias", Lobo said.

The police supplied gas at a price higher than that freely available on the market but forbade residents from buying gas outside the area. The threat of invasion from the drug traffickers based in City of God – which was controlled by the Red Command – helped keep the residents on board. They were not in a position where they could refuse to pay. And all this was organised with the tacit approval of the 18th battalion of military police, which took advantage of its partnership with the militia to earn money and add firepower [for its battles with the gangs].[11]

Lobo told Paes Manso that the connection between his paramilitary unit and the local military police was very close. Even though he had never qualified as a policeman, Lobo wore a uniform and his group took part in joint operations with the 18th battalion. They were able to use the police's own heavy weaponry when they made incursions into the City of God favela. "I [went to the headquarters of] the 18th and picked up a weapon. We went out and were in total control."[12]

"Violence was justified because it was a way of defending the interests of good people who were threatened by criminals", wrote Paes Manso. "Lobo was proud to have been an assassin and worked for the Rio paramilitaries. He had seen a war against crime, and the killings, the beatings and the violence were tools of the trade." Lobo, who openly admitted to killing various people, spoke as if the victims were guilty of their own deaths – as if they, the killers, "were simply acting according to the rules of the local community".[13]

As the Rio das Pedras model spread to the north, west and across the lowland areas of Rio state known as the Baixada Fluminense, something else became evident. The militias' businesses were more sustainable than those of the drug gangs. Whereas the Red Command or Amigos dos Amigos relied on receipts from drug sales, the militias earned income from sales of gas, electricity, cable TV and from the minibuses that provided transport to the centre of the city. On top of that there were protection fees from shopkeepers and small businesses. Essentially, the paramilitaries were establishing and running small local monopolies, overcharging for basic items and using strong-arm tactics to keep out competition. And whereas the drug gangs had to pay off informants and policemen to secure their strongholds, the paramilitaries enjoyed the willing cooperation of local military policemen.[14] A former Red Command leader interviewed by Paes Manso calculated that the militias could earn many times more from these services than the gangs could from drug sales. "Nobody is going to get rich selling drugs."[15]

The same interviewee calculated hypothetical incomes earned by drug gangs and militias in a community of 18,000 families. The militias would typically charge protection fees of R$10 per family, while businesses such as shops and bars – of which there might be a couple of hundred in such a neighbourhood – would pay R$50 per month. "And they can still make additional money on gas, water, electricity, transport and land sales and rents." By contrast, the drug gang would have been reliant on the margins it made from sales of cocaine and crack cocaine. "A trafficker would pay a supplier R$8,000 for a kilogram of crack cocaine and make maybe R$11,000 on sales. Cocaine would offer only slightly more attractive margins", suggested the same former Red Command leader. "The gang would have to sell up to R$500,000 of drugs to make R$200,000." And it still faced the burden of covering the costs of its arms, ammunition, bribes for the police and wages for its 'soldiers'. There would be little money left to invest. The partnership with the police was another big advantage for the paramilitaries. "If I am a paramilitary there is no chance of me being picked up by the police. This is a huge advantage. Militia members are not hunted down, as occurs with traffickers, and they don't get involved in battles. They are accepted and they form part of the state."[16]

Political connections

The militias had also developed connections with Rio de Janeiro's political establishment. Militias were well placed to offer the votes of their residents in exchange for the promise of money and services. Deals of this kind helped cement relations with a number of aspirant politicians. Luiz André Ferreira da Silva, for example, a local representative for the Republican Party, which is close to the Universal Church, helped the militias expand in favelas such as Bateau Mouche, Chacrinha, Mato Alto and Bela Vista, in the west of the city.[17]

Powerful senior politicians also provided encouragement. In particular, Cesar Maia, a centre-right reformist politician who was mayor of Rio for twelve years in the 1990s and 2000s, defended the militias, arguing that many of their original members were policemen or firemen[18] who lived in poor areas and had been threatened by the drug gangs. In his third mandate as mayor, Maia had tried to decentralise many government services and treated the militias as self-defence associations, an example of the sort of community organisation that it was good to encourage. As late as 2007 Maia told a journalist that the militias could compensate for the absence of the state. "The militias are better than the drug traffickers", he argued.[19]

Jair Bolsonaro and his family were also defenders of the militia cause. As we saw in Chapter 1, Bolsonaro first came into politics when he was elected as a *vereador* (councillor) for the assembly of the city of Rio de Janeiro back in 1988. He had relied heavily on the votes of former colleagues in the armed forces, their friends and their families. Two years later the former captain moved to Brasília to assume a seat in Congress. But he took care to protect the political capital that he had built up in Rio. Bolsonaro first backed the candidature of his wife, Rogéria Nantes Nunes Braga, to take over his own seat. Then in 2000, after the couple had divorced, Bolsonaro persuaded his second oldest son, Carlos – nicknamed 02 – to run against his mother. Meanwhile, Flávio Bolsonaro, the oldest son or 01, became a deputy in the legislature of Rio de Janeiro state in 2002. Both sons continued to work closely with their father, nurturing his contacts and reputation among the military and building new links with the state's police officers. In his first speech to the city legislature, Carlos, who turned 18 only after the election took place, said that he was speaking "not in the name of the Progressive Party [on whose ticket he had been formally elected] but in the name of the Party of Daddy Bolsonaro".[20]

Flávio, meanwhile, worked hard to retain the backing of the family's supporters in the police and security forces. Between 2003 and 2018, as a state legislator, he sponsored hundreds of motions lavishing praise on policemen and soldiers and awarding them decorations. Among those lauded in this way were twenty-three who were subsequently convicted of crimes ranging from homicide to money laundering and involvement in fraudulent tenders. Some policemen who had been closely involved with the militias were also singled out for distinction.[21] Flávio Bolsonaro downplayed the importance of his relationship with the errant police and soldiers, arguing that he had "always acted in defence of agents of public security". He had, he said, "conceded hundreds of honours [and] those that made mistakes are responsible for their actions".[22] Even so, the Bolsonaros were always happy to defend the actions of militias. Repeatedly during the 2000s both Flávio and his father spoke out in their favour. When in 2003 the lower house debated death squad killings in the north-eastern state of Bahia, Jair Bolsonaro was as provocative and belligerent as ever. "A little while ago I heard a legislator criticise the death squads. I want to say that as long as the state does not have the courage to adopt the death penalty, the crime of extermination, as far as I am concerned, is a very welcome thing."[23]

Flávio too was outspoken. In a debate in the state assembly four years later he said:

> you can't simply stigmatise the militias, about which we have heard so much in the press. A militia is nothing more than a disciplined getting together of military and other policemen, organised along certain hierarchical lines, with a view to purging criminals from the heart of the community. In all these militias there is always one, two or three policemen who live in the community and count on the

support of their colleagues to try to guarantee a minimum level of security for their own neighbourhoods.[24]

By 2008 – as we will see shortly – the militias had become much more controversial, but Flávio continued to defend them. As he explained in a speech to the state assembly,

> the militias are a consequence of the state's neglect, the miserable wages that our policemen are paid ... They need other sources of income and look to other activities that are reprehensible from the point of view of public opinion and in the press. In many communities where policemen and firemen live, they organise themselves so that the drug traffic doesn't have the run of the place, without looking for profit, without charging anything. Just ask people in Rio das Pedras ...[25]

The Bolsonaros had other links too. In 2007 Flávio Bolsonaro asked Fabrício Queiroz, a former sergeant in the military police who had served in the 18th battalion at Jacarapeguá, to administer his office in the Rio de Janeiro state assembly. Queiroz had been a family friend since meeting Jair Bolsonaro in the army in 1984. Flávio, then a child of three, had referred to him as 'Uncle'. After leaving the army, Queiroz had joined the military police and got to know Adriano Magalhães da Nóbrega. As policemen, both of them had been involved in actions against gangs in City of God, and Da Nóbrega had eventually become a militia leader in Rio das Pedras.

Queiroz employed Danielle Mendonça da Costa, Da Nóbrega's wife, and from 2016 until 2018 his mother, Raimunda Vera Magalhães da Nóbrega, in Flávio Bolsonaro's office. According to state prosecutors in Rio de Janeiro, wages paid to these and other assistants were illegally channelled back to the family, in a corruption scheme known as *rachadinhas* (little cracks). The revelation followed investigations by a special anti-corruption unit. Queiroz, who allegedly coordinated the scheme, was arrested in June 2020. A separate group of investigators pursuing militia leaders in Rio das Pedras ordered the arrest of Da Nóbrega in January

2019. The former policeman fled north to Bahia and was killed in a shootout with state police units a few months later. Early in November 2020 state prosecutors in Rio de Janeiro confirmed that Flávio Bolsonaro, a senator in Brasília since 2019, was under investigation over the *rachadinhas* affair.[26] The charges concerned the period between 2003 and 2019 and involved payments made to parliamentary advisers being transferred to the deputy. Fifteen other advisers – as well as Quieroz – were also named.

Tackling the militias

Rio's militias went from strength to strength during the 2010s. By 2018 they ran eighty-eight neighbourhoods, compared to forty-one in 2010.[27] One recent survey, published by the Federal Fluminense University and based on calls to a crimestoppers line, estimated that the militias could control more than half the city.[28] In recent years some of the militias have begun to diversify into the drugs trade themselves. Increasingly there are examples of militias cooperating with the drug gangs, in particular the Pure Third Command. "For both the militias and the Third Command their main enemy is the Red Command. It makes sense."[29]

The scale of the militia problem had first begun to emerge in 2008 when, in the wake of the widely publicised detention and torture of three local journalists, the state assembly of Rio de Janeiro set up an inquiry. In May 2008 a reporter, a photographer and a driver for the newspaper *O Dia* went undercover in the Batan neighbourhood of north-west Rio to prepare a report on the daily lives of a community run by a militia. The three were discovered and held for nearly eight days, during which time they were beaten, asphyxiated with plastic bags and given electric shocks.

More recently, public concern was heightened by the controversy surrounding the murder of a popular black politician, Marielle Franco. Franco, who was assassinated along with her driver in March 2018, had been closely involved in political actions aimed at tackling police and militia violence. She had worked as an adviser to Michel Freixo, a state deputy for the PSOL, who had coordinated the investigation which eventually requested the indictment of 266 politicians, policemen, prison guards and firemen. "This was when the penny dropped in Rio de Janeiro. After they started torturing journalists nobody had the courage to say they were a necessary evil", said Simone Sibilio, the Rio prosecutor.[30]

Franco had grown up in the Maré, a complex of favelas, and was studying sociology when she started working with Freixo. She too had joined the far-left PSOL and in 2016 won an impressive number of votes to become a city councillor. Fearless, Franco had been looking into land-titling scams in a number of favelas in the north of the city. It must have sometimes seemed an uphill struggle though. Few of the tougher policing procedures recommended by the inquiry were implemented and the militias continued to extend influence and power. By 2016 poorer Brazilians were beginning to see the militias as a bigger problem than the drug traffickers. During 2016 and 2017 for example, 65 per cent of complaints received by the crimestoppers line were about the militias.

Franco's murder – committed during the first weeks of a military intervention into the state's security that had been ordered by President Temer and was designed to tackle rising violence among the drug gangs – seemed to epitomise the militias' impunity. As both a lesbian and a black woman Franco represented a new kind of identity politics that, although embryonic in Brazil, had international resonance. Moreover, initial press reports pointed to police collusion in the killing. The security cameras at the site of the shooting had been turned off and police units responsible for investigating the case had been slow to act in the first few days. In March 2019 investigators eventually arrested two men – both militia members – for Franco's murder. The trial is due to go ahead in 2021.[31]

In spite of this particular legal advance, the militias have continued to tighten their grip over many communities. A Datafolha survey conducted early in 2019 suggests that this has been the case for a while in the favelas. The survey found that while a majority of those interviewed "from all backgrounds" were still more fearful of the drug gangs, 29 per cent of those living in favelas feared the militias more, while only 25 per cent were more worried by the drug gangs.[32] For Sibilio, the Rio prosecutor, the pace of the militias' recent expansion and their growing unpopularity have brought these organisations to the top of her agenda. When I talked to her in November 2020 she told me that militias "began with a certain amount of popular support but they don't have that sympathy any more. It has been proved that they kill, they rape and they impose punishments on communities. Even if favela residents have a little stall they have to pay the militia."[33]

In addition, though, Sibilio said investigators have had to compensate for the fact that in the past the situation was not tackled in the way it should have been. Militia leaders such as Ronald Paulo Alves Pereira, a major in the military police, and Da Nóbrega had been "active for more than twenty years. It was one of the reasons why we gave the name *Intocáveis* (Untouchables) to our inquiry into the Rio das Pedras militia", said Sibilio.[34] In any event, Sibilio was in little doubt that the fight against militias was now the priority for her organisation. It will not be an easy one to win, partly because of the connections the militias have with the police forces. In fact, it is hard to separate out the battle in Rio from a broader national fight to make the police more accountable.

The challenge of police reform

Police reform has been on Brazil's political agenda for a while, but progress has been very limited. Ombudsmen and community councils have been established to make relations with local communities more harmonious but have worked well in only a few places. As we saw in Chapter 7, the ambitious UPP experiment in community policing in Rio de Janeiro was a failure. Police culture is notoriously resistant to change and the involvement of policemen in politics has made matters worse. A growing number of policemen have been elected as congressmen at a national and local level, but overwhelmingly these representatives support a hard and repressive approach towards crime.

The cultural issues are deeply rooted. Since 1985 both the larger military police – responsible for patrolling and responding to crimes – and the smaller civil police (which investigates and does detective work) have been under civilian control. They are both subject to the orders of elected state governors.[35] However, the police are "still more the maintainers of governmental order than they are crime-solving organisations".[36] Their history has a lot to do with this. The military police forces originated as autonomous armies that served provincial governors during Brazil's first republic (1898–1930). They were subjected to increasing control by the federal government and especially the army during the presidencies of Getúlio Vargas (1930–45 and 1951–54). The civil police grew out of judicial investigators attached to the imperial crown in the nineteenth century, but both forces were modified under the military dictatorship of 1964–85. The military police were put under army control and deployed in the repression of political opponents and dissidents, while the civil police lost some of their investigative capacity. The 1988 Constitution legitimised a conception of the public order that was based on the idea of the national security doctrine – the same body of ideas that saw the world as divided into two blocs and treated political dissidents as internal enemies.[37]

The military police also retains the rigid hierarchies, disciplinary codes and legal structures that stem from the period of military dictatorship and are based on army practices. "You can be punished because you don't shave or give up your seat on a bus to a superior. Does that make sense?", Samira Bueno, the executive director of the Forúm Brasileiro de Segurança Pública, told the BBC in 2017.[38] Military courts – separate from the national justice system – rule on all cases involving policemen, apart from homicides. The defensive corporatism of both the military and civil police is so strong that it impedes the two forces from working together effectively, said Bueno. This helps explain why only about 8 per cent of homicides are ever solved.

The big complicating factor is the emergence over the last twenty years of the police as an aggressive and noisy political lobby. In the first part of the twentieth century the police tended to rely on their relationships with retired governors who had been elected to the senate. These politicians deployed the police forces and could veto bills that threatened their interests. The initial impetus for change was the emergence of police unions after a number of police strikes in the 1990s. These unions represented "not just individual forces but also ranks within them. They began to organize collectively to elect members to municipal and state legislatures and to the National Congress."[39] Seven former police officers were elected in 2002, but only four in 2006 and 2010.

In the 2000s the emergence of a congressional lobby on security issues was shaped by the debate about gun control. Indeed, the term *bancada da bala* or bullet caucus originally denoted legislators funded by the Brazilian firearms industry as it lobbied to combat the Lula government's proposed tightening of rules on the owner-ship and use of firearms. Brazil restricted gun ownership in 2003, but in a 2005 referendum Brazilians voted against banning the sale of guns and ammunition to civilians. Subsequently the bullet 'bench' or caucus has become more associated in the public mind with the defence of a hardline approach towards crime and a defence of the corporate interests of the police – both themes that echo the concerns of Bolsonaro and his allies.[40]

However, during the Rousseff administration police organisa-tions became more strategic about encouraging and supporting candidates. The number of policemen and former policemen run-ning for the federal Congress and state assemblies rose to 1,250, the highest to date. In 2014 eighteen were elected to Congress. The *bancada* included Jair Bolsonaro and his youngest son, Eduardo, who before running for election in 2014 had spent four years as an administrative officer in the federal police. Four policemen-turned-deputies – Éder Mauro from Pará, Waldir Soares de Oliveira from Goiás, Moroni Torgan from Ceará and Alberto Fraga from Brasília – were among those who received most votes in their states. Ten of the thirty Brazilian municipalities with the highest homicide rates in 2017 were to be found in Pará, Ceará and Goiás, indicating, as we suggested in Chapter 7, that the hardline approach has a particular attraction in areas where crime rates are high.[41]

During 2018 this tendency's campaign went into overdrive. With anxieties about crime mounting, right-wing parties actively sought to recruit police officers. Police associations made much use of WhatsApp groups and other social media to promote candidates – nowhere more so than in Rio, where Wilson Witzel, a former naval officer and federal judge, came from nowhere to win the race to become governor of the state. A military police commander, Fabiana Silva de Souza, was one of eight Rio-based officers elected to either the state assembly or the federal Congress. Having earned national fame by using her weapon to control a crowd in Rio's Jacarezinho favela after crime gangs had set a bus on fire, she won election as a deputy for Bolsonaro's PSL. But elsewhere too, police officers – celebrities by virtue of their social media fame – came to prominence. Corporal Kátia Sastre, the off-duty policewoman whose shooting of an armed robber outside her daughter's school in the São Paulo suburb of Suzano was mentioned in the introduction to this book, was another PSL deputy. In 2018 the numbers of this group doubled. Now thirty-two members of the lower house and five senators had a background in the police forces.

The police lobby was evident too in the municipal elections, and many police officers were vocal in their support for the president during his first two years in office. The authors of one recent study describe these radical right-wing policemen as "Bolsonaro's shock troops".[42]

9

AND GOD TOLD ME TO VOTE FOR BOLSONARO

Fashionably dressed in a dark red shirt and plain dark slacks, Antônio Pires did not look like a typical evangelical preacher. Yet in December 2019 Pires and his wife – who is also a pastor at the Pentecostal Church of Jesus Christ the Nazarene – welcomed me warmly into a church decorated with posters that extolled the "plenitude of God". The church, a humble affair made from breezeblocks and topped with an aluminium roof, was barely distinguishable from the neighbouring shacks on the dusty tracks of Glória, a favela on the eastern edges of the central city of Uberlândia, but the atmosphere inside was cheerful. As a group of women banged out gospel songs, we sat on white plastic chairs in a dimly lit corridor and Pires, a slim, fit and muscular man of 43, told me why a year previously he had cast his ballot for Jair Bolsonaro. "Each Christian, each person, started to pray. And I, Antônio, started to pray and I asked God who I should vote for", said Pires, as if he were reading a biblical text. "And God showed me that I should vote for Bolsonaro. If you ask me why it was because of this revelation: Christians can't act on the basis of emotion but follow what God directs. The Workers' Party did good work here but it was not right for them to continue."

I was meeting Pires and other evangelical preachers in Glória because Igino Oliveira, the distraught left-wing labour lawyer who we met in the introduction to this book, was convinced that the evangelical churches were a big reason why his Workers' Party had done so badly in the 2018 election. Glória, an informal settlement of simple one-storey houses and unpaved roads established on land owned by the local university, was one place where the party really ought to have done well. Home to 15,000 people, most of whom were migrants from rural areas in the centre of the country, the favela had survived demolition only by dint of a party campaign. But large numbers of residents had voted for Bolsonaro. This had contributed to an impressive win for the right-wing candidate in the city, where Bolsonaro won 63 per cent against 37 per cent for the PT in the second round run-off, 8 percentage points more than the national average. "The evangelical church was one of the main reasons for our defeat", said Oliveira, who reckoned that 70 per cent of Glória's population attended evangelical churches of one form or another.

> These churches sink such deep roots into these communities. When squatters occupy land or the occupation develops almost at the same time you get these evangelical and neo-Pentecostal churches branching out. They have a powerful appeal that you just can't ignore. It is incredible. Various people say they have spoken with angels and talk about revelations from God. And when you are arguing against a revelation and God said Bolsonaro was better what can you say?

Pires's church had been built three years earlier, mostly with money painstakingly collected from followers, and would have been knocked down if the clearance had been allowed to go ahead. It was one of no fewer than twenty-two evangelical churches that had sprung up in Glória in only eight years, highlighting the dynamism of a religion that is transforming many parts of Brazil and seems to be particularly vibrant in the poor outskirts of Brazilian cities. In Uberlândia all the big evangelical churches were present – the Baptists, the Methodists, the Assemblies of God and homegrown Brazilian churches such as the Universal Church of the Kingdom of God, which we will take a detailed look at later in this chapter. But there were also literally dozens of tiny churches, which seemed to be emerging more or less spontaneously.

Many of these evangelicals had voted for or were sympathetic to Bolsonaro. It wasn't always easy to pin down the reasons though. After talking to Pires for more than an hour I was still not sure – save for the divine revelation – why he had voted the way he did. He said that he had always voted for the PT in the past. So had another preacher I met – a wild-eyed, 48-year-old domestic cleaner, Maria Aparecida Rodrigues de Oliveira. Neither had much time for the individualistic prosperity theology that forms a big part of the message promoted by the big neo-Pentecostal churches. Instead they were keen to improve social conditions in their community. In fact, the smaller and newer churches – like the Nazarene and Rodrigues's Evangelical Kingdom Church – seemed to have been formed precisely in order to establish close relationships with their flocks, or at least closer than the bigger and more institutionalised churches managed. They were particularly supportive to communities that lacked basic social provision and that were often at the mercy of drug gangs. The women singing gospel at the Nazarene had just visited a member who had not been seen for a few weeks and were trying to tempt her back. The Evangelical Kingdom Church donated food and petrol to unemployed or hard-up members and encouraged them to keep away from drugs and alcohol.

In fact there is nothing inevitable about the evangelical church's alliance with the political right. Former left-wing president Luiz Inácio Lula da Silva was able to fashion an alliance with evangelical churches.[1] His vice-president, José Alencar, himself converted to the evangelical church towards the end of his life. But from 2009 onwards, the alliance between the PT and the evangelicals had come under increasing pressure, partly as a result of the growing prominence of gender and identity politics within the Workers' Party. By 2016 the leaders of all the biggest churches had broken with the PT, and in 2018 all explicitly advocated a vote for Bolsonaro.

So it wasn't too surprising that some of the evangelicals I met in Glória were unhappy about the PT's support for homosexuality and gender identity, which they argued breached Christian teachings. Rodrigues harangued me on the evils of gay sex. "It's disgusting, disgusting", she told me. "For me a man is a man and a woman a woman. I'll tell you something. If a gay person came to me to be baptised I wouldn't do it." She tended to see the PT's involvement in corruption as part of the same process of moral collapse. She drew a parallel between Bolsonaro and Nebuchadnezzar, a sixth-century BC king of Babylon who, according to the Bible, was sent by God to clean up corruption and reverse moral decay. "God used Nebuchadnezzar to teach people a lesson. I don't know whether [Bolsonaro] will rescue Brazil but he will start something. Already it's changing."

Oliveira was convinced that gender issues had been a decisive factor in his party's defeat.

> One woman had the courage to tell me her motive for voting Bolsonaro. I said to her Dona Maria if this guy wins he'll knock down your house. Can't you see that they are against us? And she replied "Better that they knock down my house than my son becomes gay. The only thing I can't accept is my son becoming gay. The government is fucking us up on these things."

Glória though is simply an extreme example of a wider trend. Across Brazil, the growing evangelical community voted very heavily indeed for Bolsonaro in 2018. Three days before the second round run-off between Bolsonaro and Fernando Haddad, the PT candidate, Datafolha conducted a poll that – in an era of polling surprises – proved to be remarkably accurate: 56 per cent of those interviewed said they would vote for Bolsonaro, 44 per cent for Haddad, fairly close to the final outcome. Datafolha found that evangelicals were much more likely than Catholics, agnostics or members of other religions to favour the former army captain. It predicted that whereas Catholic voters were likely to opt for Bolsonaro by a very narrow margin, the evangelical camp favoured Bolsonaro by more than two to one.[2] "Without a doubt the evangelicals have been transformed into a decisive political force", commented José Eustáquio Diniz Alves, a professor of demography at Brazil's statistics institute, the IBGE.[3]

Why and how evangelicalism has grown in Brazil and the way it has contributed to a moral backlash against liberalism and to the strengthening of the conservative right is the subject of the rest of this chapter.

The resonance of evangelicalism

Ever since it was a colony, Brazil has been predominantly a Catholic country. Initially introduced in the nineteenth century by European and North American missionaries, Protestantism grew slowly at first. As recently as 1980 only eight million Brazilians – the equivalent of 6.6 per cent of the population – said they were Protestants. By 2010, when the IBGE published its most recent census, the number had risen to 42.3 million or 22.2 per cent. We won't know for certain until the next census is out, but according to a January 2020 poll by Datafolha there could be as many as 65.9 million Protestants in Brazil, or 31 per cent of the country's total population.[4]

What is more, while the number of Protestants is rising as a percentage of the population, the number of Catholics is falling, so much so that Protestants are forecast to become a majority of Brazil's population by the middle of the century. Diniz Alves at IBGE said that between 1990 and 2010 the Catholic population had declined at 1 percentage point per year, while the number of Protestants has grown at an average rate of 0.7 per cent each year. Since 2010 the trend has become even more marked, with the number of Catholics declining at a rate of 1.2 per cent, and the number of Protestants rising by a yearly rate of 0.8 per cent.[5]

It is not just the sheer number of Brazilian Protestants that is notable, however. Brazil has seen the rise of a particular kind of Protestantism, known as Pentecostalism. Historically, Protestantism has been a broad and multi-faceted phenomenon. It includes the modern descendants of the original Anglicans, Lutherans and Calvinists, the reformists who in the sixteenth century shook Western Christianity apart by rejecting not only the supremacy of the Pope, but all the centralised structures and ritual of the Roman Catholic Church. And then Protestantism produced the Methodists, Baptists and other so-called 'non-conformists' of the late eighteenth and nineteenth centuries who emerged as a reaction to the perceived bureaucratisation and conservatism of existing churches. This tension between the institutional conservatism of an established church and the radicalism of grassroots preachers wanting a return to simpler and purer Christian values has been a constant feature of a movement that is well known for its fractiousness. The most important of these schisms from a Brazilian perspective was the emergence on the US west coast at the beginning of the twentieth century of Pentecostalism.

Pentecostalism places special importance on the Holy Spirit, an invisible divine force (the third 'person' of the Christian divine Trinity) that binds Christ's followers or disciples to God. This religious tradition derives its name from Pentecost, when according to the biblical Acts of the Apostles the Holy Spirit infused the spirits of Jesus' followers shortly after his death. A black churchman called William Seymour claimed an ability to interpret this spirit. He and other followers, who set up their first church in Los Angeles in 1905, also developed the ability to go into a state of trance and make speech-like sounds that have no discernible meaning and are from no identifiable language. Adherents believed this 'speaking in tongues' was a transmission of divine influence. They also claimed to be able to channel these spirit forces in order to 'heal' – to cure diseases or physical conditions.

Two Swedish missionaries brought Pentecostalism to Brazil in 1911, establishing the first Assemblies of God church in the city of Belém on the Amazon. The Assemblies of God, which itself is divided into various competing factions, is still the biggest Pentecostal church in Brazil, with more than 12 million members, and is especially powerful in the north. As we shall see, the church – especially the branch led by Silas Malafaia, the Assemblies of God Victory of Christ Church in Rio de Janeiro – has been politically influential. Other Pentecostal churches include the Quadrangular, which takes its name from the Four Square Church of the US – so-called to reflect the four aspects of God as man, lion, ox and eagle that were revealed in a vision to the Old Testament prophet Ezekiel and encompassing the four aspects of Christ: saviour, baptiser with the Holy Spirit, healer and soon coming king. Another is the homegrown Brazil for Christ, which was one of the first churches to use radio and television and to hold prayer meetings in football stadiums and cinemas.[6]

Pentecostalism resonated in poor communities. Its emphasis on spirits, cures and miracles is perhaps closer to traditional popular forms of Latin American religiosity, including popular Catholicism, than the more mainstream Protestant creeds dominant in the developed world. The idea of the trance and possession by spirits figure in traditional belief systems, possibly – as one Latin American theologian suggests – to help deal with the nightmare of slavery or the lesser trauma of migration. Brazil's vast rural-to-urban migrations from the 1940s onwards broke up traditional patterns of social relations, producing a rootless urban population for whom Pentecostalism provided hope and comfort.

In Brazil, for example, good and bad spirits – invoked or spurned by a priest – are a central element of Candomblé and Umbanda, syncretic creeds that link elements from Catholicism and African and indigenous cults. Similar ideas are found in Spiritism, a belief system that reached its peak elsewhere in the world in the first two decades of the twentieth century, but that is still popular in Brazil.[7]

Pentecostalism also draws on the popular Catholic traditions that flourished in Brazil in the eighteenth and nineteenth centuries, in part because of acute shortages of clergy.[8]

Neo-Pentecostalism takes off

From the late 1970s onwards the spread of Pentecostalism was super-charged by the growth of an entirely new kind of locally evolved Pentecostal church that was more flexible than its older and more staid counterparts. These new churches, which became known as neo-Pentecostals, at first held services in warehouses, disused cinemas or old shops. Services had no fixed end time. Preachers learned their trade quickly, eschewing the theological colleges and long training courses typical of older churches. Neo-Pentecostal preachers spoke in the same dialects and used the same idioms as their followers, and were quickly able to establish emotional bonds. Churches were open all the time. Music and popular culture were used to attract followers. The new churches were less prescriptive about dress styles and lifestyles and much more aggressive about winning converts. They never recruited as many members as the Assemblies, but neo-Pentecostals proved to be exceptionally dynamic, financially powerful and politically influential.

I learned quite a bit about them from Marcello Rodrigo Peres Ramos, a 50-year-old sales executive who spent several years as a senior figure in one of the most dynamic neo-Pentecostal churches, Renascer em Cristo (Rebirth in Christ). Ramos had grown up in the Pentecostal church, attending an Assemblies church in São Paulo, and described an institution that was inward-looking and rigid in its customs. "The Assemblies were stuck between four walls. Many people didn't want to get involved before because they thought the church would stop them from going to the beach or playing football."

Ramos discovered Renascer as a teenager. The approach adopted by new churches was much more appealing to younger, more urban groups. "The preacher had rented a theatre hall, installed ramps there and invited kids to use their skateboards. At the end of the afternoon he got all the kids together and offered them a quick sermon. It really made on impression on me", Ramos told me. Renascer, launched by a former marketing executive for Xerox, was following in the footsteps of the Universal Church of the Kingdom of God, which was originally based in the offices of a funeral parlour in the Rio suburb of Abolição. Its founder, Edir Macedo, was a clerk at the Rio state lottery, who had done much of his early preaching in a disused porn cinema.[9]

But neo-Pentecostalism wasn't just about form. The new churches embraced an entirely new kind of religious thinking that had been imported from the United States. Pentecostals have traditionally insisted that austere living and self-sacrifice are necessary to achieve salvation in the afterlife, but the new ideas were quite different. Rather than shun material wealth, believers were urged to embrace money, commercialism and business success in what became known as the theology of prosperity. The traditional tithes – the regular contributions that Christians from all Catholic and Protestant churches pay – assume particular importance in the neo-Pentecostal church since they effectively allow the believer to buy into prosperity. In Brazil, these payments are known as a *dízimo* or a tenth (reflecting the fact that church members are expected to donate a tenth of their income). Additional contributions are called for, with the scale of commitments generally seen to reflect the depth of a congregant's faith.[10]

Macedo, who had been a Catholic and had dabbled with Spiritism in his youth, made the idea a guiding principle for his Universal Church of the Kingdom of God, which – along with his brother-in-law Romildo Ribeiro (or as he is better known RR) Soares – he formed towards the end of 1978. "Just as blood is necessary for the human body, so money is needed for the works of God", he once said.[11]

The *dízimo* is a guarantee of abundant material life and spiritual prosperity. It is necessary to give what you can't afford. The money that you keep in your savings account for a future dream this is what has importance [for God], because if you give something that you don't miss and doesn't have value for you, it has no value for God either.[12]

The new denominations grew quickly. Their organisation was highly centralised, with power residing in the figures of charismatic leaders. At the Universal Church, senior figures who might have challenged Macedo were quickly moved on. Two of Macedo's closest colleagues left the church to form rival organisations. Barely had the Universal Church got off the ground before Soares was squeezed out and freed up to form his own version, the International Church of the Grace of God. Another disciple of Macedo, Valdemiro Santiago de Olivares, followed suit a decade or so later with the World Church of the Power of God.

At the churches' grass roots, modestly paid clerics were obliged to follow instructions. Pastors were expected to work long hours and were judged on their ability to raise money from congregations. One observer described a "competitive climate" and said pastors were constantly moved around "to avoid any dissidence".[13] Everything was geared up to achieve continuous expansion. And the churches did this by broadcasting their messages on radio and TV. The preachers wanted to reach as many people as possible. Again the Universal Church set an example that newer churches such as Renascer em Cristo followed. A few months after launching the Universal Church, Macedo had stretched its finances to breaking point by renting a 15-minute spot late at night on Rádio Metropolitana, one of a number of popular radio stations in Rio de Janeiro. The church formed clubs to bring listeners together who they would then invite to regular services. With the money raised from the new congregants, the church bought more time from stations in different cities.[14] As soon as a new deal was signed, the church's pastors again formed a new circle of supporters and potential new members, and so the process went on.

By 1989, eleven years after its formation, the Universal Church was borrowing heavily to buy Record, a struggling São Paulo-based television station, reflecting the steady build-up of the evangelical presence in Brazil's media. Within a few years broadcasting was becoming integral to all the new neo-Pentecostal churches. It was almost a matter of survival. Ramos remembered that in 1999 when his own Renascer was acquiring Rede Gospel, the search for funds was so frantic that the church persuaded members to make big one-off donations; his wife had given up her car, a recently bought Fiat. Media was crucial for the churches as they sought to increase the number of followers and income. Increasingly, media appearances were dominating the lives of evangelical leaders. By 2008 Ramos was a bishop in Renascer, based in the university city of Campinas, and was spending his days driving between one radio station and another in order to give sermons or take part in live Bible discussions. "In Campinas I'd do a programme between 9 a.m. and 11.30 a.m., drive to São Paulo to do the Bible Debate programme there from 2 p.m. and return to Campinas for an evening show there."[15]

Other evangelical churches too have put a lot of emphasis into their media organisation, and overall they now boast a media presence way bigger than that of the Catholic Church. According to one recent analysis the evangelical church has 963 radio stations, four times the number of the Catholic Church.[16] The Universal Church alone has more than sixty-four radio stations and a complex network of regional TV channels and local franchises. As well as Renascer's Rede Gospel, the Igreja Mundial do Poder de Deus acquired Rádio Mundial and the Sara Nossa Terra church owns Rede Gênesis. All of these stations dedicated a certain section of their programming to religion, but fairly soon they began to broaden their non-religious output. Record began to employ

professional journalists and administrators to run its various operations in the early 1990s, for example.

As they acquired wealth, the neo-Pentecostal churches started
to build huge temples in the centres of cities, a physical manifes-
tation and symbol of power every bit as emphatic as the great
cathedrals of Western Christianity. The churches eschew the
classic nave, tower and steeple Christian model. The biggest
and most spectacular of the Universal churches, the Temple of
Salomão in São Paulo, completed in 2014 and based on the original Jewish temple of the first millennium BC in Jerusalem, caters
for 10,000 worshippers. Features include a conveyor belt system
designed to carry congregants' *dízimo* contributions directly to a
safe room.[17]

In many ways the giant Pentecostal churches resemble other
Brazilian businesses. Figures are hard to come by because few
churches publish how much they earn. But as long ago as 2006 –
the last year the figure was made public – the Universal Church
earned $750m from members' contributions.[18] *Forbes* magazine
estimated Macedo's personal wealth at $1.1bn, making him one of
the world's richest religious leaders.[19]

Stories that the churches sell items such as amulets and holy
brushes that have been blessed by a cleric – to sweep away evil
spirits – or, as during the coronavirus pandemic, holy gel often
turn out to be apocryphal, but are occasionally based in fact. In
any case, the intangible package of advice and motivation that is
sold with the promise of future wealth does amount to a product of
sorts. Not for nothing is the Universal Church sometimes labelled
Magic Inc., a company that sells magic products and services.[20]
The commitment of many neo-Pentecostals is dependent on the
benefits obtained, in the same way that customers might have
expectations of a health insurance contract or gym membership.
And that means there is high turnover. "There is so much passing
trade", said Ramos, who left the Renascer church in 2010. "Since
prosperity theology was introduced you've seen the gospel become

a commodity. It is as if the church were something you buy in a shopping mall."

Not surprisingly, these Pentecostal and neo-Pentecostal churches took root in poor communities. As we have seen, their theology had a popular appeal. The newer neo-Pentecostals were particularly flexible, but all the evangelical churches tended to move fast compared with their sluggish Catholic rival. And as migration produced new communities in poorer, more remote areas such as Glória or along the agricultural frontiers of the Amazon and the centre-west, the Pentecostals and neo-Pentecostals were often the first to be up and running. "I used to joke that after a new favela was set up a Pentecostal church would be in place the day after and five Pentecostal churches by the end of the week", Paul Freston, a British sociologist of religion, told me. "But it would take a year for the first Catholic one to be built."[21]

A 2003 study of Rio de Janeiro noted how much more numerous the Pentecostal members were in poorer neighbourhoods. Less than 8 per cent of the wealthy South Zone was Pentecostal, while in the poorer, more remote areas Pentecostals made up between 14 and 17 per cent of the population.[22] By 2006 in poor neighbourhoods in Rio de Janeiro, such as Belford Roxo, Duque de Caxias and Nova Iguaçu, Pentecostals comprised roughly 30 per cent of the population, making these areas the most Pentecostal regions of the country.

In general the evangelicals were perhaps more likely to offer their followers contacts and advice about how to acquire new skills. By discouraging the consumption of alcohol and drugs, the new churches might help their followers develop the confidence, motivation and personal skills that are essential in the service economy where most of them find work.[23] So close was this connection between Pentecostalism and poor and marginal communities that some sociologists drew parallels with the way non-conformism in the late eighteenth and early nineteenth centuries became entrenched in the new working class of Britain.

Pentecostalism might not offer the same recipe of hard work and frugal consumption as its older Protestant counterparts, nor did it help adherents learn the obedience and punctuality necessary to work in a factory. But it might to some extent – as Freston put it – impart "greater optimism, self-belief and new patterns of honesty, sobriety and diligence". David Martin, another British sociologist, talks about how the new religions allow a "psychic mutation" towards independence and individual initiative.[24]

The Church wins political power and influence

As the financial power and social presence of the evangelical churches grew, so inevitably did their political influence. In the past many evangelicals had treated politics with a certain amount of disdain. Until well into the 1980s pastors at the Assemblies of God used to tell followers that "believers don't mess with politics", for example.[25] But all this began to change when Brazil was swept up in a debate about how the country should govern itself, as the generals prepared to go back to the barracks. And the evangelical churches entered the discussions in a particularly noisy way, quite different in tone from their Catholic rivals.

Catholic clerics had traditionally been forbidden from involvement in political parties and had instead moved quietly among local and national elites, forming part of a conservative establishment and exercising influence from behind the scenes. Liberation Theology, which emerged in the late 1960s and in which radical clerics linked up with community organisers and trade unionists to form so-called base communities, disrupted this pattern to a degree. But by and large the conservative Catholic hierarchy retained control perhaps to a greater extent than elsewhere in Latin America.[26] The two largest Pentecostal churches – the Assemblies and the neo-Pentecostal Universal Church – both endorsed and supported candidates in the constituent assembly elections that took place in 1986, with the Assemblies coining the slogan "Brother votes for Brother". In the 487-member legislature the Pentecostals had helped elect nineteen deputies. Evangelicals from the Methodist, Baptist and Presbyterian traditions backed a further fourteen deputies. At successive elections after that the evangelical representation continued to rise.

The churches formed links with particular parties. Initially, the Social Christian Party was closely linked to the Assemblies of God, for example. Subsequently, the Republican Party, now renamed the Republicans, became a vehicle of the Universal Church. The Liberal Party, a right-wing party close to the government of Lula da Silva between 2003 and 2010, and the Social Liberal Party, another socially conservative grouping that came to prominence with the election of Bolsonaro, both had connections to the Universal Church.

But the churches also worked in a broader way, providing support for candidates who were prepared to back their ideas and preferences irrespective of which party they belonged to. A coordinating group in Congress – registered as the Evangelical Parliamentary Front and nicknamed the Bible caucus – was formed in 2003. In 2017 the eighty-four members of the Front came from twenty-one different parties, nineteen separate religious denominations and twenty-three Brazilian states. A large number of its members came from the various evangelical denominations, but – as the political scientist Amy Erika Smith notes – a significant number of Catholics have also joined the caucus, which has come to represent religious conservatives more broadly.[27]

As we have seen in earlier chapters, the weakness of Brazilian political parties and the 'open list' electoral system encourages candidates to cultivate their own connections with lobbies, especially those – like the evangelical churches – that can provide funds and guarantee votes. "They have a huge influence over their members", Ramos, the former Renascer bishop, told me. "If a preacher recommends a vote for a certain candidate people get the message and they vote that way." Academic studies have provided some nuance. Smith found that evangelical clergy do strongly influence their voters, although she cautions that the majority of church members also believe clergy shouldn't be too overtly politically, which limits what they say.[28]

The evangelical lobby has been effective also because it is concerned to promote two very clear priorities. First, it has been anxious to preserve and potentially extend the fiscal advantages granted to the church in the 1988 Constitution. Second, the evangelical churches – even more than the Catholic Church – have been concerned to protect conservative social values. The lobby's overwhelming priority has been to oppose gay marriage, any relaxation of strict limitations on abortion and liberal sex education in schools. It was this stance more than anything else that made the evangelical lobby so sympathetic to Bolsonaro's social conservatism and so active in his cause.

It has not always been like that though. The evangelical churches were very happy to support the left-wing Lula government between 2002 and 2010. Like other conservatives, evangelical leaders were seduced by Lula's shift to the political centre ahead of the 2002 election. Lula followed up by inviting José Alencar, a prominent industrialist and leader of the small right-wing Liberal Party, to be his deputy, further appeasing potential evangelical opponents. Alencar was a Catholic but close to the Universal Church, and began to attend their services towards the end of his life (he died of cancer in 2011). "When Lula started to appear as Little Lula (Lulinha) of peace and love our fears began to dissipate", Ramos told me.

The Lula government's relationship with one church in particular, Edir Macedo's Universal Church, was especially warm. Macedo positioned his growing TV station – TV Record – to benefit from the distrust between the PT and the conservative Globo media group. Globo had opposed Lula's candidature in previous elections, and with the former trade unionist in power, Record won a growing share of government advertising revenues.

Macedo recommended that the church vote for Lula in 2006 and for Dilma Rousseff in both 2010 and 2014. In 2011 one of Macedo's most important lieutenants in the church, his nephew Marcelo Crivella, became a minister in the Rousseff government, taking over the fishing portfolio. The church preserved its position in 2014, when another federal deputy from the Universal Church, George Hilton, became minister of sports.

The Universal Church was out of sync with fellow evangelical churches on some aspects of sexuality (although the church has made relatively few pronouncements on the subject recently). Macedo is equally as conservative about homosexuality as his evangelical peers. He has said that the church can "cure homosexuality", echoing the controversial positions of evangelical legislators. But he has argued that legalising abortion would "help people have better-quality lives, less violence, less death, less infant mortality and less disease. What's better – an abortion or a child begging in the street or living among rubbish? The Bible says it's better that a person not be born than live in hell."

Slowly, however, this connection between the PT and the evangelical churches became frayed. Just as in other parts of the world, the vexed issue of identity politics was a flashpoint. Back in 1993 the United Nations had recommended that national governments introduce human rights plans. Initially these plans covered the relatively uncontroversial areas of civil and political rights, and later the only slightly trickier areas of social and economic rights. In 2009, however, the UN extended its human rights definitions to cover questions of gender and family, recommending the decriminalisation of abortion and new protections for LGBTQ people. The shift in international norms coincided with an uptick in campaigning by LGBTQ groups in Brazil itself, with the PT becoming one of the movement's strongest allies in Congress.[29] The evangelical lobby became alarmed at these trends.[30]

Proposed legislation would have made it illegal for pastors to condemn homosexuality and prompted energetic campaigning.

"It was a huge thing", said Ramos. "They were telling pastors that they could no longer say homosexuality was a thing of the devil. They came out fighting." Lula's government yielded to this pressure, but confusion about Dilma Rousseff's stance on abortion prompted a number of high-profile preachers to drop their support. As in most of Latin America, abortion in Brazil is illegal except in cases of rape or when the mother's life is in danger. Rousseff caused some controversy in 2009 when she said that although abortion "is not an easy thing for any woman, this could not be used to justify not legalising it". Subsequently the country's National Human Rights Programme contained a proposal to decriminalise abortion. Rousseff, who was chief of staff at the time, subsequently stepped back from endorsing legalisation, although she had already prompted protests from religious right-wingers. Both Catholic and evangelical churchmen came out to openly oppose the decriminalisation idea and the proposal was dropped from government plans.

Silas Malafaia, who led a Rio-based faction of the Assemblies frequented by Michelle Bolsonaro, the president's third wife, was especially prominent among the critics. Malafaia labelled the human rights project "a plan for human shame". During the second half of 2010, as campaigning got under way, billboards – paid for by Malafaia's church – sprang up all over Rio de Janeiro, calling for "the defence of the family and human beings". As the dispute raged, polls showed that Rousseff was losing the support of evangelical voters; among this group she lost 7 percentage points between August and September.[31]

Rousseff was never able to dispel completely the impression that she favoured abortion. One adviser who worked in the government and was close to Rousseff told me: "These accusations had a tremendous effect. She knew it wasn't politically feasible but always suffered the consequences of being seen to be in favour."

Another development then disastrously undermined the PT's standing among evangelicals. By 2014 Rousseff was losing support across the country, as a result of a deteriorating economy and the beginnings of the Lava Jato corruption scandal. She faced opposition not only from the centre-right PSDB but from an alternative left-wing candidate, Marina Silva, a former member of the PT, an environment minister in Lula's government and – as luck would have it – a senior member of the Assemblies of God, who took a conservative position on family and sexual issues. Silva performed well in the run-up to the first round of the election (in which she won 20 per cent of the vote), and in order not to lose the votes of its own left-wing supporters, the PT took a more radical position during the campaign. "On gays and women the party emphasised our differences and that meant that the evangelical churches started to say, 'you see she's as bad as we thought'", said the same adviser. "In order to win, in order to get the vote out, she lost the middle ground." This rebounded disastrously among evangelicals, for whom the PT was establishing itself as the party of "gender ideology".

In 2018 the PT's problems with the evangelicals deteriorated another notch. By choosing Fernando Haddad, a former education minister, as their candidate as soon as it became clear that the imprisoned Lula would not be allowed to stand, the PT was backing a man who had clashed directly with the powerful Universal Church. As mayor of São Paulo between 2012 and 2016, Haddad had opposed the establishment of a university in the city by the Universal Church and fined it over irregularities in the construction of its huge temple of Salomão in the São Paulo suburb of Brás.[32] Initially the Universal Church opted for Geraldo Alckmin, the candidate of Brazil's traditional centre-right party, the PSDB. But after Alckmin's campaign failed to take off, Macedo announced at the end of September that his church would throw its weight behind Bolsonaro. The Universal Church was the last Pentecostal church to campaign for Bolsonaro, but provided him with powerful support. Record gave airtime to Bolsonaro and the Bolsonaristas accused the traditionally socially conservative

Globo of running soap operas (*telenovelas*) that were presenting too positive a picture of gay and transsexual characters and were generally far too upbeat about non-traditional families.

Sensing how unpopular these issues of gender rights were, Bolsonaro's media campaigners began to exploit every opportunity. Back in 2011 Haddad's brand among evangelical voters had been damaged by controversy over the so-called 'gay kit'. Haddad had been the minister of education when legislators proposed that education materials be produced to help teachers tackle homophobia in schools. The materials – three videos and a learning pack – had been commissioned from an NGO at a cost of R$1.8m, but never distributed. Bolsonaro's campaign team continued to insist that they had been. Carlos Bolsonaro and Malafaia made heavy use of the story in their social media feeds, so much so that Brazil's electoral court eventually prohibited Bolsonaro from using videos that associated Haddad with the gay kit. The evangelicals got hold of an entirely different set of materials designed to tackle HIV and sexually transmitted diseases among lorry drivers that was phrased in more explicit language, and claimed that these materials were intended for use in schools. Haddad, in a piece written for *Piauí* magazine in 2017, said "we were obviously framed".[33]

But by then the damage had been done. According to Google Trends, in September 2018 the search for the words 'gay kit' was the most popular in the country. After the first round paved the way for a two-way run-off between Bolsonaro and Haddad, the Bolsonaro media team went into overdrive, pumping out social media material that distorted the left-wing team's support for gender rights and for a more open discussion of sexuality. Haddad was falsely accused of a relationship with a minor. Social media posts claimed that pacifiers shaped like penises were being distributed to younger children. Other posts made much of the alleged efforts of Marta Suplicy, a senior politician who had recently left the PT, to promote the discussion of childhood sexuality in schools. Manuela D'Ávila, the young Communist Party militant who was running as deputy to Haddad, was accused of proposing the end of Christian holidays and proposing to fly the multi-coloured LGBTQ flag alongside the Brazilian colours. In mid-to-late October an average of two fake news items per day were being circulated, the vast majority against Haddad.[34]

Back in Uberlândia, it was clear that this campaign had had a big impact among evangelicals. A ten-minute taxi drive away from Glória in a better-off working-class area, I met Domingos de Souza Guimarães, who a few years ago left mainstream Methodism to form his own church, the Christian Vision Missionary Church. Guimarães styled himself as a right-wing patriot, and said he had voted for Bolsonaro, whose social media offensive may well have influenced his views. "Today you place a kid in front of a couple having sex and say its art – this is degradation", he told me, an apparent reference to a 2017 controversy about a performance art exhibit at the Museum of Modern Art in São Paulo, in which Brazilian dancer Wagner Schwartz lay naked on a plinth and invited visitors to the show to manipulate his body.[35] At some point a fellow artist had taken her four-year-old daughter and the young girl had been filmed touching the man's leg (in the presence of her mother). The images were circulated on social media and caused a furore.

But I got the sense that Guimarães, who described himself as a Christian in the Wesleyan tradition, would have voted the way he did irrespective of fake news. His church had strong social commitments, offering classes of all kinds, and at weekends the church's better-off members got together to offer free legal advice, medical and even dental care to members. But Guimarães was alarmed by social liberalism and bitterly opposed in principle to abortion, gay marriage and sex education in schools.[36] Bolsonaro had shown the "kind of thinking that evangelicals were looking for. What has happened is that after fourteen years of the PT, conservatives have risen up."

10

"ENVIRONMENT, ENVIRONMENT, IT'S A JOKE ..."

Crisnel Ramalho didn't really want to talk when I arrived at his home in a grubby corner of Boa Vista, a five-minute drive from the city's derelict yacht club. A small, wiry, dark-skinned man wearing blue jeans and a beige bowling shirt, the 74-year-old miners' leader was frank about his support for Brazil's right-wing president. "I voted for him with pleasure. I campaigned for him and I'm not sorry. I've put faith in Bolsonaro to change things." But like many staunch Bolsonaristas, he was distrustful of the media.

We eventually sat down on rough wooden chairs in a dusty yard at the back of his house, as two small mongrel dogs and a litter of recently born puppies yapped at our feet. And Ramalho came across as something of an embattled figure. Since leaving home in a dirt-poor district of the north-eastern state of Maranhão, he had worked in the Amazon for fifty years, first cutting down trees for logging companies, then running a hotel for migrant workers, and finally panning for gold in informal mines carved out of the rainforest. But Ramalho was bitter. He believed that Brazil undervalued his experience and had betrayed men whose skills and bravery it once celebrated.

"Environment, environment", he lamented. "It's a joke. I am the environment. You are the environment. I have to make this very clear. My house is my environment. Your car, your flight or your work is your environment. I'm in favour of preservation.

I want to preserve my family, my health, my morals, and my character." Roraima's indigenous reserves where illegal invasions by *garimpeiros* have generated serious social conflicts were a nuisance. "The Indian is still here, ignorant, rotting away. Dying in misery, isolated, he doesn't know about anything", said Ramalho, again echoing themes that have peppered the discourse of Brazil's president.[1]

I'd come to Boa Vista at the end of January 2020 to look more closely at Bolsonaro's appeal in the Amazon. Wedged between Venezuela and Guyana, Roraima is Brazil's deepest intrusion into the northern hemisphere. Even if the state is in some ways atypical, it seemed like a good place to start. Over the last few years thousands of desperate migrants have come in from Venezuela, swelling the population to more than 600,000, but that is still less than in any other of Brazil's twenty-seven states. Indeed, for much of its history Roraima was a no-man's land occupied by a handful of indigenous groups, where the British, Spanish, Dutch and Portuguese vied for influence. Only during the Second World War did the Brazilian government (under pressure for security reasons from its US allies) bother to establish control, setting up a new federal territory that was upgraded to the rank of state in 1988.

Today few places offer better insights into Bolsonaro's policy towards the Amazon. The state's political and economic elites have embraced wholeheartedly the commercially aggressive and expansionist approach to the Amazon backed by Bolsonaro's government. About four-fifths of Roraima consists of savannah and a substantial number of the new arrivals were attracted by cheap land. Many have made money by growing soya, a sector set up from virtually nothing over the last two decades.

Seven out of every ten voters in Roraima had opted for Bolsonaro in the presidential contest, the third highest of any Brazilian state. Acre, another Amazonian state, was the highest, and Santa Catarina, in the far south of the country, the second. They had also elected as governor Antônio Denarium, himself a soya farmer and former banker, who is so avowedly pro-private sector that he has adopted a surname that in its original Latin means money.

Roraima also reflected, in a particularly acute form, the general dilemma shared by all of Brazil's Amazon states. It has abundant natural wealth – fertile land, plentiful water and rich deposits of gold, diamonds and other valuable minerals – but its ability to take advantage of this is limited. More perhaps than anywhere else in Brazil, businesses and political elites in Roraima have felt hampered by the country's commitments to protecting its environment and the rights of diverse indigenous populations, all of which has over the course of the last thirty years been underpinned by international agreements.

Just as the evangelical Christians in Chapter 7 railed against new global norms protecting LGBTQ rights, so the farmers and *garimpeiros* I met in Boa Vista denounced what they called environmentalism and "indigenism". Even moderates in Roraima thought there was something illogical about a policy that put so much emphasis on protecting trees, plants and animal species, and so little on the development of opportunities for the Amazon region's 25 million inhabitants. "People just want to preserve, preserve, preserve", said Gustavo Viera, who had worked as communications adviser for the previous PSDB government in Roraima and was not a Bolsonaro fan. "But how are these 25 million people going to live?"[2]

During the 2018 campaign, Bolsonaro had struck a chord with voters by criticising the way the indigenous reserves had stifled the state's economic development, labelling the policy "separatist" and "dooming Roraima to economic failure".[3] Two indigenous reserves in particular – those established for the Yanomami to the north-west, where Ramalho's *garimpo* was established in the late 1980s, and the more recently created Raposa Serra do Sol to the north-east – had for various reasons proved particularly controversial and unpopular. I'll explore the stories of both, but first it's useful to return to Ramalho and retrace some of the broader recent history of the Amazon.

From the chain saw to the *garimpo*

Back home in Maranhão, Ramalho had heard old miners talk about how they'd sought their fortunes in lawless mining camps. "They used to tell us it was very risky and that you had to be very macho. And anyone who knows the Amazon will tell you. You put yourself at risk there." Then in the 1960s he had been attracted by the opportunities created by the military government's expansionary policies. There had been prosperity in the Amazon before, notably in the late nineteenth and early twentieth centuries, when a rubber boom brought great wealth to the cities of Belém and Manaus. The rubber barons built an opera house in Manaus and engaged in an orgy of conspicuous consumption, although tales about them sending clothes to Paris to be laundered are possibly apocryphal. Cheaper rubber from elsewhere and alternative synthetics brought the boom to an end. Other governments had made efforts to develop the region. From the 1930s, presidents such as Getúlio Vargas (1930–45; 1951–54) and Juscelino Kubitschek (1956–61) had tried to stimulate growth, but none had made such concerted efforts as the military administrations of the 1960s and 1970s. This was partly because Brazil's military saw settlement of the thinly populated Amazon states as the best way to protect borders and national resources and ease social pressures elsewhere in the country. Borrowing a line from nineteenth-century Zionism, President Emílio Médici promised in 1971 that Brazil would open up "a land without men for a people without land".[4]

Ramalho was one of thousands of migrants who flooded the Amazon in the 1960s and 1970s. His first job was on the river border dividing the vastness of Pará from the smaller eastern state of Amapá, which lies below French Guiana and has Brazil's only northern coastline. The Jari Project was a giant forestry plantation and pulp and paper mill set up in 1967 with military encouragement by Daniel K. Ludwig, a prominent US shipping magnate and billionaire. Ramalho was one of 35,000 workers at the site, where he learned to operate a chain saw, a tool that would play a crucial role in the uncontrolled deforestation of the 1980s and 1990s. According to the geographer and explorer John Hemming, along with aircraft and the bulldozer, the chain saw was one of three inventions that "destroyed the tranquillity of the Amazon. The world's richest ecosystem might have continued as a pristine paradise."[5]

Ramalho saw things differently, however. Skilled chain saw operators were valued because the job of cutting down giant hardwood trees was difficult and dangerous. The chain saw – introduced to Brazil by the American managers at Jari – was more efficient than traditional tools. "You had to know how the wood would fall, and whether it would fall with the wind or against the wind", he told me. A small miscalculation and the tree could fall on top of the woodsman. "There were so many sad stories, the best operators died with trees falling on top of them. My friend Boneta was an animal with seven heads with the motor saw. He was respected across the Amazon, but he was crushed." Like a fighter pilot or the captain of a giant oil tanker, Ramalho took pride in his ability to control powerful equipment and in his mastery of a hazardous process. "Even with my small build I was very skilled. I was seen as a hero, a hero of the jungle", he said.

During the 1970s, as the Amazon started to open up, Ramalho plied his expertise around the region. An extensive network of roads had been built, making it easier for him to move around. The Rodovia Bernardo Sayão – the BR 010, named after the agricultural engineer who oversaw it – cut north for 1,250 miles from Brasília to the Amazonian port city of Belém. The 2,700 mile BR 364 – popularly known as Rodovia Marechal Rondon in homage to the military officer who had explored the western Amazon – linked the south-east to the far west. Most significantly, the Transamazônica sliced across an area of semi-arid land and rainforest for 2,500 miles from the north-east state of Paraíba to the western state of Amazonas. These roads opened up the region to migration. Thousands of farmers and farm hands displaced by mechanisation from southern states such as Rio Grande do Sul moved northwards along these arteries. "The Transamazônica is the route to a gold mine", claimed government propaganda in the 1970s. "There is a treasure waiting for you … Enough of legends, Brazil is opening up the Amazon and offering profits for anyone who wants to take part in this great enterprise."[6]

Soon the discovery of real treasure would cement the region's attractions. In the late 1960s, huge iron ore reserves were found at Carajás and the then state-owned Company of the Valley of the Rio Doce was invited to exploit them. But what did most to influence perceptions of the region was the discovery of gold in 1979 at a farm in the Serra Pelada about 30 miles east of Carajás and 55 miles south-west of Marabá, a town which had grown rapidly around a nexus of new highways. Just a few months later in January 1980 gold prices surged to a record high of $850 an ounce. Investors spooked by the Iranian Revolution, the rise in oil prices and the Soviet intervention in Afghanistan were buying the metal as a safe haven from global economic uncertainty and rising inflation. Soon tens of thousands of people flooded to the Serra Pelada site in a movement similar in scale to the great Californian gold rushes of the nineteenth century. Hunger for gold became frenzied. In appalling conditions, up to 100,000 half-naked miners wielding pickaxes and shovels gouged out a vast muddy crater, unearthing up to a ton of gold each month. In Marabá, shopkeepers took payment in gold and deployed precision scales to measure what became a new currency. At the hotel in the town where buyers gathered to buy the mineral gold, particles of the precious metal were scattered so widely that "in the evenings the kids who swept out the rooms collected small glasses full of gold dust".[7]

When word of these events reached Ramalho, he was logging at a farm halfway between Altamira and Itaituba, along a stretch of cleared rainforest that had been opened up by the Transamazônica. Ramalho said that a manager persuaded him to stay but stories of the money made at Serra Pelada left a lasting impression. Within a couple of years Ramalho had abandoned his chain saw and had moved west, first to the state of Rondônia and then north to the booming diamond and gold mining regions of Roraima. "I left the farm and I said to myself. Do you know something? I'm not working on farms any more. That is enough of cutting down trees. I don't want to do it any more. From then on it was *garimpo, garimpo, garimpo*."

Roraima had a long history of informal mining that was legal for most of the twentieth century. Back in the 1960s the state's governor had commissioned a 7-metre-high sculpture celebrating the *garimpeiro* to be built and placed in the main square of Boa Vista. The statue – a figure bent over his gold pan above a mirrored pool – is still there, adopted in 2007 – long after the activity was declared illegal – as the symbol of Boa Vista. Many Roraima families had connections with mining, and thousands – like Ramalho – were originally attracted to the state to seek their fortunes. As mining took off – triggered by the discovery in 1985 of a giant gold deposit – the miners enjoyed official backing too. "It was another world then, even for us Brazilians. To get to Roraima you had to cross the entire Amazon", said Ramalho.

Between 1987 and 1990, 30,000–40,000 *garimpeiros* arrived in the state. Airforce personnel helped them establish the first airstrips, and in 1987 a military policeman helped organise invasions. Two governors of Roraima, Roberto Klein and Romero Jucá, both defended *garimpeiro* activities even in indigenous territories. For military strategists, the activity helped consolidate national territory. As one academic put it in a detailed study of the Roraima *garimpeiros*: "The strategists were seeking to promote the integration of western Roraima with the rest of Brazil, and the 'living frontier' of *garimpeiros* moving into the area helped them achieve this goal. In supporting the rush the military saw an opportunity to further its own geopolitical agenda."[8]

But towards the end of the 1980s the *garimpeiro* presence became increasingly controversial. Much of the mining had taken place in territories traditionally regarded as a homeland by the Yanomami people, one of the most numerous of northern Brazil's indigenous groups. And as worries about the impact of mining on these groups increased, Roraima – like the wider Amazon – was becoming a subject of growing international concern.

The tide turns

Slowly the debate about the impact of untrammelled development was becoming more heated. In part this was a product of international pressure. The apocalyptic images coming out of Serra Pelada had raised awareness considerably. Images of the Serra Pelada mine captured by the Brazilian photographer Sebastião Salgado became iconic and synonymous with the greed and exploitation of the age. According to the photo editor Peter Howe, when the photos were first seen at the *New York Times* there was complete silence. "In my entire career at the *New York Times*, I never saw editors react to any set of pictures as they did to Serra Pelada."[9] Equally explosive was the campaign that ensued in response to the murder in 1988 of Chico Mendes, a leader of traditional rubber tappers in the western Amazonian state of Acre. Mendes had led opposition to loggers, establishing links with both the Workers' Party and international environmental organisations such the World Wildlife Fund and the Environmental Defense Fund.

Much of this initial pressure stemmed also from concern about the fate of Brazil's one-million strong indigenous population, many of whom live in the Amazon states. The Portuguese settlement of Brazil had been devastating for the 2,000 or so indigenous groups, who at the time of the conquest amounted to perhaps as many as three million people. Hundreds of thousands died from disease. Many thousands of others were captured, sold as slaves, or lost their lives in violent incursions by the so-called Bandeirantes of the seventeenth and eighteenth centuries, military raiding parties set up to secure colonial control over Brazil's interior.[10] During the twentieth century Brazil began to establish reserves, but it wasn't until the 1970s and 1980s that indigenous activists – supported by radical Catholic clerics influenced by Liberation Theology – began to press for the rights of these groups to retain and develop their own identities without pressure to assimilate. This view proved influential during the debates surrounding the adoption of the Constitution in 1988, when legislators voted to streamline the legal process through which indigenous reserves were created.

All of this was hugely important for Roraima. Efforts to delimit a reserve for the Yanomami – who inhabited the west of the state and southern Venezuela – had begun in the late 1970s, stimulated in part by the pioneering reporting of the British journalist Norman Lewis. The Yanomami had suffered badly from Amazon expansionism. In the early 1970s, when the government decided to build a road along the northern frontier with bulldozers, two villages were wiped out by diseases to which they had no immunity. A commission – the initiative of another journalist, the Swiss-Brazilian Cláudia Andujar – started work in 1978. And in the mid-1980s Severo Gomes, a liberal Brazilian politician, took up the cause and began lobbying Congress to provide the Yanomami with greater protection.

Roraima's settler population resisted at first. In the late 1980s, for example, the municipal council of Boa Vista declared Gomes *persona non grata* after he urged the Yanomami to defend themselves. President José Sarney sought to defuse conflict by expelling the NGOs from the region, and by restricting the Yanomami reserve to more than a dozen separate islands of territory, between which the *garimpeiros* were free to move as they wished. But slowly the tide of international and national opinion was beginning to leave *garimpeiros* such as Ramalho more isolated.

Two developments were crucial. First, between 1988 and 1990, 1,500 mainly Yanomami people died in a malaria epidemic, a disease that NGOs claimed had been brought into the reserve by the *garimpeiros*. Clashes between *garimpeiros* and Yanomami villagers left more than two dozen Yanomami dead. There were disputes too about the use by *garimpeiros* of mercury, which was polluting water supplies. According to Survival International, the British campaigning group set up in the wake of Lewis's reporting, 20 per cent of the Yanomami died in just seven years. In the autumn of 1990 Severo Gomes took Davi Kopenawa, a Yanomami leader, on an international tour to denounce the treatment of the Yanomami, finding support not just among human rights activists but from the US administration and European governments. Britain's Prince Charles became an enthusiastic and hugely influential advocate for the indigenous cause, taking the Royal Yacht to the Amazon early in 1992.

In 1989, in another election surprise, Brazil voted a relatively unknown liberal politician into office, Fernando Collor de Mello, who was committed to freeing up the economy and rehabilitating the country's international image in order to attract investment. As his administration stumbled and ran into political opposition to its mainstream economic plans, Collor became all the more eager to impress his international friends by presenting his government as a protector of indigenous rights. During 1991 federal police were ordered to bomb illegal landing strips used by the wildcat miners and remove them from the area. Clashes between the police and *garimpeiros* were frequent and – according to Ramalho – several deaths resulted. "When [Collor] came in they killed *garimpeiros*. I saw the bodies of *garimpeiros* with bullet holes. They'd been shot point blank by the police", he told me. Within months the government was pressing ahead with proposals to make the whole area a Yanomami reserve in which wildcat mining would be banned.

By 1992 Collor had created more than 200 other reserves across the country and handed new powers to the National Foundation of the Indian (Funai).

In Roraima, local politicians, farmers and businessmen joined the dispossessed *garimpeiros* to demonstrate against the creation of the reserve. In 2020, more than thirty years later, Ramalho viewed the shift in Brazilian government policy in the late 1980s as a bewildering and vicious act of betrayal. "Collor stopped the *garimpo* because he said he was going to legalise it, but he did the opposite", said Ramalho. Over the next couple of decades, as the web of international agreements connecting environmental protection and the rights of Roraima's indigenous minorities grew denser, that sense of grievance began to affect the thinking of the state's political class.

"We undermine our own potential"

In his office in the modest headquarters of the *Folha de Boa Vista*, Getúlio de Souza Cruz, the newspaper's publisher, explained to me how "environmentalism" and "indigenism" were "kidnapping" his state's development. "Foreigners are sometimes surprised about the way we undermine our own potential", Souza Cruz told me. Since the state's creation, four new national parks have been established, increasing the amount of land in conservation areas by more than 50 per cent. In 1988 there were ten indigenous reserves, but over the last thirty-two years, twenty-three new ones have been created. Overall, he claimed, more than 90 per cent of the state's land area is protected in one way or another.

As Souza Cruz presents it, Roraima's history over the last three decades has been a constant and recurring conflict between business and burdensome regulation imposed by national governments faithful to international conventions and policed by agencies such as the Brazilian Institute of the Environment and

Renewable Resources (Ibama) and Funai, and NGOs backed by the Catholic Church.[11] Souza Cruz detailed the many frustrations suffered by local business. Efforts to improve communications and power supplies have frequently stumbled into opposition from the environmentalists. Two huge hydroelectric projects have been mothballed since the 1980s. Even a less ambitious move to build a transmission line from Manaus to Boa Vista, which would have allowed Roraima to buy electricity generated by the Tucuruí dam in neighbouring Amazonas state, had been blocked. Plans to build roads had also run into opposition from activist magistrates. Each night indigenous groups in the Waimiri–Atroari reserve to the south of Boa Vista ran a chain across the road to Manaus, regularly limiting the use of a transport connection that is perhaps Roraima's most important with the outside world.

In the last two decades, however, one particular controversy has served to radicalise conservative opinion in Roraima: the creation of the indigenous reserve of Raposa Serra do Sol in the north of the state in 2005 and the expulsion from that area of a handful of farmers who had been very successfully cultivating rice. The affair has became something of a *cause célèbre* not just for Roraima but for Bolsonaro and his supporters. The decision to create the reserve – which covers a thinly populated 1.7 million hectare area of scrubland – was contentious for several reasons. First, the indigenous presence was uneven. To the east near the border with Guyana in the Raposa section of what became the reserve was a group of about 1,000 Ingarikó, who survived mainly through subsistence farming. To the north-west was the village of Serra do Sol, and isolated groups of Macuxi and Wapixana, and other communities, who had begun to raise cattle during the 1970s. In between these areas were groups of immigrant farmers, often from the far south of Brazil, who had established soya and corn farms and cattle ranches of their own. And on the clay soils of the gently undulating hills of the Raposa region fifteen farmers had established prosperous rice farms, with dozens more making a decent living by farming rented land. The rice farmers occupied 70,000 hectares – about 4 per cent of the reserve's area – but contributed significantly towards a sector that accounted for 6 per cent of the whole state's economic output.

In Boa Vista, I met Genar Luiz Faccio, a 63-year-old business-man who was one of those forced to abandon the area. Faccio had evidently recovered from the loss. He ran a business called Prato Chic from comfortable offices in Boa Vista, farming grains, rais-ing cattle, and producing processed rice and other foods for sale in the region. However, he was not representative of an entrenched and blinkered oligarchy. Faccio was 21 when he left his home in 1979, joined an uncle in Roraima, and started work in order to save money for university. Back home in Pelotas, in the state of Rio Grande do Sul, Faccio's family had grown soya and raised pigs for three generations, but as the family expanded, the size of inherited plots diminished and land prices rose, forcing younger family mem-bers to look for cheaper land elsewhere. He was one of thousands of natives of Rio Grande do Sul – *gaúchos* as they are known in Brazil – who migrated to the productive centre-west and subsequently to the newer and more precarious frontiers of the Amazon.

The move worked well for Faccio. He gave up on the idea of returning home to study and eventually joined forces with his uncle to start farming rice on rented land. By 2000 they had saved enough capital to buy a 4,500-hectare farm near the Surumu River. Armed with a land title dating from 1924 – a huge length of time by Amazonian standards – they were confident about the future. During the 2000s their business was expanding at a rate of 20 per cent a year.

The creation of the indigenous reserve of Raposa Serra do Sul disrupted all this. Initially the government had proposed to form several smaller indigenous reserves, based on each of the half-dozen or so ethnicities present in north-eastern Roraima, allowing the farmers active in the state to retain their land and continue producing. However, indigenous rights organisations, backed by the Catholic Church, argued for a more comprehensive reform along the lines already introduced in Yanomami territory to the west, arguing that the alternative would allow Roraima's traditional elites to preserve their socio-economic influence at the expense of the indigenous communities. For ten years the issue was batted back and forth by different elements of Brazil's judicial system, before – at the beginning of May 2009 – the fuller reserve was established and the rice growers expelled.

The order was controversial. General Augusto Heleno, then commander of the Amazon and subsequently secretary of Bolsonaro's Institutional Security Cabinet, explicitly criticised the decision to create the reserve, lambasting the Lula government's indigenous policies as "lamentable not to say chaotic" and "completely dissociated from the historic process of colonisation".[12] This public dissent paved the way for Heleno's removal, his eventual retirement three years later, and his subsequent re-emergence as an important ally of Bolsonaro.

The Raposa Serra do Sol seems decided. Most of the farmers involved – like Faccio – have re-established their businesses elsewhere in the state or in other corners of the Amazon. But there are lasting legacies. For Roraima's elites the affair continues to cast a shadow over investment. Faccio said, "there are producers who want to invest here that are holding back [because they worry it might happen again]". And then there is the political fallout. As Faccio put it: "80 per cent of the population agreed with us. Bolsonaro backed our cause and people agreed with him and that has contributed to Bolsonaro's popularity."

11

THE AMAZON IS BURNING

In the mid-afternoon of 19 August 2019 the skies over the largest urban sprawl in the Americas turned black. At the heart of this darkness, drivers in downtown São Paulo turned on their headlamps, streetlights lit up three hours early, and Paulistanos started to make apocalyptic comparisons on social media with Tolkien's Mordor or the Gotham City of Batman. "It was as if the day had turned into night", one resident told a reporter. "Everyone commented because even on rainy days it doesn't usually get that dark."[1]

Some thought there was a smell of smoke, and the idea was soon abroad that it was smoke from fires in the Amazon. Not all weather forecasters were convinced, but one meteorologist from the popular website Climatempo told Globo TV that a cold front had indeed brought smoke from areas of the Amazon that were ablaze. "The smoke [comes] from very dense and broad fires that have been burning for several days in [the state of] Rondônia and Bolivia", she said. The cold front changed direction and its winds carried the smoke to São Paulo.[2]

Within hours the hashtag #PrayfortheAmazon was being attached to hundreds of thousands of tweets. Soon the internet was awash with alarm, as one celebrity after another signalled their concern for the environment. Madonna, Lewis Hamilton, Jaden Smith, Leonardo DiCaprio and Cristiano Ronaldo all posted their own pictures of burning forests, some from many years before, others not even from Brazil, a few not even from Latin America. Leonardo DiCaprio called on his nearly 34 million Instagram followers to become more environmentally conscious in a post warning that "the lungs of the Earth are in flames". Amid the media frenzy, Bolsonaro flailed around, at one point even suggesting that NGOs themselves had started the fires to discredit his government. "The question to ask about these Amazon fires – which in my view might well have been started by NGOs because they lost money – is what's the motivation behind them? It's to cause problems for Brazil", he told a steel industry congress in Brasília.[3]

Soon the issue was at the top of the international agenda, dominating a G7 summit in Biarritz that opened a few days later. Emmanuel Macron, the French leader, took direct issue with Bolsonaro, accusing the Brazilian government of what he described as "ecocide". "The Amazon rainforest – the lungs which produce 20 per cent of our planet's oxygen – is on fire", Macron tweeted. The French leader asked world powers to help Brazil and its neighbours fight the fires. The German chancellor Angela Merkel called the fires "shocking and threatening". Boris Johnson, Britain's prime minister, was "deeply concerned", and Finland, which held the EU presidency, called on the European Union to ban imports of Brazilian beef, a development that threatened to capsize a trade deal painstakingly negotiated only a few months previously with Mercosul, the trade bloc formed by Brazil, Argentina, Paraguay and Uruguay.

Whether or not the dark clouds over São Paulo had actually come from the Amazon might have been open to question. More serious conflagrations in 2004 and 2014 had attracted no comparable international interest. As Carlos Nobre of Brazil's National Institute of Space Research (Inpe) and Thomas Lovejoy of George Mason University wrote: "2019 was not the worst year for fire or deforestation but it was the year when fires garnered global attention".[4]

We'll return to Nobre and Lovejoy – the scientists who have perhaps done most to stress the growing urgency of the crisis in the Amazon – but it's worth pausing for a while to assess what had actually happened and how Bolsonaro's election had affected developments. During the dry season in the Amazon – which typically begins around April – farmers burn brush and waste in order to clear land for pasture. But satellite data collected by Inpe showed that deforestation has been rising. Inpe monitors forest cover on both a monthly and an annual basis, using two separate satellites. The annual measure – gathered from the Landsat satellite as part of the Amazon Deforestation Calculation Program ('Prodes') – takes images of a higher resolution and is more accurate, but the monthly figure – based on the Real Time Deforestation Detection System ('Deter') and picked up by a sensor aboard the Sino-Brazilian satellite – provides a reasonably precise early warning and is particularly helpful in policing operations. The latter system – introduced in 2004 – was upgraded in 2016 and now monitors units of land of as small as 6.25 hectares.

2019 started relatively quietly, but monthly data showed steadily escalating amounts of deforestation as the April–November dry season got underway. By August, when the black clouds were drifting towards São Paulo, the Deter data indicated that deforestation was running at three times the rate of the previous year. Inpe's 'deforestation year' – which confusingly runs from 1 August to 31 July – was the worst since 2010. And numbers have continued to run at high levels since then. In September 2020 the amount of tree cover lost – on a trailing twelve-month basis – was lower than in 2019, but fires were running at all-time highs.[5] A letter written by eight former environment ministers in May 2019 proved to be prescient. "We're facing the risk of runaway deforestation in the Amazon. We need to strengthen its environmental protection measures, not weaken them."[6]

During the first year and a half of the Bolsonaro government there were signs of a pick-up in deforestation in all sorts of places.

Adalberto Veríssimo, a researcher at Imazon, an NGO, pointed to new areas of activity in the extreme west of Pará and all across the north of the Amazon, a remote sub-region that had been less badly hit in the past.[7] In March 2020 reporters for the *Folha de São Paulo* visited the reserve created for the rubber tappers of Acre.[8] They discovered that growing numbers of rubber tappers – or *seringueiros* – inside the Chico Mendes reserve were cutting down trees to create pasture land for cattle. It was a massive irony. The reserve had been created thirty years before to block the expansion of ranchers, and the *seringueiro* leader Chico Mendes had been assassinated by a cattleman. Francisco Diogo da Silva, a rubber tapper for fifty-eight of his seventy-two years, had just burned his last Brazil nut tree to create pasture. None of his ten sons were deploying their traditional skills. Five were in the nearby city of Rio Branco and five were ranching. The rubber tappers in the region voted heavily for Bolsonaro in 2018.

Brazil gets a grip on deforestation and then loses it

How had this happened? In a way it is part of a longer-term development. After the big Amazonian expansion of the 1970s, deforestation proceeded apace in the 1980s and 1990s. Until the early 1990s incentives and subsidies – originally established by the military government in order to stimulate economic development and job creation – remained in place. Road building continued too, with extensions to the Amazon highways. By 1986 the BR-364 was asphalted and extended from Porto Velho in Rondônia to Rio Branco in Acre. Between 1978 and 2001 the amount of deforested land increased fourfold to 60.3 million hectares. Economic development had attracted millions of migrants from the poor north-east (such as Ramalho, the *garimpeiro* we met in the last chapter) and the increasingly competitive south and south-east (such as Faccio, the rice grower). Overall, the population of the Amazon had increased from only 2.9 million in 1960 to 25.5 million by 2010.

For the newcomers, clearing occupied land for pasture was the best way to secure title, and the quickest route to prosperity. "The main change of land use is unquestionably the huge additional area devoted to planted pasture which by 1995 covered 70 per cent of the deforested area", concluded one study.[9]

Logging had also thrived, especially in the 1990s as Asian demand for hardwoods such as mahogany grew quickly. Sawmills – often operating illegally – sprang up all over states such as Pará. One writer who spent a lot of time in the Amazon during this period wrote that "the roads were full of trucks piled high with the trunks of mighty trees that had once towered over the forest canopy and been home to thousands of creatures. Every Amazonian river seemed clogged with endless rafts of logs."[10]

Clearing land by logging or burning and then setting up a ranch and bringing in cattle was often a complex process that provided work and opportunities for thousands of people. Middlemen identified areas where tree cover could be removed, provided security for occupiers and traded the cleared land. With values changing quickly, speculators – nicknamed *grileiros* or grasshoppers – were also attracted. Fraud and extortion were rife. When Brazil's environmental agency examined title deeds in the Amazon, it cancelled over 60,000 of them. Roberto Mangabeira Unger, a left-wing philosopher, found the Amazon high up his agenda when he took over as minister of strategic affairs in 2007. "I was shocked to discover what the fundamental problem was. It was land tenure", he said.[11] "When I came in 4 per cent of the land in private hands had clear legal title. No one knew who had what. In that situation pillage is more attractive than either preservation or production." Legislation was approved but, according to Mangabeira, its implementation "went very slowly", partly because of opposition from the Workers' Party. Mangabeira left the government in 2009.

International pressure on Brazil over its management of the Amazon had grown during the late 1980s, initially triggered by concern for the fate of the country's indigenous populations. At the same time the relationship between deforestation in the Amazon and global warming was beginning to emerge as a new focus of concern for environmental activists. Brazil's governments began to channel more resources into the area. Momentum picked up significantly following the election in 2002 of Lula da Silva. Lula's environment minister – Marina Silva – was herself from the Amazon state of Acre and had been a union leader alongside Mendes. Under this new leadership, Brazil's regulatory agencies sharply stepped up enforcement actions. Environmental crimes were taken more seriously. In 2003 Inpe began the monthly monitoring outlined above, allowing quicker action to clamp down on illegal loggers and fires.

The Ibama environmental agency was given new powers to levy fines, confiscate equipment and block bank credit. In 2008 Lula even sent troops to Tailândia, Pará's logging capital, after sawmill workers expelled Ibama inspectors. The pace at which new indigenous reserves and conservation areas were established was stepped up. Overall, Brazil made impressive progress during this period. According to the Inter-Governmental Panel on Climate Change, the reduction of deforestation between 2004 and 2012 was one of the biggest initiatives made by any country against global warming. By 2012 the rate of annual deforestation had fallen to 4,400 square kilometres, down from 27,700 square kilometres in 2004. Over an even shorter timespan – from 2003 to 2009 – roughly three-quarters of the world's new protected areas had been created in the Amazon.[12]

But these advances came to a halt in 2013 when the rate of deforestation began to tick back upwards. A change to Brazil's forest code – which stipulated how much original vegetation farmers were obliged to preserve on their properties – was one of the main reasons, according to environmentalists. Under rules dating back to 1965, farmers had been obliged to preserve (or restore) 50 per cent of their properties in original vegetation. That had been increased in 1995 to 80 per cent. Pressure from the agribusiness lobby to relax these restrictions grew, and in 2012 President Dilma Rousseff, who was desperate to halt a decline in economic growth, buckled and softened the regulations. The new code contained an amnesty provision that cleared landowners of any responsibility for illegal deforestation before 2008. The amount of land that landowners were obliged to restore was reduced from 80 per cent to 50 per cent, but only in states where 65 per cent of overall land was in conservation areas, indigenous reserves or otherwise protected. Some registration and certification requirements were tightened.

Agribusiness interests claimed that the new code was still onerous and more demanding than legislation elsewhere. For example, the new rules introduced the idea of a register and environmental certification of land, with the information to be collected by state administrations. Environmentalists, however, said the new code, combined with constraints in funding that limited control and policing efforts, paved the way for a slow upward trend in deforestation. Under the Rousseff administration, environmentalists suffered other setbacks too, with the president responding to demands from the agribusiness sector. The demarcation of indigenous reserves, which had been advancing steadily under Lula, stopped.

Rousseff championed the Belo Monte hydroelectric dam on the Xingu River, an Amazon tributary, facing down opposition from local indigenous groups. An independent, multidisciplinary report condemned the project, which is located on the Xingu 40 miles downstream from the city of Altamira, as a social, environmental and human rights calamity in the making. Rousseff attached greater priority to the additional electricity generation capacity created, however.[13]

All this had happened in part because behind the scenes, the parliamentary lobby representing the interests of farmers was increasing its strength. Colloquially known as the 'ox bench' (*bancada do boi*), the lobby registered support from 192 deputies and 11 senators after the 2010 election in which Rousseff took office. Four years later the lobby increased its weight, with 228 deputies and 27 senators joining. And by 2018 the agribusiness interest was further strengthened, with 243 deputies and 37 senators. As the front lobbied for changes – such as the relaxation of the forest code – environmentalists were alarmed. "This group always wielded economic and political power but now it has moved to the centre of things", said Marco Astrini, Greenpeace Public Policy coordinator.[14] By 2018, with Bolsonaro's victory, the agribusiness lobby had achieved unparalleled influence in government.

The consequences of denialism

Jair Bolsonaro and his more radical supporters have never sought to hide their disdain for the idea of global warming. Like one of their most important political mentors, Donald Trump, the Bolsonaristas are unremittingly sceptical about the science. Ernesto Araújo, Bolsonaro's foreign minister, went so far as to claim that what he called "climatism" was inspired by left-wing ideology.[15] Ricardo Salles, a São Paulo lawyer who became the new environment minister, said climate change was merely a secondary question as far as he was concerned. One prominent Bolsonaro supporter, Dom Bertrand de Orléans de Bragança, has even compared environmentalists with communist insurgents.[16] Statements of this kind have done much to encourage grassroots supporters in the Amazon such as Ramalho.

One of the best examples came in the weeks before the apocalyptic afternoon in São Paulo that opened this chapter. Prosecutors in the state of Pará found evidence that in order to demonstrate support for Bolsonaro, small farmers from the southern Amazonian town of Novo Progresso had deliberately set fires. Novo Progresso is one of those towns that was made possible by the military government's huge road-building programme. Built in the 1980s alongside the BR-163 highway that runs more than 2,000 miles from Brazil's far south to the north of the Amazon, Novo Progresso is full of smallholders, land developers and property speculators. So much so that farmers from this town of 25,000 people were rearing 600,000 head of cattle. In other words, like Boa Vista in Roraima, Novo Progresso is a classic example of the kind of 'wild west' frontier town – part of the vast *interiorzão* – that provided such bedrock support for the president. In October 2018, 80 per cent of the municipality's voters cast their ballots for Bolsonaro.

Over the last few years, locals – enjoying the support of local politicians – have steadily expanded the land available for pasture and development, often eating into the protected territory of the Jamanxim National Park created by the Lula government in 2006. Early in August 2019 the town's newspaper, the *Folha de Novo Progresso*, reported that a group of seventy local farmers had formed a WhatsApp group in order to coordinate what they called a "fire day". They had even held a whip-round to collect money for the petrol required. Within days federal police and state lawyers had launched an investigation. "The data suggests there is a deliberate and premeditated effort to burn the forest", said Paulo de Tarso Moreira Oliveira, a Pará public prosecutor. "There are people in these areas who have been pressing to take control of [protected] land and these people are the targets of our investigations", he said, adding that the effort seemed designed to frustrate inspection. "No inspection is capable of checking so many outbreak sources at the same time."[17]

More than a year later the legal case was still inconclusive. Agamenon Menezes, the president of the Novo Progresso farmers' union and one of those allegedly involved, claimed the affair was a press invention thought up to discredit the president. Menezes, like Ramalho in Boa Vista, was downright dismissive of his environmental critics and their concerns. Global warming was "a farce" invented by "2,500 scientists", he said. "There are 3,500 scientists in Brazil publishing material against this." NGOs have "no interest in resolving anything here. They simply want to blow things up."[18]

Visiting Novo Progresso in September 2019, the *New York Times* was invited to a barbecue set up by the town's farmers for Nahban Garcia, the head of land affairs at the agriculture ministry and a firm advocate of Amazon development. The film that the newspaper made at the event shows speaker after speaker brazenly rejecting environmental rules.[19] The town's mayor, Ubirici Soares, who is an enthusiastic advocate of the farmers' cause, was himself fined for violations of environmental law, having cut down 780 acres of trees inside the Jamanxim National Park in two separate incidents in 2009 and 2017. The film shows Garcia egging on the farmers. "We are not going to accept NGOs conspiring against Brazil", he said.

This was not just about encouraging radical supporters, though. Bolsonaro and his ministers did their best to undermine the institutions that have done so much to tackle environmental destruction. Bolsonaro's own stance on such matters was neatly illustrated by an incident in January 2012 when a team of inspectors from Ibama caught the future president fishing in a protected area near Angra dos Reis in Rio de Janeiro state. Bolsonaro argued with the agents, refused to identify himself and refused to pay the fine that was levied. When he was elected the fine was rescinded. Three months into his presidency the agent who had led the Ibama team that day found himself demoted.[20]

In office, the new president failed to follow through on his radical promise to scrap the environment ministry and make it a dependency of the more business-oriented agriculture portfolio. But his ministers chipped away at the powers of virtually every public body in the sector and starved them of funding. After the appointment of Salles as environment minister, two issues that had been a central part of the ministry's work – climate change and forestry – disappeared from its agenda. Since 2015 the ministry had coordinated the work of nine other ministries on the issue of deforestation, but now this function was dropped. "The theme was diluted. Salles suggested that the orchestra would have to play without a conductor", reported Bernardo Esteves.[21]

In a detailed piece based on interviews with dozens of officials, Esteves exposed a climate of insecurity and intimidation that he said had paralysed work schedules. "Officials feared they were being monitored by Salles. I heard stories of bugged phones, leaked WhatsApp conversations and spies posted in meetings of officials."[22] A document circulated by the minister's cabinet chief recommended that employees leave their office blinds open when they were at work. Several staff were sacked. Others found their participation in overseas conferences abruptly cancelled. Salles said that he was simply finishing with the "spree of agreements [with other countries], endless studies, conferences and speeches". Esteves said he had "met an official who had been asked to talk about projects without using the terms climate change or indigenous people". Two of the ministry's agencies that have traditionally enjoyed significant autonomy – Ibama and the Chico Mendes Institute for Conservation and Biodiversity (ICMBio, which manages protected areas) – were in the front line of the attack.

Salles oversaw Ibama and ICMbio press operations. "The minister speaks badly of us and we can't say anything", said one Ibama inspector. Many positions at these agencies were left vacant. On the ground, Ibama inspectors met fierce resistance, with loggers, farmers and wildcat miners acting, as Esteves put it, "with impunity, as if environmental infractions were no longer considered crimes".

Budget cuts further undermined the ability of the agencies to work effectively. Ibama's funding was cut by a quarter in 2019. Another third was withdrawn in 2020. Suely Araújo, a former head of the organisation, said that even the reduced budget of 2019 was not fully implemented. The 2020 budget was so small that it was insufficient to cover the cost of renting the trucks and helicopters used to carry out inspections in the Amazon. Ibama's ability to police deforestation was being seriously weakened. Inpe – through its Deter system – had in the previous twelve months issued 44,000 alerts detailing sharp falls in forest cover. But the agency's 800 agents could only act on a few hundred.[23] ICMBio faced similar difficulties. At the beginning of April a group of military officers were brought in to senior positions. Funding for the conservation areas administered by the agency was cut sharply. "The funding cuts underlined the way in which governance in this area was being dismantled and the environmental agencies de-legitimised."[24] Even before Bolsonaro's election, the fines levied by Ibama and ICMBio had usually been contested in court, and only about 5 per cent of them were actually collected. Now the number of fines levied began to fall sharply.[25]

This offensive extended further in July 2019. After Inpe published its latest monthly deforestation figures, Bolsonaro publicly accused the space agency of lying. Ricardo Galvão, the agency's chief executive, accused the president of cowardice. The 71-year-old physicist, whose previous job had been to head up a team at the University of São Paulo that researched nuclear fission, was offended by what he described as "bar-room language". A month later he was sacked and replaced by an airforce officer who was happy to admit that climate change was "not my thing". As Esteves put it, not content with weakening control and prevention, "the government was now attacking the messenger".[26]

The Bolsonaro administration was contributing to deforestation in other ways too. In spite of the setbacks under Rousseff and her short-lived successor Michel Temer, one of the areas where Brazil continued to make progress was in the relationships forged by the private sector with environmental organisations. A group formed to limit soya production in the Amazon in 2006 had been a great success. From the outset, though, the new government's environment team played down such cooperation. Edson Duarte, the minister under Temer, said his department had prepared a

document outlining all the environment programmes and part-
nerships to ease the transition, but found that it was ignored by
the incoming administration.[27] At the end of 2019, *Valor Econômico*,
the São Paulo-based business newspaper, reported that Salles had
pressed the associations of coffee, sugar and cattle to abandon an
industry coalition that had pressed for progressive climate change
policies.

The justice ministry agency responsible for indigenous groups,
Funai – once described by Bolsonaro as a "nest of rats" – was
weakened as well.[28] Its new chief executive, Marcelo Xavier da
Silva, was a former federal policeman who had once been an
aide to Nahban Garcia, he of the Novo Progresso barbecue. The
appointment was followed by a string of lower-level changes that
generally involved the appointment of soldiers or ex-soldiers. Luís
Ventura, who works with Cimi, an NGO based in Roraima, told
me that the agency was being "militarised. You go to Funai and
more than one regional coordinator has been substituted by a
military guy."[29]

Under Bolsonaro the government froze the procedures
whereby new reserves are recognised. And the defence of existing reserves has been weakened. In 2019, for example, the military abandoned two river outposts that had been set up to keep
garimpeiros out of the Yanomami reserve in Roraima. Meanwhile,
funding cuts have hampered Funai's ability to protect existing
reserves. Funding for 2020 was 40 per cent less than in 2019,
limiting the ability of Funai's inspectors to service distant communities. Reporters at the *New York Times* who visited the Uru Eu
Wau Wau people in Rondônia in April 2020 reported that money
was no longer available to pay for teachers and that a new school
building was seldom used. Doctors and nurses visited only rarely.
The community was concerned about invaders – mainly illegal
loggers – establishing a permanent settlement in the 6,850 square
mile territory.[30]

Global warming concerns widen

Policy was weakening at exactly the time that scientific concerns about the impact of deforestation on global warming were multiplying. During the 1990s, and especially from the beginning of the twenty-first century, policymakers had come to worry about deforestation in the Amazon mainly because of the way that it directly released large amounts of carbon into the atmosphere. In simple terms, dense forests store huge amounts of carbon. Burning them down releases carbon dioxide. Environmentalists were also increasingly concerned about the impact of deforestation on bio-diversity. The tropical rainforests contain thousands of animal and plant species, many of which are undiscovered.

More recently, scientists have also begun to worry about the way deforestation could affect rainfall patterns. In the 1970s and early 1980s a Brazilian physicist named Eneas Salati carried out research on the region's hydrological cycle that showed how the rainforest generated approximately half of its own rainfall. He argued that, as air masses moved east to west from the Atlantic Ocean over the Amazon basin, they picked up and recycled mois-ture from the trees between five and six times. Typically, the same air masses would hit the Andes mountain range to the west and then deposit rainfall further south, helping to water the farms of southern Brazil and Argentina. In effect the Amazon functioned as a giant pump, pushing water above the tree canopy and creating what has come to be known as a 'flying river', as large in volume as the Amazon on the ground.

When deposited on to the savannahs and grasslands of south-ern Brazil, Paraguay, Argentina and Uruguay, the rainfall has been essential to the success of grain and soya farmers. In this sense the Amazon was not only a carbon sink but a core part of the continent's climate system. Carlos Nobre, a Brazilian scientist who originally wrote about this aspect of the Amazon, calls it the "flywheel" of the continent's climate.[31]

High levels of deforestation would disrupt this system, however, reducing rainfall and triggering longer dry seasons in the Amazon and in turn reducing the level of rainfall further south. Beyond a certain level of deforestation this "flywheel" would stop working, and the Amazon would gradually get dryer and begin to reach a point of no return. In 2007 Nobre and his fellow scientists estimated that this tipping point would be reached when 40 per cent of the rainforest had disappeared. Since the 1970s about 17 per cent of the rainforest had been lost through deforestation and fire, so in 2007 calamity still seemed some way off, giving policymakers time to adjust.

The pattern of climatic events more recently, however, has made scientists much more concerned. In recent years dry seasons (which usually last from July to November) in the Amazon basin have become longer and hotter. Species that thrive in wet climates such as toucans or giant Brazilian otters are beginning to die at a faster rate. A study of bird species in a part of the Amazon north of Manaus by Professor Philip Stouffer at Louisiana State University found that the musician wren – a South American bird known for its tuneful whistle – and the wing-banded antbird, known for its foraging strategy of tossing leaves aside, which both thrived in humidity, were both in decline as conditions become drier. Stouffer argued that biodiversity was being eroded because this part of the Amazon now has hotter and drier dry seasons.[32]

Extreme weather events have also become much more likely. In at least three years – 2005, 2010 and 2015 – the Amazon experienced droughts of unprecedented severity. Severe floods occurred with much more frequency as well (in 2009, 2012 and 2014), suggesting that a stable and predictable climatic pattern is a thing of the past. As a result Nobre and his colleagues think that the tipping point could be much closer than they hitherto believed, with deforestation of little more than half their original estimate of 40 per cent triggering this catastrophic change. There is plentiful recent scientific research to back up this alarming picture. One particularly influential study by a big network of international scientists, known as Rainfor, has collected data from 106 different one-hectare plots over the last thirty-five years. It showed that species adapted to a wet rainforest climate are dying out, while drought-resistant species are on the rise. Adriane Esquivel Muelbert from Birmingham University, a participant in the research, said that this shift is already well advanced, especially in the worst-hit regions such as the southern Amazon. "We are seeing very high temperatures and very long dry seasons. If the species change then the changes are more permanent."[33]

"We believe that negative synergies between deforestation, climate change and widespread use of fire indicate a tipping point – a flip in rain forest eco-systems in East, Central and Southern Amazon – is 20–25 per cent deforestation", wrote Nobre and Lovejoy in February 2018. In their follow-up piece in December 2019 they added an even more urgent note. "The tipping point is here. It is now."[34]

12

TILTING AT WINDMILLS

Early in his presidential campaign, Jair Bolsonaro took to the floor of Congress to angrily denounce what he called a "crime against the nation". He warned that China was acquiring too much control over Brazil's niobium, an obscure but valuable mineral that can be added to steel to make it lighter and more resistant. Bolsonaro claimed that Brazil's 85 per cent of world reserves could make it one of the most prosperous countries on the planet if they were properly harnessed. "We can't let China come in here and buy up land, buy niobium, as if it were just another mineral! No!", he thundered, standing in front of a Brazilian flag. "That's like giving the Chinese billions of dollars!"

Bolsonaro lambasted the 2016 acquisition by the China Molybdenum Company of a small niobium mine at Catalão in the state of Minas Gerais, and even made a short film on the subject, in which he argued that Brazil should develop a "niobium valley". But as president, Bolsonaro has discovered just how difficult it is to separate niobium and other commodities from China's tight embrace. The Brazilian company that accounts for most of the country's niobium production, Companhia Brasileira de Metalurgia e Mineração (CBMM), depends on exports to international steel companies. "China accounts for more than half of world steel production and we couldn't be outside this main market", Eduardo Ribeiro, the company's chief executive, told me when I met him early in 2019 at his office in Faria Lima, in São Paulo's financial district.[1]

Brazil's Moreira Salles family owns a controlling interest in CBMM, but five Chinese steel companies – Bao Steel, CITIC, Anshan Iron & Steel, Shougang and Taiyuan Iron & Steel – acquired a 15 per cent stake in 2011. Bolsonaro vehemently criticised that deal as well. But in practice it has benefited all parties, helping the Chinese guarantee future supplies while allowing CBMM to shape future applications of niobium-based steel alloys in sectors such as construction, motors, and oil and gas. Ribeiro described the deal, which also saw Japanese and Korean steel groups buy another 15 per cent of CBMM's shares, as "strategic".

The connections have paid off in other ways. Partly because of a change in Chinese regulations requiring builders to use stronger steel girders, sales of ferro-niobium ingots – one of CBMM's most popular products – surged by 26 per cent in 2018. The CBMM mine and smelting installations in the former spa town of Araxá were busier than they had ever been, with the company's 2,000 workers operating at full capacity.

The niobium controversy epitomises a much broader dilemma for Brazil. During the campaign Bolsonaro made it very clear that he wanted to realign foreign policy, establish closer ties to the United States and distance Brazil from China and other emerging powers. In many ways the stance was identical to the one adopted by former US president Donald Trump. Anti-China rhetoric dovetailed neatly with the campaign's firmly anti-PT and anti-communist themes. Olavo de Carvalho, the US-based guru to the new Brazilian president who we encountered in Chapter 2, suggested that China formed part of a broader "cultural Marxist" trend that during thirteen and a half years of rule by the left-wing Workers' Party had pulled the country away from the conservative values embraced by its population.

In February 2018 Bolsonaro became the first presidential candidate to visit Taiwan since Brazil recognised the People's Republic in the early 1970s. During electioneering Bolsonaro portrayed China as a predatory economic power, arguing that China – in sectors such as mining and energy – was not just "buying in Brazil it is buying Brazil". Chinese diplomats – who had watched their country develop extremely close relations with the PT governments of Lula da Silva and Rousseff – started to worry. "There were some strong declarations and this caused a lot of concern in China", Reinaldo Ma, a Brazilian lawyer with São Paulo-based firm Tozzinifreire, told me.

Brazil's growing China dependency

Yet these tensions arose at a time when China was becoming more pivotal than ever to Brazil's stability and future growth. Since China joined the World Trade Organization in 2001 it has been more open to business with the world. China still heavily restricts foreign companies' access to its own markets, but its international trade, within a market-based system and subject to the WTO's rules and judgements, has expanded dramatically.[2] This reshaped economic relations all over the world, but had a particularly important influence in Latin America, whose raw materials were essential to China's manufacturing boom and build-up of infrastructure.

Over the last twenty years China has become the biggest export market for Chilean and Peruvian copper, for example. Oil exporters such as Venezuela and Ecuador sold to China. China's demand sucked in Argentinian soya and wheat. But Brazil was transformed by its new trade relationship with Beijing. As we saw in Chapter 3, China provided a huge market for the iron ore mined by Vale, the big privatised mining giant. As it slowly started to exploit the vast oil reserves it had discovered in the 2000s, Petrobras, the state-controlled oil company, saw its sales to China rise sharply. Above all, Chinese demand for products such as beef, pork, chicken, sugar, coffee and especially soya brought unprecedented prosperity to Brazilian farmers. The soya fed the Chinese pigs and poultry reared to meet a change in consumption habits. The better-off city dwellers spawned by the country's epic urban migration wanted more protein in their diets.

The prices of many commodities had fallen during the period from 2012 to 2016, but Brazil's China trade continued to grow. When Rousseff was impeached and the thirteen years of PT government ended in 2016, exports to China amounted to $35.6bn, which represented about 19 per cent of that year's total exports. But in the following three years to 2019 sales to China doubled, and Brazil's trade surplus with Beijing increased from about $5bn to $28bn. In other words, just as Bolsonaro and his more ideological supporters stepped up their rhetorical attacks on the Chinese government, the country's trade dependence was becoming ever more stark.[3]

In 2020 the reliance on the Chinese market deepened. China's early recovery from the COVID-19 pandemic allowed its economy to grow much faster than the depressed economies of the US, Europe and South America. Sales of soya climbed steadily and were given an additional boost by the trade war that reduced sales from the US, hitherto an important rival supplier. In September 2020 Brazil exported 7.25 million tons of oil seed to China, compared to 4.79 million tons in the same month in 2019. In the first ten months of 2020 China absorbed 33.6 per cent of Brazil's exports.

By the end of 2020 Brazil's two other major exports, oil and iron ore, also seemed to be becoming ever more prominent. In 2018 Brazilian oil provided 8 per cent of Chinese imports, up from only 2 per cent in 2014. By October 2020 Brazil was on course to be the third largest exporter of oil to China (after Russia and Saudi Arabia). Chinese imports from Brazil were running at 1.1 million barrels per day in September 2020, up from 723,000 barrels per day a year earlier. Overall, in the first nine months of 2020, oil exports to China had risen by an average of 15.6 per cent.

Iron ore – mined from Vale's enormous open pit facilities in the Amazon and despatched by train and ship to China – remained an export mainstay. In October 2020 Vale signalled expectations of further expansion when it struck a $500m investment deal with the Chinese state-owned port operator Ningbo Zhoushan Port to create additional handling capacity at Shulanghu Port. New deep berths would be able to accommodate Vale's giant Valemax carriers, which are as big as some skyscrapers and can carry 400,000 deadweight tonnes, much more than normal iron ore transport vessels.[4]

But China was interested in far more than trade. Since the beginning of the century, China had also been an investor and lender, with commitments designed to ensure the long-term security of supply of raw materials and also win a share of Brazil's growing market. Investment levels were relatively modest. China had invested $55.7bn in Brazil by the end of 2018. Flows reached a high point of $10.7bn in 2017, but then dipped sharply amid the uncertainty ahead of the 2018 election and Bolsonaro's anti-Chinese stance. Activity recovered in 2019 when $1.9bn of investment was made, but remained fairly modest compared to Brazil's total inflows of FDI.[5]

Chinese investment in Brazil was never as prominent as it was in some other developing countries. In a number of African countries, for example, Chinese construction companies had been allowed carte blanche to build big infrastructure projects, often bringing in thousands of their own workers. At the end of 2009, for example, I visited Luanda, the Angolan capital, and saw Chinese trucks driven by Chinese drivers clogging the roads that took me to my hotel. Construction sites across the capital were covered with Chinese signs, flags and brightly coloured banners. Clad in their blue overalls, Chinese workers were all over the place.

Brazil had always insisted that Chinese investors comply with the country's restrictive labour laws. Compared to its overt and upfront presence in countries such as Angola, China has a low-key, much more sophisticated way of doing things in Brazil. Chinese companies have typically taken over or bought stakes in existing businesses, rather than setting up so-called green field operations. Local management and staff have been retained. Sometimes the company has retained its Brazilian brand and very often the only sign of Chinese control is the regular video meeting with Chinese staff.

However low profile its presence though, China has slowly been gaining access to strategic sectors such as energy and communications. This push is in line with the Chinese government's Belt and Road initiative (BRI), a mammoth $1,400bn international investment plan launched in 2013. The plan is of an unprecedented scale, at least seven times larger, measured in today's dollars, than the Marshall Plan, the US initiative to rebuild Europe after the Second World War. As Daniel Yergin, one of the world's leading energy writers, puts it:

> Infrastructure investment has served for decades as an economic growth engine for the country's development, which can be revved up when growth appears to be waning. An initial impetus for Belt and Road was the expectation, following the global financial crisis, of slower global economic growth for China. Development in Eurasia, reflecting the Asian and European focus of policy, would stimulate growth, create new markets for Chinese industries suffering from extensive overcapacity, support jobs in China, and create new opportunities for Chinese firms.[6]

Another writer argued that the BRI is more like an ambitious development policy launched in response to the growing difficulties experienced by a strategy based on low wages, technology transfers from the West and heavy state investment that had underpinned China's very fast growth rates since the 1980s. In contrast, the government now insisted on the importance of developing high-productivity industries and encouraged its companies to go abroad and build businesses in a range of appropriate sectors.[7]

Brazil is not formally a member of BRI, although it could become one, and the infrastructure investment initiative launched by President Xi Jinping in December 2019 would chime with its potential future membership. Several Latin American nations are part of the Belt and Road plan, although the majority are small and relatively weak Central American and Caribbean countries where China has been battling fiercely for influence against Taiwan.

China's Brazil investment thrust has focused heavily on energy and communications. Huawei, the Chinese company that makes telecommunications equipment, has been in Brazil since 1998; it has factories in two Brazilian cities (Manaus and Sorocaba) and supplies all four of Brazil's big mobile phone companies (Oi, Vivo, Claro and TIM), relationships which, as we will see, could make it difficult to dislodge Huawei from the race to build 5G capacity.

Chinese giant state oil companies have all made big commitments to Brazil's efforts to exploit its reserves. The China National Offshore Oil Corporation (CNOOC) and the China National Petroleum Corporation (CNPC) have minority stakes in consortiums to exploit several fields. In 2018 CNPC bought a 20 per cent stake in the Comperj refinery in Rio de Janeiro state, allowing work at the facility to resume three years after it was interrupted at the height of the Lava Jato scandal. And in 2020 CNOOC and a CNPC subsidiary were the only companies to bid in another auction of rights to exploit the same deep-water reserves. No other international company made a bid, but the Chinese participation meant that the deal raised nearly R$70bn.[8]

Deals in the power-generation sector have also highlighted Chinese interest. In 2019 the China General Nuclear Power Corporation paid US$783 million for the total solar and wind energy assets already in operation of the Italian group Enel in Brazil. And State Grid, which we will look at in more detail shortly, invested $1bn in a 46.7 per cent share of CPFL Renováveis, the leading renewable energy company in Brazil. The focus on renewable energy chimes with another significant aspect of the Belt and Road initiative – the attempt to dominate segments of value chains in highly productive new technology sectors. Chinese companies dominate the global supply chains for wind turbines, solar panels and the lithium-ion batteries used in electric cars. Huawei's prominence in the telecoms equipment market reflects this approach. And there is a technological element to the expansion in Brazil of State Grid. Another well-informed writer explains Chinese thinking as follows:

> In this new age it pays to think across national boundaries [...] What a country wants is to pick and choose the best elements in each value chain [...] In truth [it is] less a question of somersaulting to the top of extant value chains than building new ones, allowing one to specialise in capital intensive and technology intensive industries. If a country wants to compete with the most advanced countries it must do so by establishing new more efficient and more dynamic value chains.[9]

In May 2015 China's State Council identified eleven sectors as priorities for international expansion: steel, non-ferrous metals, construction materials, railway equipment, power generation and infrastructure, resource development, textiles, motor vehicles, information technology, aviation and shipbuilding.

In a series of deals since 2012, State Grid has gradually built up its presence and has about 20 per cent of Brazil's transmission market. In 2015 State Grid outbid international competition to win a $2.2bn contract to build a 2,500km transmission line from the Belo Monte hydroelectric project in the Amazon to Rio de Janeiro. And in 2016 it paid $4.1bn to acquire control of Companhía Paulista Força e Luz, a privately owned and listed utility. The investments are significant because China sees them as part of a broader global plan – known as the Global Electricity Interconnection (GEI) – that aims to develop a global electricity grid. So-called ultra-high-voltage transmission lines, being deployed by State Grid in Brazil in the transmission line between the Belo Monte dam and Rio de Janeiro for the first time outside China, are an important element of GEI, since they allow more electricity to be transported over longer distances and with lower levels of loss than conventional power cables. Typically losses on conventional lines using alternating current average between 6 per cent and 21 per cent, compared to between 2 and 3 per cent for UHV lines using direct current. China originally developed this technology to shift electricity from hydroelectric dams in its remote mountainous interior to coastal cities, but GEI – a brainchild of a former State Grid chairman – sees broader potential global applications, linking, for example, Congolese dams to the developed economies of southern Europe. According to industry specialists the technology is not unique, but China has become a leader in the sector.

Risks and lobbies

China's penetration into Brazil presents some policy challenges. First, there is the sheer weight of the trade dependency. Without the China trade surplus to cushion its current account deficit, Brazil would have much greater financing needs. "The administration knows that if things were to go wrong China might punish us and our trade surplus would be reduced to peanuts in six months time", a former official in the Rousseff administration told me.[10] Then there is the potential unpredictability of the Chinese presence. With plentiful cheap finance and encouraged by a government anxious to win business for Chinese suppliers, China's energy and infrastructure companies are often more able to take a longer-term perspective than their Western competitors. State Grid undercut rivals when it forged its way into the Brazilian market, for example.

But equally, Chinese companies can sometimes prove to be remarkably fickle. Take, for example, the case of China's foray into the business of making tractors, diggers and other equipment used in construction projects. During the period between 2010 and 2013, Chinese companies in this sector quickly built up market share by offering cheaper products than their rivals. "They priced their tractors, dump trucks and bulldozers at 70 per cent of the rate of local competitors", one Brazilian academic who studied the sector told me.[11] Having quickly built up a market share of 20 per cent, the companies unveiled ambitious plans to expand, throwing their more established rivals into turmoil. But just as quickly, as Brazil's economy slowed down, these plans were abandoned.

Perhaps the biggest concern is that Chinese investments and economic ties will cause companies and politicians to act in ways that are counter to Brazil's national interest. The level of direct political influence over Chinese companies varies, but it is relatively strong in the big utility companies such as State Grid and Huawei. In both companies, high-level committees – known as workers' fronts – help ensure that company decisions follow guidelines set down by the Chinese government. "They [the Chinese] see this as an industry which can give them strategic influence across the board. [The fronts] are to ensure that all oarsmen are rowing in the same direction", one US analyst told me.[12] Investors in CPFL, the renewables business bought by State Grid in 2016, were sometimes surprised to find that two people – one from Brazil and one from China – were appointed to senior positions in the company after its takeover. "People used to joke that everybody has a shadow", said one fund manager who traded the shares of the company.[13] These risks led some governments in the developed world – Australia and Germany among them – to block Chinese acquisitions in the energy sector. Not only former US president Donald Trump but several other developed country governments blocked Huawei from participating in the auctions of new 5G licences. Until recently this restrictive approach towards China was in sharp contrast to that adopted by Brazil.

Under the PT governments of Lula and Rousseff, Brazil not only welcomed Chinese investment but saw Beijing as a more welcome ally than any of the developed countries. While Lula did move to block big acquisitions of land by Chinese and other foreign investors, the architects of the Workers' Party's foreign policy saw China as a valuable partner in their efforts to promote an alliance among the poor countries of the south. Membership of the BRICS – the group linking Brazil with China, India, Russia and South Africa – was enthusiastically embraced. "It was always very friendly. It was quite clear there was a partnership between both governments", said a former government official who attended several high-level meetings between Brazilian and Chinese leaders. By the end of the Rousseff government, Brazil was "the biggest western economy to maintain an open investment policy towards China", according to Cebri, a Brazilian think tank.[14]

This has evidently begun to change under Bolsonaro. But there is a world of difference between rhetorical attacks on "Maoist China" – a phrase favoured by foreign minister Ernesto Araújo – and actually putting an effective policy into place. Part of the problem faced by the Bolsonaro administration is that powerful vested interests are now in favour of closer links to the Chinese. Take Huawei and the upcoming 5G auctions (at the time of writing, due to take place in late 2021), for example. Huawei has supplied between 40 and 50 per cent of the equipment used by Vivo, Claro, TIM and Oi – the four dominant telecoms companies – in the development of their 4G networks, and Vivo is already working with the Chinese on the development of its first commercial 5G network. Ericsson of Sweden and Nokia of Finland compete with Huawei, but are generally regarded as more expensive. Not surprisingly, perhaps, the Brazilian companies appear to be resisting pressure from the US to change course.

The other very big problem for Bolsonaro is that a significant part of his support base in the powerful agribusiness lobby is fearful that too robust an approach towards the Chinese could lead to retaliation and a potential loss of market share. It is impossible to overemphasise how bound up the fortunes of many Brazilian farmers are with China. Over the last couple of years, I have met a number who have benefited from the China trade. Pedro Cervi, a 55-year-old agronomist from Curitiba in southern Brazil, was one example. In the early 1990s Cervi bought 28,000 hectares of land in a north-east region of Brazil known as Mapitoba, whose name derives from the first two letters of each of the four states it straddles – Maranhão, Piauí, Tocantins and Bahia. Mapitoba is an expanding agricultural zone made up of savannah and scrubland that has seen a dramatic increase in its maize, cotton and soya output. Cervi exported 80 per cent of his harvest to China, with produce carried by trailers from his farm to the port of São Luís in Maranhão. "China is really important for Brazil especially on these new frontiers", he said. Like many other big farmers, Cervi voted for Bolsonaro in 2018 but is hoping that nothing will be done that damages his business.

In Boa Vista I met Jay Edwards, an American now naturalised as a Brazilian, who has farmed soya in Mato Grosso and more recently in an expanding soya zone on Roraima's savannah. Edwards, who farmed several thousand hectares on behalf of a group of individual investors, was part of a cooperative that aimed to sell directly to Chinese buyers, rather than going through one of the large trading companies. Farmers such as Cervi and Edwards voted for Bolsonaro for various reasons. Rural security was one big issue. Fearful of land invasions by squatters or straightforward theft of petrol or fertiliser, farmers were anxious to be allowed to protect their land and wanted to be free to use their guns to defend themselves. While happy to comply with environmental rules, they frequently argue that agencies such as Ibama are arbitrary in the way they implement and enforce rules.

There was an implicit assumption that China needed Brazilian soya so much that it was virtually impossible for the trading relationship to be interrupted. "It would be irrational to damage our biggest trade partner", said Cervi. "Bolsonaro was my option but his thinking [on China] was a bit hasty. He wasn't well-informed." When in January 2019 I interviewed senior figures at the National Agricultural Confederation, the trade body that represents farming interests, I got a similar sense that the lobby felt it was sufficiently well organised to protect its China interests. "We don't want to segregate or distance ourselves from China. To be a great player we need pragmatism. We can't be taken by ideologies."[15]

Tensions of this kind between the ideological and pragmatic wings of the Bolsonaro government over issues such as China and the environment were to pop up repeatedly during the first year and a half of the Bolsonaro administration. It is to a broader examination of these divisions that we now turn.

13

A PRESIDENT UNDER PRESSURE

On the surface, everything about the two-hour cabinet meeting that took place on 22 April 2020 seemed ordered and calm. Two dozen ministers and senior officials – most of them men wearing dark suits and ties – sat around a conference table. The blurred outlines of Brasília's skyline were visible through the Planalto Palace's blinds as General Walter Braga Netto, the president's chief of staff, explained how the government should coordinate its response to the coronavirus pandemic.

At first the tone was bland, low-key. Braga Netto, sitting next to Bolsonaro, had prepared a few slides. The name of the recovery plan – Pro-Brazil – was emblazoned on a large flatscreen TV. Ministers were asked to make short responses, detailing their policy plans. But every time Bolsonaro spoke, the atmosphere changed. The president was agitated and at times it seemed he could barely contain his anger. He raged against the press, and hurled invective at local government leaders who had imposed quarantines earlier in the month. He seemed to think they were doing it to score political points.

Wilson Witzel was one of the extreme right-wing outsiders who had surfed a wave of anti-establishment sentiment to win the governorship of Rio de Janeiro in 2018. Many of the hardline police officers and evangelicals who provided the Bolsonaro family with such firm support in the state had voted for him. Now after declaring a lockdown, Witzel was derided as "a piece of dung". Bolsonaro launched a furious attack on João Doria, a conservative politician from São Paulo, who had also backed him in the second round of the election. Now Doria was a "shit" for telling the residents of Brazil's biggest city to stay at home. The mayor of Manaus, another conservative, who had just had to order the digging of mass graves to cope with the growing numbers of victims, was also "a piece of shit". The president stopped short of a full-frontal attack on the Supreme Court judges who a week previously had given local governments the freedom to impose quarantines, but one of his lieutenants had no such compunction. "If it was up to me I would put these bums in prison", said Abraham Weintraub, his education minister.

In the style of a bar room brawler, Bolsonaro said he would not be bound by any restrictions. He would mix with whom he wanted and ignore pettifogging virus tests. "I am not going to walk around with my tail between my legs", he said, banging his fists on the table.

> I am not having these mayors stopping people moving about. I'm the chief of the armed forces and that's it. I'll interfere where I want. Ponto Final [End of argument]. If I have to go down one day [it will be for] a good reason. Not a stupid anti-virus exam.

Eighteen months on from his election win, it seemed that the broad political alliance that linked his hardcore extremist supporters to the middle-class supporters of Doria and anti-PT business groups was falling apart. The economy was beginning to tank and it was taking Bolsonaro's ratings with it. His eldest son, Flávio, was under judicial investigation. The popular health minister Luiz Henrique Mandetta, whose profile had risen during the first weeks of the crisis, had just been sacked. And now – judging from the evidence of this meeting – the president was beginning to doubt the loyalty of other members of his government. "Our ship is going I don't know where. It could hit an iceberg", he insisted.

You have to be on side. Anyone who is not prepared to accept what I stand for – family, God, Brazil, arms, freedom of expression and the free market – is in the wrong government. Some people say one or two ministers are doing well despite the government – what is that about? The president gets a kicking but the minister is praised. Fuck me. I pick the fucking team.

Sérgio Moro, the one-time star judge of the Lava Jato investigation, was one minister whose allegiance looked likely to come into question. Moro had controversially joined Bolsonaro's team in 2018 to take over the justice portfolio. He had argued that his presence in the administration was the best guarantee that the clean-up of political corruption would continue. He had had a turbulent time since then, suffering all manner of setbacks. As we saw in Chapter 6, his credibility had been badly knocked by leaked text messages suggesting that he had not been impartial in conducting the case against former president Lula de Silva. Rather than presiding over a stronger and more coordinated campaign against corruption, Moro had watched as Bolsonaro chipped away at the independence of the judicial system. Since 2003 Brazilian presidents had allowed public prosecutors to shape the selection of the chief public prosecutor, an arrangement that meant that their investigations were more likely to proceed without political interference. But Bolsonaro had broken with convention. Augusto Aras, the new chief public prosecutor, was picked because he was a right-winger.[1] Moro's attempt to streamline the fight against corruption and organised crime faltered. The Financial Activities Control Council, which monitored suspicious financial transactions and oversaw money laundering cases, was handed to Moro's justice ministry, but was then taken away again and passed to the Central Bank, where critics said it would be subject to greater political interference. The courts had even rolled back some of the reforms that had made the Lava Jato case effective. Above all, Bolsonaro had pressed Moro to make changes to the leadership of the federal police. Critics had argued that the meddling was designed to protect Bolsonaro family members from investigation. "Unfortunately a minor issue, one of the most banal crimes involving politicians (allegedly committed by Bolsonaro's son) is hampering the fight against corruption in Brazil", said the former leading Lava Jato prosecutor, Carlos Fernando dos Santos Lima.[2]

Yet in spite of all this, Moro remained a popular minister. In January 2020 a poll by Datafolha showed that Moro was the most trusted of twelve leading Brazilian politicians. These included former presidents Lula da Silva and Cardoso, as well as Bolsonaro and his vice-president, Hamilton Mourão. Moro was also the most popular of Bolsonaro's cabinet members. It was perhaps not surprising then that at the 22 April meeting, the justice minister's body language suggested he was frustrated. Moro sat with his arms folded and head bowed, as he heard Bolsonaro say,

> I will not wait for them to fuck with my family or my friends for the hell of it. There'll be a change. If we can't switch [an official] we'll switch his boss. If we can't change the boss, we'll change the minister. This is going to end. I am not joking.

Two days later, it did end. Bolsonaro sacked the head of the federal police, Maurício Valeixo, and within hours Moro had resigned. Valeixo had been one of Moro's right-hand men: he had been with the federal police in Paraná in 2009 and 2011, and again from 2017. In April 2018 he had coordinated the imprisonment of Lula da Silva. Many Brazilians concluded that Bolsonaro had taken the action to protect his sons from prosecution. Flávio Bolsonaro, the eldest son and now a federal senator, was under investigation over the *rachadinhas* cases, in which money earmarked for political advisers in the Rio de Janeiro state assembly had been skimmed off. The *Folha de São Paulo* also reported that police had targeted the president's second son, Carlos, for his involvement in fake news schemes both during and after the 2018 election.[3]

Amid the controversies surrounding COVID-19 and quarantine, pro-Bolsonaro social media campaigners – what Supreme Court judge Alexandre de Moraes called the "digital militia" – had begun to directly attack the eleven judges of the Supreme Court itself.[4] Bolsonaro supporters – including a group of activists who called themselves Brasil 300 – were also being investigated for staging demonstrations against democracy. Pro-Bolsonaro activists had even threatened to kill and dismember judges and their families. Late in May police seized the hard drives and mobile phones of a number of pro-Bolsonaro bloggers.[5]

Within minutes of Moro's resignation there were signs that support for Bolsonaro was sliding, with "deafening pot-banging protests erupting in major Brazilian cities, including in strongly pro-Bolsonaro areas of Rio de Janeiro. '*Fora Bolsonaro! Fora Bolsonaro!*' ('Bolsonaro out!'), dissenters cried from their windows and balconies as they pounded their saucepans."[6] The Supreme Court's judges stepped up their actions. They began an investigation into allegations that Bolsonaro had interfered with the police and blocked Bolsonaro's first nomination for the post of director general of the federal police. And they released the video of the 22 April meeting, the video that had, in the words of one newspaper columnist, "exposed a government that was totally out of control".[7] By the middle of 2020 there were at least forty separate motions before Congress calling for Bolsonaro to be impeached. "The president is digging his own grave", tweeted former president Cardoso. "May he quit before he is removed, and spare us, on top of the coronavirus, from a long impeachment process."[8]

An uneasy alliance

Tensions had been evident in the Bolsonaro government pretty much from the beginning. As we have seen, the political alliance that brought Bolsonaro to office was a broad one, uniting social conservatives and radical right-wingers with more moderate middle-class and business interests who had seen the former army captain as the best bet to defeat the left.

Bolsonaro's first cabinet had a haphazard and patched-up feel about it. The president had little connection with any of Brazil's largest political parties. His adherence to the conservative Social Liberal Party had been negotiated as recently as January 2018. It was the latest of the seven parties with which he had been affiliated during his three decades in Brazilian politics. The party for him was nothing more than a shell required for legal reasons. In any case, Bolsonaro had rejected the traditional deal-making approach – the give and take (what Brazilians call the *toma lá, dá cá*) of congressional politics which had, as a result of the Lava Jato case, become intimately connected in the public mind with corruption.

Some ministers emerged through their links to Bolsonaro's three sons and their coterie of Olavo de Carvalho associates. Like Carvalho, each of Bolsonaro's sons tended towards an intensely ideological, anti-liberal view of the world. Bolsonaro and his sons admired the United States, and Donald Trump in particular. They shared Trump's narrow nationalism and his scepticism about global warming and gender politics. They were instinctively distrustful of political pragmatism, authoritarian in their instincts and looked to promote Bolsonaro through social media.

Carlos Bolsonaro had been running his father's Facebook and Twitter accounts since 2010 and had built a small team of digital activists, in which Filipe Martins, a star student of Carvalho, played a prominent role. The team, nicknamed the cabinet of hate (*gabinete de ódio*), allegedly occupied offices in the presidential palace in Brasília (although the Bolsonaros denied this). One commentator labelled them *Bolsolavistas*: "[These activists] hack social media pages, create false news and employ robots – or bots – that multiply the tweets of 'social influencers' like Eduardo Bolsonaro."[9]

One of their most important representatives in government was Ernesto Araújo, the foreign minister, previously a mid-level official in the foreign ministry who had come to the notice of Martins by virtue of an article he had written praising Trump. Araújo had attacked "globalist cultural Marxism", arguing that it "promotes both a dilution of gender and a dilution of national sentiment: it calls for a world of 'gender fluid', cosmopolitan people with no country, denying what is for everyone the biological fact of birth in a particular gender and in a particular historical community".[10]

Ricardo Vélez Rodríguez, the short-lived education minister, and his immediate successor, Abraham Weintraub, were both followers of Carvalho. Vélez's signature initiative was to have school children filmed singing the national anthem, and then have the videos sent to his ministry.[11] Damares Alves, the minister of women and human rights, was a Baptist preacher and a social conservative hostile to abortion and "gender ideology". After Bolsonaro took office Damares famously proclaimed that "the new era has begun. Now a boy will wear blue and a girl will wear pink."

For more moderate government supporters, who had voted for Bolsonaro mainly because he represented the best hope of finally defeating the threat from the political left, two ministers in particular provided reassurance. Moro, as we have already noted, remained the most popular minister in Bolsonaro's cabinet, even though his first year in the justice portfolio had not been a sparkling success. Paulo Guedes, the economy minister, boasted orthodox liberal economic credentials. He had been taught by Milton Friedman at the University of Chicago, had been a co-founder of a Brazilian investment bank, Banco Pactual (now BTG Pactual) and advocated far-reaching state reform and deregulation.[12] Alongside him, a number of figures who had formed part of the Temer government continued to play important roles.

Several ministers were members of the Democrats, the latest incarnation of a mainstream conservative trend that had provided support for the military governments of the 1960s, 1970s and

1980s. Onyx Lorenzoni, who was Bolsonaro's first chief of staff, Tereza Cristina Corrêa da Costa Dias (widely known simply as 'Tereza Cristina'), who took over as agriculture minister, and Luiz Henrique Mandetta, the health minister until April 2020, were all members.

Finally, and momentously, the Bolsonaro government marked the most significant involvement of the armed forces in Brazilian politics since the 1980s. Several senior generals were still distrustful of Bolsonaro on account of his trade union style activities of the 1980s, but the high command as a whole shared the political and business elite's disenchantment with the Workers' Party. And Bolsonaro had won support from the top brass for his opposition to the Truth Commission established by former president Rousseff. Even sceptical generals shared this common enemy. Seven of the twenty-two ministers in Bolsonaro's first cabinet had been senior officers, and that number rose further with the appointments in 2020.[13] And at lower levels too there was a considerable military contingent. In July 2020 the Tribunal de Contas da União, Brazil's public accounts body, calculated that 6,157 officers – both retired and active – occupied positions in the administration, double the number that there had been under Bolsonaro's predecessor, Michel Temer.[14]

For those concerned about the health of Brazilian democracy this was clearly a disturbing trend. The armed forces were after all not directly accountable to voters. Bolsonaro had brought soldiers back to the table "to the degree that many Brazilians think of his administration as a military government in all but name", wrote one commentator.[15] Luiz Roberto Barroso, one of the eleven judges on the Federal Supreme Court, even drew parallels with Venezuela, where since Hugo Chávez's election win of 1998 the armed forces had played a growing role; he bluntly stated that "Brazil's government was experiencing a 'Chavezisation'".[16]

But the politics of the involvement of Brazil's armed forces in government are complex. In some ways the military ministers tended to straddle the divide between the Bolsonarista ideologues and the pro-business, anti-PT pragmatists. That the military was opposed to the PT there seems to be little doubt. In one key incident during the extended legal case against Lula da Silva, the high command might well have tipped the balance in the exclusion of the left-wing leader – then still ahead in the polls – from the 2018 election. Lula's conviction on corruption charges was controversial and his lawyers had appealed a subsequent ruling confirming his exclusion from the race. With the eleven judges of the Supreme Court about to give their judgment on that appeal, General Eduardo Villas Bôas, then commander of the army, tweeted that the army "rejected impunity" and remained "attentive to its institutional mission". One judge described the intervention as an "insurgency of a prae-torian nature". Less obliquely, a mid-level officer told Brian Winter that the tweet "announced the military's return to politics".[17] Some generals, though, still had scruples about backing Bolsonaro. In the first round of the 2018 election eight of the army's seventeen four-star generals voted for two candidates from the centre right, Geraldo Alckmin of the PSDB and João Amoêdo of the small New Party (Partido Novo). But faced with Haddad in the run-off, the top brass threw their weight behind Bolsonaro.[18]

A number of senior and mainly retired officers – who were to occupy powerful positions in the new administration – did share Bolsonaro's extreme right-wing views on a number of matters. Prominent among them were two retired generals, 67-year-old Hamilton Mourão, who became deputy president, and 73-year-old Augusto Heleno, who was invited to be minister of institutional security. Both had been members of the paratroop regiment and had met the new president at the Agulhas Negras military acad-emy in the 1970s. Heleno had been an instructor and Bolsonaro a cadet competing in the military pentathlon (shooting, swim-ming, cross-country running, grenade throwing and an obstacle race). "Their love of athletics, hatred of the left and irreverent style brought them together", according to one account of the

Bolsonaro government's turbulent first year.[19] Heleno had clashed with the Lula administration about its decision to create the indigenous reserve at Raposa Serra do Sol in Roraima, which he had labelled "lamentable not to say chaotic".

Mourão, who had also slated the incompetence and corruption of PT governments, in 2015 called for a "patriotic light" to lead the fight against them, and subsequently defended the idea of a coup in certain circumstances, and proposed the formation of a constituent assembly made up of the great and the good and without popular participation. A barracks under his command had commemorated as a hero the notorious torturer Colonel Brilhante Ustra, under whom he served during 1978 and 1979. "There was a war here in Brazil and Ustra was one of those who defended the democratic system", Mourão had said. "They said he tortured a few. Well, it was a war."[20] Although Mourão said he found some of Bolsonaro's ideas too radical, he was wont to be similarly provocative on social issues, calling single parents "misfit factories", for example.[21]

Equally, there was an institutional dimension to the military's participation. Mindful of their reputation for effective and clean administration, many senior officers were simply concerned to bring greater efficiency to the government machine. There tended to be a sharp distinction between the more interventionist retired older officers like Heleno, and the generation currently in command of troops. And however extreme their views, Mourão and Heleno had – as we will see – enough experience to be pragmatic and cautious. With the president loyal to his younger and stridently ideological sons and their Bolsonarista friends, the old guard's steadier hands would be needed to steer the ship whose course their captain was so unsure of.

The "president of small things"

In January 2019, shortly after assuming office, Bolsonaro travelled to Davos, the Swiss resort where each year the World Economic

Forum invites international politicians and business leaders to discuss issues of global importance. The new Brazilian president was asked to make the keynote speech, which offered an excellent opportunity to introduce himself and his plans to investors. Business groups in Brazil had welcomed his election victory and were enthusiastic about the new economic team's support for fiscal reform and privatisation. But international business leaders were sceptical, especially about the potential impact of Bolsonaro's policies in the Amazon. For the heads of big multinational companies, commitment to the environment, women, minorities and transparency was now simply what you did. There were doubts that Bolsonaro understood this, and at the meeting he did nothing to assuage their concerns. His speech lasted only six minutes and left the audience perplexed and unimpressed. "The previous year Macron had spoken for 45 minutes. Donald Trump for 25 minutes. Temer for 20 minutes", wrote Thaís Oyama. When interviewed by Klaus Schwab, the executive chairman of the forum, the Brazilian president answered in monosyllables. And during a dinner that night, photographers caught Bolsonaro looking lost while the conversation between Paulo Guedes, Schwab and Apple CEO Tim Cook swirled around him. Earlier that same day he had been caught lunching alone in a self-service restaurant in a Zurich supermarket.[22]

Back at home, the president showed little sign of coming to grips with the complex matters with which he was faced. Bolsonaro sometimes seemed to be in another world. Minor matters obsessed him. Officials and political allies, in particular Rodrigo Maia, the president of the lower house, were desperately trying to persuade Congress to approve a pension reform. Investors regarded this as absolutely necessary in order to bring spending under control and increase confidence. Unless Brazil could limit the payments it made to public-sector workers, especially better-paid groups such as top civil servants and judges, the country's deficits would soon be unmanageable. Michel Temer, Bolsonaro's predecessor, had done much to swing public opinion around and in favour of the reform, but now a final push was needed. It was possibly the most crucial economic challenge that the country faced.

While it was being discussed, Bolsonaro dedicated his time to a plan to raise the number of traffic infraction points drivers could incur before losing their licence. There were other issues that obsessed the president as well. In July 2019 *O Estado de São Paulo* reviewed the video presentations – or *lives* – that Bolsonaro had made every week since March.[23] The most popular subject for these *lives* was fishing and in particular the tilapia. The president also busied himself with some cultural issues that were perhaps closer to the interests of his supporters. He ordered the state-owned Banco do Brasil to take down publicity that promoted racial and sexual diversity, for example, and supported an education ministry plan to reduce budgets for sociology and philosophy departments. One columnist called him the "president of small things".[24]

In her colourful account of Bolsonaro's crises, Thaís Oyama notes that big – and perhaps more abstract – policy questions were of no interest to Brazil's leader. She quotes an adviser who saw Paulo Guedes try to explain macro-economic ideas to Bolsonaro during the election campaign. "It was as if Paulo was talking with a bored adolescent. Bolsonaro simply changed the subject in the middle of the conversation."[25]

Behind the scenes, meanwhile, Bolsonaro's sons and their associates continued to press an ideological agenda that fairly soon found them in conflict with the more pragmatic elements of the government, whether military or civilian. Israel was one such issue. The ideologues favoured moving the Brazilian embassy to Jerusalem, just as Trump had done, in spite of the damage this would do to Brazil's standing with the Emirates, Egypt and other Arab nations which had become significant customers for agricultural exports.

China was another crunch issue. The foreign minister Ernesto Araújo wanted to reduce ties with China and talked about promoting links with India, Japan and South Korea. Bolsonaro himself had protested during his campaign that China was buying up Brazil and had objected to the way it was making strategic investments in areas such as minerals and energy. But mindful of the growing weight of the China trade and the importance of Chinese investment, pragmatists were anxious to maintain good relations with Beijing. Eduardo Bolsonaro, the family member who took most interest in foreign affairs, was prone to insult the Chinese, heedless of the damage that this could to Brazil's economy. He claimed, for example, that the Chinese Communist Party was responsible for the coronavirus.

There were also clashes over the environment. Ricardo Salles, the ideological environment minister, cut funding for agencies such as Ibama and ICMBio. The resulting increase in deforestation has been a major concern for local agribusiness groups, worried about their potential loss of access to markets and capital. At the 22 April cabinet meeting, Salles had suggested taking advantage of the fact that the coronavirus pandemic was dominating the attention of the media; with journalists looking elsewhere it was, he said, a good time to press ahead with plans to loosen environmental controls in the Amazon. When the video was published, environmentalists immediately seized on the comments as fuel for their campaign to unwind the trade deal agreed the previous July between the European Union and Mercosul. Anna Cavazzini, a German MEP and spokeswoman for the European Greens, said that the statements confirmed "that the Bolsonaro government is dismantling, step-by-step, the regulations protecting the Amazon, while the world fights the Coronavirus".[26]

Led by his son Carlos, Bolsonaro's media campaigners were relentless in their criticism of ministers concerned by the implications of these controversies. During 2019 two leading figures in the government, the deputy president Mourão and the leader of the lower house of Congress, Rodrigo Maia, were targeted. According to Oyama, Carlos was particularly "obsessed" with Mourão. She claims that Carlos's jealous defensiveness was at the root of many of his father's problems.[27] Mourão was excoriated by the radicals for allowing himself to be photographed with former president Cardoso after an innocent and accidental meeting at Harvard University, where both were involved in the same conference.

Maia's success in winning congressional support for pension reform was the Bolsonaro government's biggest achievement in its first two years in office. But as one commentator wrote, the politician still "came under relentless, frequently vulgar attacks on Twitter from Carvalho and Bolsonaro's sons for supposedly being part of Brasília's corrupt old guard".[28] The same commentator noted that "Maia reacted with exasperation, calling the government 'a desert of ideas', urging Bolsonaro to stay off social media, and lamenting 'this radical environment where they have to feed meat to the lions every single day'".[29]

With Bolsonaro always prone to side with his sons and the Olavista part of his base against any criticism, these kinds of issues proved very disruptive. The military could claim some successes. They had avoided budget cuts and protected their pensions, for example. But "many [soldiers] have expressed shock at his government's perpetual disorganization, penchant for constant conflict, and narrow emphasis on topics they view as secondary – or completely irrelevant – to Brazil's well-being".[30] In June 2019 these frictions deepened the rift between the radicals and the military. One episode led to the departure of General Carlos Alberto dos Santos Cruz, the highly rated chief secretary, who left the government after failing to rein in the radical Bolsonaro media activists. General Villas Bôas had memorably labelled Olavo de Carvalho "a true Trotsky of the right" and warned that "replacing one ideology with another does not contribute to concrete solutions for Brazil's problems".

But the sniping from the radicals continued. In 2020 these tensions were to focus on major battles between Bolsonaro and his hardcore supporters, and Brazil's Supreme Court. And they were aggravated by the controversy surrounding the government's response to the pandemic.

COVID clashes

When in February 2020 Brazilian doctors diagnosed the country's first cases of COVID-19, Luiz Henrique Mandetta, the health minister, led efforts to limit the spread of the disease. But Mandetta, a doctor from the conservative farming state of Mato Grosso do Sul who had specialised in orthopaedics, found the government unreceptive to his advice. Bolsonaro showed "contempt" for instructions to use hand gel or wear a face mask, wrote Mandetta in a memoir published after his departure from government.[31] From the outset, Bolsonaro and his supporters refused to take the disease seriously, calling it a "little flu".

> The health minister indicated one path, the president sent a message suggesting the exact opposite. Every time we talked he said he would let me work, organise the system, put in place what needed to be done. But then he did exactly the opposite, continued to meet people, got people to get together, and gave speeches against social distancing.[32]

After meeting Donald Trump at the US president's Mar-a-Lago resort early in March, Bolsonaro's denialism about the disease became more pronounced, even though several members of his delegation became infected. Like Trump, Bolsonaro refused to embrace the idea of social isolation and argued that it was more important to protect his country's economy. Also, in a further echo, he condemned the recommendations of the World Health Organization and the regional multilateral, the Pan-American Health Organization, which advocated quarantine. Funding commitments to the PAHO were suspended. And in the same way as his North American counterpart, Bolsonaro attached huge faith to chloroquine and its cousin hydroxychloroquine, anti-malaria treatments that have also been used to treat autoimmune conditions such as lupus and that some thought could ease the symptoms of coronavirus.

As the death rate climbed, Bolsonaro became ever more blasé about the disease. When told by a journalist that the death toll had passed 5,000, he said, "Well, I'm sorry, but what do you want me to do about it? My second name is Messiah but I can't work miracles." Most of Brazil's political and judicial class took a different view, however. On 15 April 2020 the Supreme Court ruled that state governors and city mayors had the right to introduce their own quarantines, closing bars and restaurants and limiting access to public transport. Bolsonaro was enraged. Mandetta was sacked after refusing to endorse the use of chloroquine.

As the disease started to spread, the president attended rallies outside military bases, where his supporters called for armed intervention to oust governors and judges who were implementing lockdowns. That was serious enough, but on 22 May Bolsonaro actually did come close to ordering troops to intervene, sack the judges and replace them with his own appointments. According to a report by Monica Gugliano, Bolsonaro had reacted with fury when Celso de Mello, one of the judges, had explored the possibility of seizing his mobile phone in connection with one of the court's fake news inquiries. "I am going to intervene", Bolsonaro said several times, according to Gugliano's interviews with four sources, two of whom had attended a meeting.[33] General Heleno killed the idea, defusing the crisis – partly, according to this report, because active army commanders took a much more cautious view than the retired generals who were closer to the president. As Dos Santos Cruz told the *Financial Times*, "The army has been quiet for 35 years. It won't be getting into party politics now."[34]

Even so, tensions persisted during the next few weeks. Before his father's election Eduardo had said that it would take one corporal and one soldier to close down the Supreme Court. Now he told a blogger that there would be an "institutional break. It is not a question of if but when."[35] But by the beginning of 2021, however, that prospect seemed less likely. The evidence suggested that senior ministers – including some generals – persuaded the president to pull back. In June and July 2020 Bolsonaro conducted a strange about-turn, forming an alliance in Congress with a series of small parties known as the big centre (the *Centrão*). There was a sudden change in style, with the government opting to change the tone of communications and cut down on the radical rhetoric. Most significantly, a very generous emergency welfare payment was extended to millions of people who had been adversely affected by the pandemic and the economic slowdown. Whether this change proves sustainable or whether Brazil is set for a further period of turbulent faction fighting between pragmatic conservatives and extreme right-wing radicals is a judgement we must make in the final chapter of this book.

14

AN UNEXPECTED BONANZA

COVID-19 triggered an unexpected bonanza for Renato Corrêa, a 41-year-old butcher who lives in the tiny village of Santarém Novo in the northern state of Pará. "I used to sell half a cow each day," Corrêa told reporters from *Veja*, the popular Brazilian news weekly, in September 2020. "Now we sell two and half cows."[1]

The additional sales were the result of an emergency welfare payment – known as the *auxílio emergencial* or emergency grant – that was paid between April and December 2020 to compensate for losses due to local COVID-19 lockdowns and the resulting interruption to commerce. The 6,000 residents of Santarém Novo suddenly had much more money to spend, and meat – a luxury for those without regular and reliable sources of income – was on the shopping list. Corrêa had cashed in, channelling extra money into additional land, a new car and even a pharmacy.

Veja magazine reported on other telling cases of unexpected prosperity in Santarém Novo. Until the pandemic struck, Iracelina Santana da Silva and her family were dependent on the R$200 she received in monthly payments from the Bolsa Família, a social welfare programme introduced more than twenty years ago and much expanded by former president Lula da Silva. With the new *auxílio* they were getting nine times as much. "She has sorted out her debts, buys all the fruit and sweets that her children want and is helping her daughter build a new one-bedroomed house nearby", wrote the *Veja* reporters. There was something of a con-struction boom going on as well. Bricks and roof tiles were piled up outside many houses and areas had been set aside for improve-ments and extensions as families were suddenly able to pursue long-delayed home improvements and expansions. Similar stories could be found across poorer areas of Brazil. From April 2020 the authorities paid R$600 a month[2] to the poorest Brazilian families or those who could prove their businesses had been adversely affected.

Novo Santarém was one of ninety-two municipalities in poor north and north-eastern states that saw their economic output rise by more than a fifth. Those working in the informal economy, potentially most at risk from quarantines and lockdowns, ben-efited most. Farm labourers and domestic servants earned 60 per cent more from the *auxílio* than they had before coronavirus struck. But the broader macro-economic and social impact of the payment has been hugely significant. Overall 67.2 million people and 44.1 per cent of Brazilian households received the benefit. By far the most generous COVID-19 assistance provided by any developing country, the grant helped 13.1 million people escape poverty, a reduction of 20.7 per cent compared to July 2019. At the other end of the spectrum, many better-off Brazilians were hit by the negative economic impact of the pandemic. As a result, the Gini coefficient – which measures social-economic inequality – fell to below 0.5, according to the social research unit of the Getúlio Vargas Foundation, a business school and research body.[3]

Brazil's economic response to the coronavirus was a policy that – as we shall see – could not really be sustained. But its impact brought short-term economic benefits. The extra spending com-bined with the impact of looser quarantines meant that the econ-omy performed more strongly than expected in the second half of 2020. In June 2020 the IMF had predicted a 9.1 per cent drop in Brazil's GDP. The actual result was a decline of 4.1 per cent.

"It was", said one writer, "a horrible result, but still less cata-strophic than any other major economy in Latin America."[4]

By the end of 2020 it was becoming clear that this policy was also yielding political dividends. Bolsonaro's opinion poll ratings, which had sunk during the May crisis to their lowest levels since he'd assumed the presidency, improved steadily during the second half of the year. The polls showed that although the president had lost the backing of some middle-class supporters, he was becoming much more popular among low-income groups who had benefited from the emergency grant. It was particularly striking how popular Bolsonaro was becoming in the north-east, the only region that in 2018 had remained loyal to the Workers' Party. A December poll by the Datafolha agency showed that 31 per cent of respond-ents considered Bolsonaro's government good or excellent, up from only 20 per cent twelve months previously. In the north and centre-west the increase in support for the president was even more marked.[5]

In effect, it seemed that the generosity of the emergency grant had allowed Bolsonaro to win over part of the PT's social base, a surprising development given that the president had in the past derided such social policies as electorally driven handouts. In a speech to congressmen in 2011, for example, he had said that the Bolsa Família took from those "who produced and gave to those who simply accept things". He also referred to the beneficiaries as "poor ignorant wretches" who were simply election fodder for the PT.[6] But if this was something of an unexpected twist, another development that began to affect Brazil's political outlook during the second half of 2020 was an even bigger surprise.

Cosying up to the 'big centre'

After the crisis of May when – as we saw in the last chapter – a beleaguered Bolsonaro had threatened to dissolve the Supreme Court, the president changed gear. Fearful that these clashes with the courts and Congress might eventually lead to his impeachment, Bolsonaro shored up his support in Congress by turning to a group of deputies well known for the deal making that he had criticised so much during his electoral campaign and his first eighteen months in office. For a leader who had ridden the wave of popular opposition to political corruption, had benefited directly from the imprisonment of former president Lula da Silva, and had appointed the popular Lava Jato prosecuting judge Sérgio Moro to be his justice minister, this represented an extraordinary shift.

The *Centrão* – or the 'big centre' – was a political alliance made up of a hotchpotch of small, mainly conservative parties. In the bewildering world of Brazilian party politics, membership of the *Centrão* varied, but the alliance usually included the Progressive Party, the Republicanos, the Liberals, the Social Liberals, the Social Democrat Party (not to be confused with the Social Democratic Party of Brazil, the PSDB – the most important party of the centre-right), the Social Christian Party and the Brazilian Labour Party, as well as two small trade union-linked parties – Avante and Solidaridade. Sometimes, too, the group included – in whole or part – the Brazilian Democratic Movement, the big centre-right party that we came across in Chapter 2, and the Democrats, the largest traditional conservative party.[7] These were essentially clientelist or what Brazilians called physiological parties, driven by their interest in positions in government and the material benefits that these could bring for their supporters. They were politically promiscuous, equally happy to provide support for the left-wing PT governments of Lula da Silva and Rousseff, the centre-right MDB government of Temer, or the far-right government of Bolsonaro in exchange for jobs. A classic *Centrão* politician was Gilberto Kassab, a former mayor of São Paulo. When in 2011 he founded his Social Democrat Party, Kassab described it as being "neither left-wing, right-wing nor centrist".[8] "[The *Centrão*'s] commitment is not with ideas but with the government machine, the machine of any government. [They have no] ideas [they are just interested] in power and extracting dividends from that", one commentator wrote, adding wryly: "We don't know who will be the next president but we know that Kassab will be in the government."[9]

Some of the *Centrão*'s most prominent leaders had been widely implicated in the political corruption scandals of the 2000s and 2010s. Arthur Lira, for example, who was to become president of Congress early in 2021, had faced charges over irregularities at Petrobras, the Caixa Econômica Federal (the state mortgage bank) and at the ministry of cities. According to public prosecutors, between 2006 and 2015 Lira was among the congressmen known as the PP gang (Quadrilhão do PP), who had been involved in a scheme involving a myriad of crimes.[10] Roberto Jefferson, leader of the PTB, another *Centrão* party, had been sacked by Congress for his part in the *mensalão* scandal of 2005, and jailed.

Bolsonaro has been a member of several of these parties in the past, attaching himself to the Progressive Party for two spells between 1995 and 2003 and 2005 and 2016, and to the Social Christian Party between 2016 and 2018. His two older sons, Carlos and Flávio, were both members of the Republicanos, though Eduardo Bolsonaro retained membership of the Social Liberals. But when Bolsonaro started to campaign for the presidency, the political mood in Brazil had changed. As we saw, Lava Jato had discredited political parties. On the campaign trail Bolsonaro had promised a break with traditional give-and-take politics, what in Brazil is known as *toma lá, dá cá*. In fact, during his first year and a half in office, Bolsonaro had governed with little reference at all to political parties. His relationship with his own party – the Social Liberal Party, which he had joined in 2018 – was fractious, and Bolsonaro left in November 2019. Efforts to form a new party – the Alliance for Brazil – led nowhere. Relations between Bolsonaro's radical extremist supporters and the conservative parties that had backed his electoral campaign and saw him as the best alternative to defeat the left were stormy.

Bolsonaro's radical followers routinely attacked Rodrigo Maia, a Democrats leader, who as president of the lower house had a huge amount of control over the legislative agenda. The president had made half-hearted efforts to work with the congressional caucuses, and especially the three conservative parliamentary fronts – the beef, Bible and bullet *bancadas* – that had been such important sources of political support during the election campaign. The fronts had selected several ministers. Damares Alves, the minister for women and human rights, had worked closely with the evangelicals, and Tereza Cristina, the agriculture minister, with the *bancada de boi* or *ruralistas*, for example.

As an aside, the set-up of Brazil's Congress made it impossible to govern through the *bancadas*. Congressional rules meant that the parties – however loose and fragmented – were the bodies that organised votes. "If you want to win votes in Congress you have to do it through the parties, not through the parliamentary fronts", Beatriz Rey, a political scientist and researcher at the American University in Washington DC, told me. Rey, who is writing her PhD on how the *bancadas* operate in Congress, pointed to the importance of the congressional rule book (the *Regimento Interno da Câmara dos Deputados*) "that tells you exactly how the chamber operates and who can do what. If you want to be effective you have to master it."[11] The evidence suggested that Bolsonaro – in his twenty-eight years in Congress – had never done that.

Not surprisingly, during his first eighteen months in office Bolsonaro had made little progress in winning approval for new legislation. His one big achievement was the approval in 2019 of an extensive reform of pensions that had been piloted through Congress by Maia, in spite of the president's lack of interest and the open opposition of many of his hardline supporters. Other economic promises were unfulfilled, however. No progress was made on tax reform or privatisation. A proposal to simplify income tax for low-income groups never got off the drawing board.[12]

Very little of the president's social agenda had been implemented either. Congress and the Supreme Court had blocked attempts to roll back liberal social legislation. For example, in spite of opposition from socially conservative legislators, the Supreme Court made homophobia a criminal offence. Congress threw out efforts to give police officers greater leeway to use their weapons and refused to back efforts to reduce the age of criminal responsibility to 16, a measure that would have allowed courts to jail young gang members and other offenders.[13]

For a president who in mid-year had seemed dangerously isolated, the deal with the *Centrão* made sense. At a stroke Bolsonaro won the backing in Congress of between 170 and 220 of the 513 deputies of the lower house, a fairly solid core of support that could block any impeachment move by congressmen, and potentially, in alliance with other right-wing parties, provide him with a congressional majority. In return for their backing, the government immediately agreed to give the *Centrão* control over three public institutions (resources destined for education, drought prevention and urban transport) that were responsible for spending more than R$70bn or about 2 per cent of the federal budget.[14]

Subsequently, when Bolsonaro opted to reform his communications strategy, a former deputy from the Social Democrat Party, Fábio Faria, took over as head of a recreated communications ministry. Faria was the son-in-law of Silvio Santos, a media tycoon who owns Sistema Brasileira de Televisão, one of Brazil's largest terrestrial television operations, and seemed to be well placed to help improve the president's relations with the mainstream media.

In November municipal elections provided evidence that their new alliance was working well for the *Centrão* parties. Even though several candidates favoured by Bolsonaro – including Celso Russomanno in São Paulo and Marcelo Crivella in Rio de Janeiro – did badly, the *Centrão* parties won large numbers of cities. Lira's Progressive Party won 167 new mayoralties, increasing the number of cities under its control to 680. Kassab's Social

Democrat Party won control of 100 additional cities to control 649. The Republicanos won 100 cities, taking its total to 207. The Liberals won 42 new cities to reach a total of 345. Add to that list cities won by Jefferson's PTB, the Social Christian Party, Solidaridade, Avante and the Patriota Party, and the *Centrão* parties now controlled about 2,400 of the country's 5,568 municipal administrations. By contrast, the result was a disaster for the PT. The party that had won 630 mayors in 2012 and even after Rousseff's impeachment still won 257 in 2016, found itself controlling fewer than 200 cities.

Early in 2021 the relationship between the *Centrão* and the government was strengthened further when Bolsonaro backed the bloc's candidates for the presidencies of both houses of Congress. In the run-up to these internal elections the government released more than R$3bn for lawmakers to spend on public works in their districts. Government opponents claimed that effectively the executive was buying the votes of congressmen.[15] When the election took place, Arthur Lira of the Progressive Party and Rodrigo Pacheco of the Democrats won handsomely: 302 deputies from eleven parties voted for Lira, 57 of the 81 senators voted for Pacheco. All this suggested that the president's relations with Congress would be a lot smoother than they had been in the previous two years.

New vulnerabilities

But Latin American politics can often be volatile, and – as this book went to press in late March 2021 – Bolsonaro looked a lot more vulnerable. In a sense a substantial part of the president's difficulties stemmed from the impact of the pandemic on the economy. Ultimately Bolsonaro's efforts to insulate business from the health crisis had not worked. The escalation of the crisis – as we will see – started to weigh heavily on the confidence of business and consumers. Foreign investors were nervous. During 2020 the real had been one of the weakest currencies in the world, and in the first few months of 2021 it continued to weaken, contributing into an uptick in prices. Politics too became more complicated, with Bolsonaro's popularity dipping steadily in the first three months of 2021, and the outlook for the 2022 election – and the president's possible re-election – was complicated by two legal judgments that potentially cleared the way for Lula da Silva to enter the race.

One of the fundamental underlying problems was that Brazil's public finances were weak. The scale of emergency grant payments in 2020 had left the administration with a gigantic fiscal hole, increasing the size of the nominal deficit from 5.8 per cent of GDP at the end of 2019 to 13.7 per cent by the end of 2020. The decision to renew the grant in March 2021 – albeit on a lesser scale and for only four months – suggested that the gap between revenue and spending was likely to remain wide. Debt had risen from 74 per cent of GDP to 89 per cent of output.[16] By November 2020 the government was having to pay more to borrow, or borrow for shorter periods of time. When Bolsonaro took office, only 16 per cent of its debt had fallen due within a year; by the end of 2020 the amount had risen to 28 per cent.[17]

Economists had warned for some time that if the government planned to keep spending on emergency aid at the rate that it was doing, it would need to save by cutting spending elsewhere, by increasing the efficiency of the public administration, raising funds from new taxes or selling off state companies. This would be a complicated operation for any government, but Bolsonaro had shown that he was at best unenthusiastic about leading such ambitious restructuring. The pension reform of 2019 had been achieved in spite of his evident lack of interest.

Bolsonaro's new congressional alliance – nailed down with the election as congressional president of Lira on 1 February 2021 – did not augur well for the prospects of such reform. Past experience had shown the *Centrão* parties to be much more interested in pushing spending projects that could boost their re-election chances. As

José Roberto Mendonça de Barros, an economist who had served in the administration of Fernando Henrique Cardoso, put it. "The *Centrão* parties have an insatiable appetite for spending. The fiscal crisis is easy to describe but in current conditions it is not feasible to manage it. It is mission impossible."[18] Early in January 2021 Bolsonaro seemed to rule out the possibility of doing anything at all about these fiscal difficulties. Quizzed by a follower as to why he couldn't follow through on promises made during his campaign, Bolsonaro replied, "Brazil is bankrupt chief, I can't do anything."[19]

The economy posed some other challenges too. True, Brazil's economy has been hit less badly than those of its Latin American neighbours, but unemployment still rose sharply during 2020, reaching 14.6 per cent in the third quarter of the year, its highest level since the current measurement began in 2012. The closure in January 2021 by Ford of three car plants highlighted the problem. It was a huge blow in its own right, costing 5,000 direct jobs and thousands of others in businesses that supplied components. Three months previously Ford, which had operated in Brazil for more than a hundred years, had closed one plant in São Bernardo do Campo, the industrial suburb where Lula had won his reputation as a trade unionist. The car industry had benefited from billions of dollars in federal subsidies, as well as enjoying other benefits. But in an industry under global pressure as a result of the shift towards electric cars, Ford was particularly hampered in Brazil by the burdens of high costs and inadequate infrastructure. Another company, Mercedes Benz, had closed a plant in December.[20] Ford's decision also reflected a broader crisis in the industrial sector, with an average of seventeen factories closing each day since 2015.[21] A poll by *Valor Econômico* at the beginning of January suggested that popular concerns about jobs were growing. More than half of those interviewed thought that the economic crisis or unemployment were their biggest problems.[22]

One of the factors that had augured well for Brazil's economy at the beginning of 2021 was the sharp rise in commodity prices in the second half of 2020. This had been fuelled largely by China's relatively rapid recovery from the pandemic, with the economy of Brazil's biggest trading partner growing in the fourth quarter of 2020. Between March 2020 and February 2021 the price of soya, iron ore and oil – Brazil's three largest exports by value – had risen by 59, 83.7 and 78.8 per cent respectively.[23] But just as its trade prospects looked brighter, Bolsonaro's idiosyncratic foreign policy cast a long shadow. Bombastic rhetoric equally critical of the liberal international consensus and the emerging power of China had been a feature of Brazilian foreign policy in his first two years in office, but the approach damaged relations with all four of Brazil's biggest markets: China, Argentina, Europe and – following the defeat of Donald Trump in the November 2020 presidential election – the United States.

The president had bet heavily on his relationship with Trump, calling the US president his "idol".[24] While much of the world recoiled from Trump's refusal to accept his electoral defeat to Joe Biden, Bolsonaro and his supporters supported their US ally's claims that a fraud had been committed. By the time Bolsonaro recognised President Biden's win on 15 December, the only other significant holdout was the North Korean president Kim Jong-un. Eduardo Bolsonaro even briefly changed his profile picture to that of the former US president.[25] The alignment invited confrontation with the new administration. During the US campaign Biden and his team had made it clear that they were concerned about the pace of deforestation in the Amazon, and the new president's nominations suggested – in the words of São Paulo-based international relations professor Oliver Stuenkel – that the "environment would be a pillar of his mandate". Biden's interior secretary Deb Haaland was one of the fiercest critics of Bolsonaro's environmental policy, for example.[26]

The spectre of boycotts by consumers and investors had already been raised during the previous couple of years and had put at risk approval of the trade accord between the Mercosul countries and the European Union. "A majority of global companies are positioning to buy fewer products that are not clearly certified as coming from good environmental practices. This is a real threat", said Mendonça de Barros.[27] As an official at the agriculture ministry told *Valor Econômico*, even companies from China were beginning to insist on environmental sustainability as a condition for their imports, investments and commercial agreements. Late in 2020 Cofco, a Chinese trading company, demanded that suppliers of soya should be able to show that their product comes from sustainable sources by 2023.[28]

More broadly, repeated attacks by Bolsonaristas such as Ernesto Araújo and Eduardo Bolsonaro had damaged relations with China. Brazil was also badly isolated in Europe. "Outside the nationalists of Hungary, Slovenia and Poland there is not one European leader who would receive an official visit from Bolsonaro", wrote Stuenkel.[29] And by the end of January it was becoming clear that Bolsonaro's approach to the coronavirus pandemic was also increasing the risk of Brazil's international isolation.

Miracle cures and conspiracy theories

Brazil was perhaps worse hit by the second wave of the COVID-19 pandemic than any other country, and criticism of Bolsonaro's denialism increased. The average number of active daily cases in the country rose by 17 per cent in the first two months of 2021, but by 45.5 per cent in the first three-and-a-half weeks of March. Over January and February, deaths from the disease averaged more than 1,000 per day, and they climbed to more than 2,000 per day in March. Overall fatalities, which topped 300,000 on 24 March, were comfortably the second highest in the world behind the United States. Brazil had still been hit proportionately less than 20 other mainly European countries. Brazil's death rate amounted to 1,438 per million compared to 1,856 in the UK, and the United States, France, Italy and Mexico were all worse affected, but by the end of March the fatalities were rising at such a rate that Brazil was climbing this macabre league table. In particular this was because in 2021 Brazil was hit by the more contagious P.1 variant of the disease that had originated in the Amazon city of Manaus.[30] This rise in cases brought into even sharper focus the wisdom of the strategy pursued by Bolsonaro and his health minister Eduardo Pazuello, which – as we have seen – was originally based on opposition to quarantines, and on the use of so-called early treatment medicines (*tratamento precoce*), such as chloroquine. The escalation of the epidemic also exposed planning failures. Manaus was again at the centre of the story. Back in 2020 the city had seized international attention when the authorities were forced to prepare mass graves. In January 2021 more than fifty COVID-19 patients suffocated in Manaus because there was insufficient oxygen to feed their ventilators.

A cocktail of early treatment medicines including ivermectin, a treatment for stomach parasites, and azithromycin, an antibiotic, as well as hydroxychloroquine had been at the core of Bolsonaro's strategy. These drugs had not entirely come out of the blue. Chloroquine is an anti-malaria drug that first appeared in the 1930s, and hydroxychloroquine – its less toxic cousin – was developed about a decade later as a treatment for diseases such as rheumatoid arthritis. Both drugs are also anti-inflammatories, and in the early days of the pandemic doctors thought they might help victims of COVID-19, which, like some other strains of influenza, sometimes triggers a fierce over-reaction by the body's immune system.[31] Subsequently, international trials failed to confirm any benefits and pointed to dangerous side effects including heart rhythm problems and even loss of vision. Regulators in the US – where Trump was also a big fan of the drug – authorised its use in March 2020, only to revoke the permission in June "following further examination of preliminary data".[32]

Bolsonaro, however, pressed ahead regardless of the scientific evidence, determined to avoid the lockdowns that he believed would damage the economy and living standards. Bolsonaro became so convinced that he ordered Brazilian laboratories to ramp up domestic production. Luiz Henrique Mandetta, who was sacked as health minister for refusing to endorse such medicines, outlined the extent of Bolsonaro's denialism. When officials told him about side effects or their doubts about how effective the drug was, "Bolsonaro didn't want to know. He just wanted to hear that chloroquine was the salvation", Mandetta wrote. "There were always cases of chloroquine on the desk but he never had masks or alcoholic gel."[33]

A local trial of chloroquine held in the city of Manaus had been disastrous: eleven of eighty-one COVID patients being treated with different doses of chloroquine and azithromycin died within a fortnight, and the trial was quickly suspended by Brazil's medical regulators. Bolsonaristas reacted by simply attacking the messenger. Marcus Lacerda, the doctor who had organised the trial, was targeted on social media. Eduardo Bolsonaro tweeted that the study had been designed to disqualify chloroquine and accused the researchers of being left-wing partisans. On his Facebook account Lacerda was labelled an "assassin", a "monster" and a "pseudo-scientist", and even suffered death threats.[34] "Your time will come", one user warned. Lacerda required armed guards for several weeks. A group of doctors who supported the use of chloroquine also began to politicise the issue and frequently seemed to invoke the kind of conspiracy theory popular among Bolsonaro's grassroots supporters. "Geo-politics lies behind the attack on chloroquine", claimed Nise Yamaguchi, a 61-year-old cancer specialist and one of a number of advocates for the drug backed by the president. "There are a series of factors that lead them to weaken their populations. We need to form a political front in order to democratise the use of chloroquine."[35]

Evangelicals were often enthusiastic supporters of these alternative treatments, and added grist to the mill of intrigue. Magno Malta, an evangelical preacher close to the Bolsonaro family, told the audience of his TV chat show that attempts to suppress chloroquine were being promoted by governments linked to China. "It was all a scheme of trickery. An empire of fear."[36] Brazilian doctors opposed to the use of chloroquine, who generally included specialists in infectious diseases, were "using the issue as a political tool to force Bolsonaro from office".[37] In June 2020 two reporters from the Bloomberg news agency witnessed a group of evangelicals noisily chanting their support for the drug.

> They knelt along city streets, spaced six feet apart, fasting and praying for the virus to go away, and gathered to chant their support of his plan to rely on an anti-malarial drug with unproven results. "Chloroquine! Chloroquine! ... I know you can cure me, in the name of Jesus!" they sang in front of the presidential palace in May.[38]

This kind of thinking also influenced the government's approach to vaccines. For most governments, the rapid development of vaccines was a huge boost, pointing to a route out of the upheaval of the pandemic. Brazil, wrote journalists in *Veja*, was the only country in the world where the arrival of vaccines was a piece of bad news for a president.[39] Bolsonaro seemed set against them. In December 2020 he told an interviewer on TV Band that "I'm not going to take the vaccine and that is all there is to it. My life is at risk? That is my problem." When it became clear that the vaccine jointly developed by China's CoronaVac and Brazil's Instituto Butantan could be successfully deployed, Bolsonaro refused to sanction its purchase. "The Brazilian people won't be anyone's guinea pigs", he announced. "It's impossible to justify a billion-dollar support that hasn't even passed its testing stage. My decision is not to buy the vaccine." Suspicion of China – whose role in the pandemic was a favourite topic for Bolsonarista conspiracy theorists – was one of the reasons. "There is a lot of disbelief because many people say that is where the virus started", the president told a radio interviewer. The fact that João Doria, the governor of São Paulo state, who had supported Bolsonaro in 2018 but had become a fierce opponent of the president and a potential electoral rival for 2022, had championed the medicine was another factor. "Dear governor of São Paulo, nobody is going to take your vaccine by force. The people aren't going to buy your vaccine", Bolsonaro told the audience for his weekly live broadcast at the end of October.[40]

But Bolsonaro's scepticism seemed to run even deeper. Pfizer, the US pharmaceutical company, had developed a vaccine with an extremely high efficacy and had had few problems rolling it out worldwide. By the end of December the UK, the European Union, Canada and the United States, and notably Israel, were all immunising large numbers of people with the Pfizer vaccine. Brazil was an exception though. Bolsonaro told an audience in Bahia in mid-December that the contract with the company took no responsibility for any side effects, claiming – bizarrely – "if you become an alligator it's your problem. If you become a superman, if as a woman it makes you grow a beard or if you are a man it makes you speak in a high voice, it has nothing to do with them."[41] Although Brazil had agreed to buy 70 million doses of the vaccine, the contract had by 21 January still not been signed, at best delaying the health authority's ability to protect the population.

Predictably, Bolsonaro's sons shared their father's cynicism. On 19 December, on a day when 49,243 new cases and 669 deaths were announced, Eduardo Bolsonaro said the "rush to develop a vaccine was not justified, because the disease was coming to its end". Anyway, he added, "when you vaccinate someone you mess with their lives. An inoculation could provoke an unexpected reaction by the immune system."

Bolsonaro's headstrong approach to the disease left him isolated internationally. Research published in 2021 by an Australian think tank evaluated the success of 98 countries in managing the pandemic, and ranked Brazil as by far the least effective. The researchers at the Lowy Institute awarded scores for the performance of each country in the 36 weeks following the confirmation of their first 100 cases. New Zealand was rated most effective with 94.4 points. Brazil scored only 4.3 points and was in last place. The survey covered data available on 9 January 2021, since when the death toll from the second wave of the disease in Brazil has risen sharply.[42]

The future of Bolsonarismo

By the end of March 2021 there were signs that the combination of economic issues and the fear and uncertainty stemming from the pandemic were influencing political calculations and potentially bringing Brazil to the edge of a new crisis. Opinion polls reflected this. Even in December 2020 Bolsonaro's presidency was still relatively well regarded, especially – as we have seen – by poorer voters who were benefiting from the emergency grant. Although an average of 35.5 per cent of those interviewed in four separate polls regarded the government as bad or terrible, slightly more – 37.25 per cent – thought the administration was good or excellent. In the first three months of 2021 this picture changed. Evidence from 14 polls showed Bolsonaro's positive ratings falling in March – the worst month for coronavirus cases since the pandemic began – to an average of 28.4 per cent. By contrast, in the same month 46 per cent took a negative view of him.

As death rates continued to increase, Bolsonaro came under increasing political pressure to change the course of his health policy. The government's mismanagement of the pandemic was leading to growing opposition from the private sector. Back in 2018 the private sector had supported Bolsonaro as the best way to defeat the PT. On 16 March 2021 Bolsonaro removed the ineffective Pazuello. Five days later an open letter signed by more than 1,500 bankers, business leaders and top economists condemned the government's record on the pandemic and pressed for more radical measures. "Brazil is the world epicentre of COVID-19", it read. "The economic and social situation is bleak ... We are on the threshold of an explosive phase in the pandemic and it is fundamental that public policies are based on data, reliable information and scientific evidence."[43] Among the signatories were heavyweight bankers and businessmen that any Brazilian president would struggle to ignore. The letter demanded that the administration provide more and better-quality masks, back quarantines and accelerate its rollout of vaccines. "We have no more time to lose in sterile debates and false news ... The government is using the resources at its disposal badly in part because it ignores or gives little weight to scientific evidence in the action it takes", read the letter.

In a series of high-level meetings and dinners over the next few days this same message was drummed home to government congressional leaders. Healthcare executives complained about the shortages of sedatives and drugs to help patients using ventilators. Bankers were concerned that the pandemic was blocking investments and making it difficult to bring companies to the stock market. Business in general was worried about the way the foreign minister's anti-Chinese message had complicated the task of importing ingredients for vaccines. The environment minister's stance was damaging relations with the US. All this – it seemed – had the potential to feed through to a new political crisis.

For the parties of the *Centrão* there was little to be gained from supporting a government that was increasingly unpopular and regarded as inept by the most powerful and wealthy interests in the country. Two decisions by the Supreme Court in the second half of March had a big impact on the political landscape ahead of the 2022 presidential election. The judgements questioned in a variety of ways the impartiality of Judge Sérgio Moro and effectively quashed the conviction of Lula da Silva, allowing the former labour leader to compete in the election and ensuring that the contest would be more competitive.

Sensitive to the importance of these changes, Arthur Lira and Rodrigo Pacheco, the president of the senate, acted quickly. After their meetings with the private-sector bigwigs, Lira told Congress that it was time for the administration to change course. "I am switching on the amber light", the president of the lower house of Congress told legislators on 24 March. "This is a warning about the basic errors being made by the government. Everything has its limit." The clear message was that if Bolsonaro stuck to his guns he could suffer the same fate as Rousseff in 2016, and another president, Fernando Collor de Mello, who was sacked by Congress in 1992. Lira did not mention the word impeachment, but few who heard his speech doubted that this was what he had in mind. "The remedies are well known and they are all bitter, some are fatal", he said. "Many times they are applied when the situation becomes uncontrollable."[44] One of Lira's congressional colleagues was even more emphatic. "Bolsonaro is walking the razor's edge. If this thing gets out of control because he's doing everything his way and ignoring the science then be in no doubt: we'll bring him down."[45]

Impeachment was by no means inevitable. Bolsonaro continued to enjoy the support of the ideological and socially conservative groups who make up his social base. Thousands of evangelical Christians, rank-and-file military policemen, small farmers and miners all remained loyal to him. Even following the decline in his popularity, nearly three in ten Brazilians thought his government had done a good job. It was by no means clear that the newly empowered Lula da Silva – now free to run in 2022's presidential election – would beat Bolsonaro if the two were to make it through to fight a run-off. In one recent poll, more than half of those questioned still thought that Lula was guilty of corruption, in spite of the court judgements that had gone in his favour. But if Bolsonaro does survive into 2022 and beyond, it will not be as the head of a government championing the kinds of liberal reforms promised during the 2018 campaign. By backing Bolsonaro and the *Centrão*, Brazilians would be opting for a grubbier and more socially conservative version of traditional politics.

The promise of liberal economic reform and more transparent and responsible politics that had featured in the campaign of 2018 had proven to be empty. Pension reform had been achieved despite, not because of, Bolsonaro. Lava Jato and the anti-corruption campaigns that had excited public opinion from the mid-2010s had run their course. At worst Brazil faced prolonged instability, increasing violence and steep economic decline. At best it was back to politics as normal: the same *toma cá, dá lá* that had proved so frustrating and so unsuccessful in the past.

ACKNOWLEDGEMENTS

Thanks to Jonathan de Peyer who heard me speak in a BBC radio interview and spotted the potential for this book; to his successor at Manchester University Press, Tom Dark, who has been an attentive and receptive editor; and to Tom's colleagues, Lucy Burns, David Appleyard and Chris Hart, who have expertly managed the complex process of producing the book and bringing it to market. Thanks also to the copy-editor, Andrew Kirk. In the last few years *Americas Quarterly*, the publication of the New York-based Council of the Americas, has backed several long reporting trips to Latin America: three in particular were especially important and provided material for Chapters 7, 10 and 12.

Several people have read drafts of this book either in its entirety or in part. Thanks to Graham Hillyard, Michael Stott, Fátima Carvalho, Dom Phillips, Helena Vieira, Jonathan Wheatley, Amy Erika Smith, Chris Sabatini, Peter West, Anthony Pereira, Elizabeth Johnson, Cuca Abbott, Richard House, John Rumsey and Andrew Downie. Graham Hillyard's impressively detailed editing work was invaluable.

I've had many helpful conversations but would like to thank (in addition to the readers mentioned above) Paul Freston, Thomas Traumann, David Cleary, Michael Reid, Lucinda Elliott, James Sinclair, Tony Danby, Elizabeth Johnson, Alberto Almeida, Oliver Balch, Wilber Colmerauer, Timothy Power, Robert

Muggah, Cláudia Rodrigues, Eveline dos Santos, Beatriz Rey, Daniel Cerqueira, Vinicius de Carvalho, Jon Lee Anderson, Sarah Maslin, Glenn Shepard and above all Brian Winter, my editor at *Americas Quarterly*. Brian has written extensively on Brazil and the book has benefited enormously from his expertise and insights.

The COVID-19 pandemic meant that I spent less time in Brazil than I had planned, but friends and family were incredibly kind when I was able to visit. Andrés Schipani and Alejandra Mejia, Elizabeth Johnson and Reese Ewing, Jesse Alves, and Miriam Hammerat were generous hosts in São Paulo. My sister-in-law Nubia Carvalho, her husband Rogério and their son Henrique looked after me during two stays in Uberlândia. Rogério also arranged a number of interviews in the city. Ray Colitt and Yana Marull provided accommodation in Brasília. My wife's family and in particular my mother-in-law Lia Carvalho have always provided a classically friendly Bahian welcome in Salvador. Jay and Kirsten Edwards and Gustavo Vieira helped me navigate my way around Roraima. Renato Roseno and his colleagues at Ceará's Committee for the Prevention of Adolescent Homicides guided me through deprived areas in Fortaleza. In Roraima João Paulo Pires was a superb fixer and helped organise a number of key interviews. Elizabeth Zechmeister and her colleagues at the LAPOP Lab at Vanderbilt University did some great research for me. Last but not least, Brenda Zach was a tireless and immensely efficient transcriber of my recorded interviews.

I've made use of a number of excellent recent books in Portuguese. I've tried to give proper recognition to each in the notes, but it's perhaps worth emphasising the importance of work by Luiz Maklouf Carvalho, André Singer, Claudia Safatle, João Borges and Ribamar Oliveira at *Valor Econômico*, Mauricio Moura and Juliano Corbellini, Thaís Oyama, Bruno Paes Manso and Camila Nunes Dias. In English Michael Reid's *Brazil: The Troubled Rise of a Global Power* remains in my view the best introduction to Brazil. I've made extensive use of both Brazilian and

English-language newspapers and magazines, but perhaps especially *Americas Quarterly* and *Revista Piauí*, the excellent São Paulo-based monthly magazine. In addition, tramping through East London and the valleys of north-west Sheffield on lockdown walks, I have listened to innumerable episodes of Brazilian podcasts, including *Estado de São Paulo*'s daily, the weekly broadcast by the English-language *Brazil Reports*, the *Americas Quarterly* podcast and in particular the weekly *Piauí* podcast *Foro de Teresina*.

Finally, I owe a huge debt of gratitude to my former employers at the *Financial Times*. In 2002 my editors agreed to let me relocate my London-based job as Latin America Editor to São Paulo and I spent six years living in Brazil. Subsequently – in the run-up to my retirement in 2015 – they allowed me to develop my interest in Brazil and Latin America by supporting the Brazil Confidential and Latam Confidential projects. To all the people who I have worked with at the paper, many thanks.

ABBREVIATIONS

MDB   Brazilian Democratic Movement (Movimento Democrático Brasileiro)

PCC   First Command of the Capital (Primeiro Comando do Capital)

PSDB   Brazilian Social Democratic Party (Partido da Social Democracia Brasileira)

PSL   Social Liberal Party (Partido Social Liberal)

PSOL   Socialism and Liberty Party (Partido Socialismo e Liberdade)

PT   Workers' Party (Partido dos Trabalhadores)

VPR   Popular Revolutionary Vanguard (Vanguarda Armada Revolucionária Palmares)

NOTES

Notes to Introduction

1 Maurício Moura and Juliano Corbellini, *A eleição disruptiva: por que Bolsonaro venceu* (Editora Record, 2019), 15.
2 Cas Mudde and Cristóbal Rovira Kaltwasser, *Populism: A Very Short Introduction* (Oxford University Press, 2017), 5.
3 Ibid., 21.
4 Néstor Kirchner (2003–07) and his wife Cristina Fernández de Kirchner (2007–15) led left-wing Peronist administrations in Argentina. Since 2019 Cristina Fernández has served as deputy president in another left-wing government led by former minister Alberto Fernández (2003–08). The current president shares the same name as his deputy, but the two are not related. Bolivia's Evo Morales held office between 2005 and 2019. In Ecuador, Rafael Correa and his left-wing PAISA party held office between 2006 and 2017. His former deputy, Lenin Moreno, won elections in 2017 but has followed a more moderate political course and has pursued a number of his former colleagues for corruption. Finally, Daniel Ortega, the former Sandinista guerrilla leader, has been president of Nicaragua since 2007. He was previously Nicaragua's president from 1979 until 1990. During this century more moderate left-wing governments have also held office in Chile, Uruguay, Peru, and briefly in Paraguay.
5 Roger Eatwell and Matthew Goodwin, *National Populism: The Revolt Against Liberal Democracy* (Pelican, 2018), 55.
6 See Francis Fukuyama, *Identity: Contemporary Identity Politics and the Struggle for Recognition* (Profile Books, 2018), Kindle edition, loc. 1641.
7 See David Runciman, *How Democracy Ends* (Profile Books, 2018), Kindle edition, loc. 834.
8 Sheila S. Coronel, "The vigilante president: how Duterte's brutal populism conquered the Philippines", *Foreign Affairs*, September–October

2018, https://www.foreignaffairs.com/articles/philippines/2019-08-12/ vigilante-president (accessed 7 December 2020).

9 See Marc Plattner, "Illiberal democracy and the struggle on the right", *Journal of Democracy* 30, no. 1 (2019): 5–19; Cas Mudde, "The 2019 elections: moving the center", *Journal of Democracy* 30, no. 4 (2019): 20–34.

10 See "Third of Brexit voters believe Muslim immigration is part of a secret plot to Islamicise Britain, study suggests", *The Independent*, 23 November 2018, https://www.independent.co.uk/news/uk/home-news/brexit-vot ers-immigration-muslims-islam-leave-remain-yougov-survey-trump-a864 8586.html (accessed 6 January 2021).

11 See Fiona Macaulay, "Bancada da bala: the growing influence of the security sector in Brazilian politics", in Conor Foley (ed.), *In Spite of You: Bolsonaro and the New Brazilian Resistance* (OR Books, 2019), Kindle edition, loc. 983.

12 Renato Sérgio de Lima and Samira Bueno, "A tropa de choque de Bolsonaro", *Piauí*, 8 August 2020, https://piaui.folha.uol.com.br/tropa-de-choque-de-bolsonaro/ (accessed 15 February 2021).

Notes to Chapter 1

1 As reported to Ingrid Fagundez, "Bolsonaro: a infância do presidente entre quilombolas, guerrilheiros e a rica família de Rubens Paiva", BBC News, 16 January 2019, https://www.bbc.com/portuguese/brasil-46845753 (accessed 7 December 2020).

2 Ibid.

3 "The life and rise and Captain Bolsonaro", *El País*, 1 January 2019, https:// brasil.elpais.com/brasil/2018/10/19/politica/1539969259_171085.html (accessed 7 December 2020).

4 Fagundez, "Bolsonaro: a infância do presidente".

5 Luiz Maklouf Carvalho, *O cadete e o capitão: a vida de Jair Bolsonaro no quartel* (Todavia, 2019), 22.

6 Ibid., 36.

7 Ibid., 43.

8 Thaís Oyama, *Tormenta: o governo Bolsonaro: crises, intrigas e segredos* (Companhia das Letras, 2020), 36.

9 Ibid., 37.

10 Timothy J. Power, "The Brazilian military regime of 1964–1985: legacies for contemporary democracy", *Iberoamericana* 16, no. 2 (2016): 13–26 (20), doi: 10.18441/ibam.

11 See Jairo Nicolau, "The open list electoral system in Brazil", trans. Plínio Dentzien, *Dados – Revista de Ciências Sociais* 49, no. 4 (2006): 689–720.

12 Power, "The Brazilian military regime of 1964–1985", 17.

13 See Scott Mainwaring, *Rethinking Party Systems in the Case of Brazil* (Stanford University Press, 1999), quoted in Power, "The Brazilian military regime of 1964–1985", 20.

14 Oyama, *Tormenta*, 11.

15 Glenn Greenwald and Andrew Fishman, "The most misogynistic, hateful elected official in the democratic world: Brazil's Jair Bolsonaro", *The Intercept*, 11 December 2014, https://theintercept.com/2014/12/11/mis ogynistic-hateful-elected-official-democacratic-world-brazils-jair-bolson aro/ (accessed 8 December 2020).

16 See "Who is Jair Bolsonaro? Brazil's far-right president in his own words", *The Guardian*, 29 October 2018, https://www.theguardian.com/world/2018/sep/06/jair-bolsonaro-brazil-tropical-trump-who-hankers-for-days-of-dictatorship (accessed 8 December 2020).

17 Ibid.

18 Jenny Gonzales, "Amazon threatened by presidential election. Brazil might follow Trump out of Paris Agreement", 21 September 2018, https://www.brazzil.com/amazon-threatened-by-presidential-election-brazil-mi ght-follow-trump-out-of-paris-agreement/ (accessed 15 February 2021); Mariana Simões, "Brazil's polarizing new president, Jair Bolsonaro, in his own words", *New York Times*, 28 October 2018, https://www.nytimes.com/2018/10/28/world/americas/brazil-president-jair-bolsonaro-quot es.html (accessed 15 February 2021).

19 See Brian Winter, "Messiah complex: how Brazil made Bolsonaro", *Foreign Affairs*, September/October 2020, https://www.foreignaffairs.com/articles/brazil/2020-08-11/jair-bolsonaro-messiah-complex (accessed 6 January 2021).

20 See Alberto Carlos Almedia, *A cabeça do Brasileiro* (Editora Record, 2007).

21 See "Latinobarómetro: Opinión Pública Latinoamericana", https://www.latinobarometro.org/lat.jsp (accessed 5 January 2021).

22 See the National Truth Commission, National Archives, Ministry of Justice and Public Security, http://www.memoriasreveladas.gov.br/ (accessed 8 December 2020).

23 Power, "The Brazilian military regime of 1964–1985", 16.

24 Ibid., 15.

25 Ibid., 16.

Notes to Chapter 2

1 Moura and Corbellini, *A eleição disruptiva*, 145–6.

2 Jairo Nicolau, "O triunfo do Bolsonarismo", *Piauí*, November 2018, https://piaui.folha.uol.com.br/materia/o-triunfo-do-bolsonarismo/ (accessed 8 December 2020).

3 Ibid. Marine Le Pen lost by 66.1 per cent to 33.9 per cent to Emanuel Macron in the second round of France's 2017 presidential election.

4 Wendy Hunter and Timothy Power, "Bolsonaro and Brazil's illiberal backlash", *Journal of Democracy* 30, no. 1 (2019): 68–82 (69), doi: 10.1353/jod.2019.0005.

5 Moura and Corbellini, *A eleição disruptiva*, 71.

6 Ibid., 74.

7 Pedro Henrique Alves, "Uma análise factual sobre Jair Bolsonaro", *Instituto Liberal*, 30 August 2018, https://www.institutoliberal.org.br/blog/politica/uma-analise-factual-sobre-jair-bolsonaro/ (accessed 9 December 2020).

8 See Chris Tenove and Grace Chiang, "The meme-ification of politics: politicians & their 'lit' memes", *The Conversation*, 4 February 2019, https://theconversation.com/the-meme-ification-of-politics-politicians-and-their-lit-memes-110017 (accessed 9 December 2020).

9 See Valdecir Becker, Daniel Gambaro and Guida Lemos Souza Filho, "The impact of digital media on Brazilian TV: ratings drop and higher turnover", *Palgrave Clave* 18, no. 2 (2015): 341–73, doi: 10.5294/pacla.2015.18.2.3.

10 Moura and Corbellini, *A eleição disruptiva*, 115.

11 Ibid., 110–66.

12 See annual surveys of Latin Barometer, https://www.latinobarometro.org/lat.jsp (accessed 6 January 2021).

13 Moura and Corbellini, *A eleição disruptiva*, 121.

14 Terrence McCoy, "He's the Rush Limbaugh of Brazil. He has Bolsonaro's ear. And he lives in rural Virginia", *The Washington Post*, 14 July 2019, https://www.washingtonpost.com/world/the_americas/hes-the-rush-limbaugh-of-brazil-he-has-bolsonaros-ear-and-he-lives-in-rural-virginia/2019/07/14/4f73dee2-8ac4-11e9-8f69-a2795fca3343_story.html (accessed 9 December 2020).

15 Letícia Duarte, "Meet the intellectual founder of Brazil's far right", *The Atlantic*, 28 September 2019, https://www.theatlantic.com/international/archive/2019/12/brazil-olavo-de-carvalho-jair-bolsonaro/604117/ (accessed 9 December 2020).

16 Moura and Corbellini, *A eleição disruptiva*, 122.

17 Brian Winter, "Jair Bolsonaro's guru", *Americas Quarterly*, 17 December 2018, https://www.americasquarterly.org/article/jair-bolsonaros-guru/ (accessed 9 December 2020).

18 As reported in McCoy, "He's the Rush Limbaugh of Brazil".

19 As reported in Duarte, "Meet the intellectual founder of Brazil's far right". Video available at https://www.facebook.com/jairmessias.bolsonaro/videos/945681038957259/ (accessed 6 January 2020).

20 Consuelo Dieguez, "Right flank, march", *Piauí*, September 2016, https://piaui.folha.uol.com.br/materia/right-flank-march/ (accessed 9 December 2020).

21 Aryovaldo de Castro Azevedo Junior and Eriza Cristina Verderio Biano, "O processo de mitificação de Bolsonaro: Messias, presidente do Brasil", *Revista Pos Eco* 22, no. 2 (2019): 88–111, doi: 10.29146/eco-pos.v22i2.26253.

22 Moura and Corbellini, *A eleição disruptiva*, 126.

23 Josette Goulart and Marcella Ramos, "Bolsonaro transfere seu sucesso na internet para a TV", *Piauí*, 31 July 2018, https://piaui.folha.uol.com.br/bolsonaro-transfere-seu-sucesso-na-internet-para-a-tv/ (accessed 9 December 2020).

24 Miguel Lago, "Bolsonaro fala outra língua", *Piauí*, 13 August 2018, https://piaui.folha.uol.com.br/bolsonaro-fala-outra-lingua/ (accessed 9 December 2020).

25 Moura and Corbellini, *A eleição disruptiva*, 126.

26 Ibid., 127.

Notes to Chapter 3

1 Jonathan Wheatley, "A bright new future is just out of reach", *Financial Times*, 6 May 2010, https://www.ft.com/content/ade07aca-571c-11df-aaff-00144feab49a (accessed 9 December 2020).

2 Rating agencies – privately owned companies mostly based in the US, although the dominant two, Moody's and Standard & Poor's, have faced competition from Europe and elsewhere in recent years – charge borrowers or bond issuers to rate their creditworthiness. Some of the biggest players on world capital markets, such as large pension funds or large life insurance companies, are restricted from buying riskier debt (classified as speculative grade or junk in the industry), so Brazil's promotion – and its subsequent relegation back to junk less than a decade later – were important steps.

3 "Acima das expectativas, Lula encerra mandato com melhor avaliação da história", *Datafolha Instituto de Pesquisas*, 20 December 2010, http://datafolha.folha.uol.com.br/opiniaopublica/2010/12/1211078-acima-das-expectativas-lula-encerra-mandato-com-melhor-avaliacao-da-historia.shtml (accessed 26 December 2020.

4 See "Brazil takes off", *The Economist*, 12 November 2009, https://www.economist.com/leaders/2009/11/12/brazil-takes-off (accessed 9 December 2020).

5 Claudia Safatle, João Borges and Ribamar Oliveira, *Anatomia de um desastre: os bastidores da crisis econômica que mergulhou o país na pior recessão de sua historia* (Portfolio Penguin, 2016), 165.

6 Most of his investment schemes proved to have been badly planned. In 2018 Batista was found guilty on corruption charges and jailed for thirty years.

7 Safatle, Borges and Oliveira, *Anatomia de um desastre*, 220.

8 See João Ayres, Marcio Garcia, Diogo Guillen and Patrick Kehoe, *The Monetary and Fiscal History of Brazil, 1960–2016* (University College London/Federal Reserve Bank of Minneapolis, December 2018). "One of the most striking features of Brazilian monetary and fiscal history is its long period of high inflation pre-1994 … Inflation rates were closely related to the growth rates of the monetary base and to seigniorage revenues."

9 The cruzeiro was replaced as Brazil's currency by the cruzado in February 1986 and the cruzado by the cruzado novo in January 1989. After my wife left Brazil, the cruzado novo was replaced by another version of the cruzeiro, and finally in 1994, the cruzeiro was replaced by the real.

10 See Michael Reid, *Brazil: The Troubled Rise of a Global Power* (Yale University Press, 2014), 142.

11 Ibid., 142.

12 Ibid., 40–147.

13 Jorge Blázquez-Lidoy, Javier Rodríguez and Javier Santiso, "Angel or Devil? Chinese trade impact on emerging markets", *OECD* Working Paper no. 252 (2004), https://www.oecd.org/dev/37054336.pdf (accessed 10 December 2020).

14 See Safatle, Borges and Oliveira, *Anatomia de um desastre*, 222.

15 Reid, *Brazil*, 199–204.

16 Author interview with Vanessa Mara, 2007.

17 See Richard Lapper and Raymond Colitt, "Brazil comes of age on the global stage", *Financial Times*, 14 September 2004, https://www.ft.com/content/689dbdf2-0681-11d9-b95e-00000e2511c8 (accessed 14 December 2020).

18 Cumulatively between 2004 and 2007, the trade surplus amounted to $165 billion.

19 See Richard Lapper and Jonathan Wheatley, "Interview transcript: Luiz Inácio Lula da Silva", *Financial Times*, 11 July 2006, https://www.ft.com/content/6d42ae3a-110b-11db-9a72-0000779e2340 (accessed 6 January 2020).

20 Reid, *Brazil*, 146–7.

21 Author interview with Helenita Santana, September 2006.

22 Back in 2003 I'd interviewed Ivo Pitanguy, a larger-than-life plastic surgeon who compared his role to that of a psychotherapist and was known as 'the Michelangelo of the Scalpel' and the 'Pope of Plastic Surgery'. "Many times when we are operating we are like therapists with a knife in

our hand", he told me. Pitanguy, who was 93 when he died in 2016, was a superstar, best known for his association with people like Jacqueline Onassis and Frank Sinatra, but his prominence as a surgeon reflected a broader Brazilian obsession.

23 See "Classe C impulsionou venda de passagens aéreas entre 2002 e 2012", Instituto Tecnologico de Aeronautica, Nucleo de Economia dos Transportes Aéreo, http://www.ita.br/noticias53 (accessed 14 December 2020).

24 Lula introduced a grant scheme (Prouni) that channelled help to hundreds of thousands of students. Subsequently, in 2010, the government introduced a loan scheme through which it offered to pay further education fees upfront and allow students to repay after they graduated, with the loans carrying negative real interest rates. The Prouni scheme was extended to technical education in 2011.

Notes to Chapter 4

1 For details of Rousseff's experiences in the guerrilla movement and prison, see Luiz Maklouf Carvalho, "As armas e os varões: a educação política e sentimental de Dilma Rousseff", *Piauí*, April 2009, https://piaui.folha.uol.com.br/materia/as-armas-e-os-varoes/ (accessed 14 December 2020).

2 Luiz Maklouf Carvalho, "Mares nunca dantes navegados: a trajetória de Dilma Rousseff da prisão ao poder – e como ela se tornou a candidata do presidente Lula à sua sucessão", *Piauí*, July 2009, https://piaui.folha.uol.com.br/materia/mares-nunca-dantes-navegados/ (accessed 14 December 2020).

3 Ibid.

4 The term was first used in December 2012 by the then secretary of political economy, Márcio Holland, in a ministry publication. Holland said the matrix was characterised by "low interest rates, low financial costs, a more competitive exchange rate and a solid fiscal result". His advisers had been cautious about branding their approach as new because – in the words of one minister – "all [our enemies] need is a label to hit us with". Safatle, Borges and Oliveira, *Anatomia de um desastre*, 93.

5 The Brazilian economy advanced by 2 per cent in 2012 and 3 per cent in 2014.

6 Safatle, Borges, and Oliveira, *Anatomia de um desastre*, 102.

7 See Carvalho, "Mares nunca dantes navegados".

8 Quoted in Safatle, Borges and Oliveira, *Anatomia de um desastre*, 260.

9 Only $0.13 of every $1 of bad debt is recovered in Brazil, compared to a world average of $0.34, according to a World Bank survey. This is

mainly because of complications in the legal system and legal protections afforded to borrowers. Banks include a provision against bad loans in their loans equal to 40 per cent of the spread.

10 In 2016 Brazil spent R$498.5bn on state pensions for 29 million private-sector pensioners (providing an average payout of R$17,080 a year), but R$110bn on just 1 million public-sector pensioners (who received average annual pensions of R$113,060). See Jonathan Wheatley and Andrés Schipani, "'Robin Hood in reverse': the crisis in the Brazilian state", *Financial Times*, 13 September 2018, https://www.ft.com/content/7555d030-9feb-11e8-85da-eeb7a9ce36e4 (accessed 14 December 2020).

11 Ibid.

12 Marcos de Barros Lisboa and Zeina Abdel Latif, *Democracy and Growth in Brazil*, Insper working paper (2013), https://www.insper.edu.br/wp-content/uploads/2013/07/Democracy_and_Growth_in_Brazil.pdf (accessed 14 December 2020).

13 See Fernando Henrique Cardoso and Enzo Faletto, *Dependency and Development in Latin America*, trans. Marjory Mattingly Urquidi (University of California Press, 1979).

14 Cardoso and Faletti wrote about the possibility of what they called "associated dependent development". See Gaylord George Candler, "Cardoso, dependency theory and Brazil", paper presented to the International Studies Association, Midwest, St Louis, 19 October 1996.

15 See Fernando Henrique Cardoso, *O presidente segundo o sociólogo: entrevista FHC with Roberto Pompeu de Toledo* (Companhia das Letras, 1998).

16 Safatle, Borges and Oliveira, *Anatomia de um desastre*, 19–29.

17 Ibid., 257.

18 Ibid., 233.

19 Ibid., 155.

20 Ibid., 229–45. Although junior to Mantega and other ministers, Augustín was nonetheless a powerful figure who enjoyed direct access to the president.

21 Twenty-to-thirty-year airport concessions assumed annual growth rates of 4.5 per cent per year, for example, a rate of expansion that would have made the airport in Brasília one of the biggest in the world.

22 Leandra Peres, "O aviso foi dado: pedaladas faz mal", *Valor Econômico*, 11 December 2015, https://www.bocamaldita.com/o-aviso-foi-dado-peda lar-faz-mal/ (accessed 14 December 2020).

23 Ibid.

24 Safatle, Borges and Oliveira, *Anatomia de um desastre*, 113.

25 Ibid., 126.

26 Ibid., 191–202.

27 Ibid., 142.

28 Ibid., 163–78.

29 Ibid., 170.

Notes to Chapter 5

1 See "Growing number of Brazilians optimistic about the economy, says Datafolha", *Invest in Brazil*, http://investinbrazil.biz/news/growing-number-brazilians-optimistic-about-economy-says-datafolha (accessed 6 January 2021).

2 Brian Winter, "Revisiting Brazil's 2013 protests: what did they really mean?", *Americas Quarterly*, 1 March 2017, https://www.americasquarterly.org/article/revisiting-brazils-2013-protests-what-did-they-really-mean/ (accessed 15 December 2020).

3 André Singer, *O Lulismo em crise: um quebra cabeça do período Dilma, 2011–2016* (Companhia das Letras, 2018), 28.

4 See "Editorial: retomar a Paulista", *Folha de São Paulo*, 13 June 2013, https://www1.folha.uol.com.br/opiniao/2013/06/1294185-editorial-retomar-a-paulista.shtml (accessed 6 January 2021).

5 Ibid.

6 See H.J. "The streets erupt", *The Economist*, 18 June 2013, https://www.economist.com/americas-view/2013/06/18/the-streets-erupt (accessed 15 December 2020).

7 Winter, "Revisiting Brazil's 2013 protests".

8 Ibid.

9 Singer, *O Lulismo em crise*, 125.

10 See Luiz Eduardo Soares, *Rio de Janeiro: Extreme City* (Penguin, 2016), 210.

11 Ibid.

12 See Singer, *O Lulismo em crise*, 110.

13 More than half of the Brazilians interviewed in Latin Barómetro's 2013 survey of political attitudes were using one or other form of social media, with Facebook by far the most popular. The proportion had climbed to nearly three-quarters when the polling agency conducted its 2018 survey.

14 Claudia Miranda Rodrigues, "Narrativas jornalísticas e midiativismo: um estudo de caso sobre as rotinas produtivas do coletivo Mídia Ninja", Masters thesis, the Pontifical Universidade Católica de Rio de Janeiro, 2016.

15 See Soares, *Rio de Janeiro*, 227.

16 Francisco Peregil, "Biggest protests in 20 years sweep across Brazil", *El País*, 18 June 2013, https://english.elpais.com/elpais/2013/06/18/inenglish/1371568124_920323.html (accessed 15 December 2020).

17 Ronald Inglehart and Christian Welzel, *Modernização, mudança cultural e democracia* (Francis, 2009), 130, quoted in Singer, *O Lulismo em crise*, 122.

18 Singer, *O Lulismo em crise*, 122–3.

19 See Soares, *Rio de Janeiro*, 210.

20 Thomas Traumann, "What Brazil's 2013 protests tell us about Chile 2019", *Americas Quarterly*, 27 October 2019, https://www.americasqu arterly.org/article/what-brazils-2013-protests-tell-us-about-chile-2019/ (accessed 15 December 2020).

21 Vladimir Netto, *The Mechanism* (Penguin, 2017), 81.

22 Ibid., 370.

23 Geanluca Lorenzon, "Corruption and the rule of law: how Brazil strength- ened its legal system", *Cato Institute* 827 (20 November 2017), https://www. cato.org/publications/policy-analysis/corruption-rule-law-how-brazil-str engthened-its-legal-system (accessed 15 December 2020).

24 See Netto, *The Mechanism*, 37.

25 See Ernesto Londoño, "Judges bid to clean up Brazil from the bench", *New York Times*, 25 August 2017, https://www.nytimes.com/2017/08/25/ world/americas/judge-sergio-moro-brazil-anti-corruption.html (accessed 15 December 2020).

26 Joe Leahy, "Sérgio Moro: the judge cleaning up Brazil", *Financial Times*, 17 May 2018, https://www.ft.com/video/2834eebb-9ebc-4677-a3be-bc6 3a39f71ce (accessed 6 January 2021).

27 Netto, *The Mechanism*, 81.

28 Ibid., 64.

Notes to Chapter 6

1 *The Trial* was written between 1914 and 1915 and published after Kafka's death in 1924. The scene was brilliantly captured in Petra Costa's 2015 documentary film *The Edge of Democracy*.

2 Singer, *O Lulismo em crise*, 189.

3 Netto, *The Mechanism*, 503.

4 Tancredo died from diverticulitis before taking office. Neves had been elected indirectly by an electoral college.

5 Malu Gaspar, "A morte e a morte de Joaquim Levy", *Piauí*, December 2015, https://piaui.folha.uol.com.br/materia/morte-e-morte-de-joaqu im-levy/ (accessed 15 December 2020).

6 Singer, *O Lulismo em crise*, 197.

7 Ibid., 199.

8 Rodrigo Janot, *Planeta nada menos que tudo: bastidores da operação que colocou o sistema político em xeque* (Planeta, 2019), 127.

9 The investigating judge is theoretically at least independent from the team of prosecutors, although both the structure of the Brazilian system

and the specific relationships between Judge Motro and the prosecution team in Curitíba have been widely questioned by critics.

10 Netto, *The Mechanism*, 266.

11 See ibid., 227–31.

12 Author interview with Brazilian journalist, July 2020.

13 Singer, *O Lulismo em crise*, 242.

14 See Janot, *Planeta nada menos que tudo*, 129.

15 See Fabio de Sá e Silva, "The trial of Luiz Inácio Lula da Silva", in Conor Foley (ed.), *In Spite of You: Bolsonaro and the New Brazilian Resistance* (OR Books, 2019), 32–46.

16 Ibid., 37.

17 See Andrew Fishman, Rafael Moro Martins, Leandro Demori, Alexandre de Danti and Glenn Greenwald, "Breath of ethics: secret Brazil archive", *The Intercept*, 9 June 2019, https://theintercept.com/2019/06/09/bra zil-lula-operation-car-wash-sergio-moro/ (accessed 15 December 2020).

18 Eight years earlier, the MDB had won 12.54 million votes in the legislative election and 24 million votes in the senate race. In the same year – even though it had been comprehensively defeated in the presidential contest – the PSDB attracted 11.48 million votes in the legislative contest and 30.9 million votes in the race for senate seats. In 2018 both parties lost between a half and a third of their voters, with the MDB down to 5.44 million in the house and 12.8 million in the senate, and the PSDB at 5.91 million in the house and 20.3 million in the senate.

19 "The demise of Brazil's great centrist party", *The Economist*, 3 November 2018, https://www.economist.com/the-americas/2018/11/03/the-dem ise-of-brazils-great-centrist-party (accessed 15 December 2020).

20 See Janot, *Planeta nada menos que tudo*, 43.

Notes to Chapter 7

1 Richard Lapper, "Against the tide: why it is so hard to stop the violence in Brazil", *Americas Quarterly*, 18 July 2018, https://www.americasquar terly.org/fulltextarticle/against-the-tide-why-its-so-hard-to-stop-the-vio lence-in-brazil/ (accessed 15 February 2021).

2 https://www.youtube.com/watch?v=JNcVoCyi8bU&t=62s (accessed 15 February 2021).

3 The PT's Camilo Santana was re-elected for a second term as state governor in 2018. Santana has recruited thousands of policemen and prison guards and spent heavily on weaponry and equipment. Since December 2018 the state government has also led a big change in prison policy, forcing prisoners from different gangs to share cells, removing televisions and electrical fittings from cells, and confiscating mobile phones. See Richard

Lapper, "This Brazilian state seems to have turned a corner on violence. But can it last?", *Americas Quarterly*, 6 August, 2019, https://www.ameri casquarterly.org/article/this-brazilian-state-seems-to-have-turned-a-cor ner-on-violence-but-can-it-last/ (accessed 15 February 2021).

4   Author interview with Daniel Cerqueira, 11 July 2019.

5   Brian Winter, "What to expect from Jair Bolsonaro", *Americas Quarterly*, 9 October 2018, https://www.americasquarterly.org/article/what-to-expect-from-jair-bolsonaro/ (accessed 15 December 2020).

6   See "Human Rights Watch World Report 1998", *Human Rights Watch*, 3 December 1997, https://www.hrw.org/news/1997/12/03/human-rights-watch-world-report-1998 (accessed 15 December 2020); Marcelo Rocha and Silva Zorovich, "Beyond overcrowding: the decline of the Brazilian penitentiary system", in Jonathan D. Rosen and Marten W. Brienen (eds), *Prisons in the Americas in the Twenty-First Century: A Human Dumping Ground* (Lexington Books, 2016), 183–94.

7   Drauzio Varella, *Estação Carandiru* (Companhia das Letras, 1999).

8   Bruno Paes Manso and Camila Nunes Dias, *A guerra: a ascensão do PCC e o mundo do crime no Brasil* (Todavia, 2018), Kindle edition, loc. 1148.

9   Quoted in Paes Manso and Dias, *A guerra*, loc. 3315.

10 César Muñoz, "Prison conditions worsen in Brazil", *Human Rights Watch*, 8 December 2017, https://www.hrw.org/news/2017/12/08/prison-con ditions-worsen-brazil (accessed 7 January 2021).

11 According to one estimate, by the end of 2012, 6,400 of the 8,000 mem bers of the PCC in São Paulo – a staggering 80 per cent of the total – were in the prison system. See Paes Manso and Dias, *A guerra*.

12 Ibid., loc. 1177.

13 See ibid.

14 Author interview with Luiz Fabio Silva Paiva, 9 May 2018.

15 Gabriel Feltran, *The Entangled City: Crime as Urban Fabric in São Paulo* (Manchester University Press, 2020), 142.

16 See Stephanie Nolen, "How Brazil's big experiment in policing failed to make Rio safer for the Olympics", *The Globe and Mail*, 2 August 2016, https://www.theglobeandmail.com/news/world/how-brazils-big-polici ng-experiment-failed-to-make-rio-safer-for-theolympics/article31222945/ (accessed 15 December 2020).

17 See Misha Glenny, *Nemesis: One Man and the Battle for Rio* (Bodley Head, 2015).

18 Feltran, *The Entangled City*, 143.

19 See Allan de Abreu, *Cocaína: a rota caipira* (Editora Record, 2017).

20 Beira-Mar was Luiz Fernando da Costa, and his nickname was derived from the Rio favela that he controlled on behalf of the Red Command.

21 See Paes Manso and Dias, *A guerra*.

22 See Gabriel Stargardter, "Brazil's gangs emerge as major cocaine exporters, flooding Europe with white powder", *Reuters*, 12 March 2020, https://uk.reuters.com/article/uk-brazil-violence-cocaine-specialreport-idUKK BN20Z1CU (accessed 7 January 2021).

23 See Fabio Serapião, "Fornecedor de droga da Família do Norte é ligado às Farc, diz MPF", *O Estado de São Paulo*, 4 January 2017, https://brasil. estadao.com.br/noticias/geral,fornecedor-de-droga-da-familia-do-nortee-ligado-as-farc-diz-mpf,10000098157 (accessed 7 January 2021).

24 See Chris Feliciano Arnold, *The Third Bank of the River: Power and Survival in the Twenty-First Century Amazon* (Picador, 2018), 139.

25 Aline Ribeiro, "A íntegra do 'salve' que explica as guerras entre facções", *Época*, 19 October 2016, https://epoca.globo.com/tempo/noticia/2016/10/integra-do-salve-que-explica-guerras-entre-faccoes.html (accessed 15 December 2020).

26 Ibid.

Notes to Chapter 8

1 Allan de Abreu, "A metástase", *Piauí*, March 2019, https://piaui.folha.uol.com.br/materia/a-metastase/ (accessed 6 January 2021).

2 Fernando de Barros e Silva, "Pastores, polícias e milícias", *Piauí*, 29 October 2020, https://piaui.folha.uol.com.br/pastores-policias-e-mili cias/ (accessed 6 January 2021).

3 Author interview with Simone Sibilio, 27 November 2020; "Rio de Janeiro's militias: a parallel power in Bolsonaro's Brazil", *Financial Times*, 25 March 2019, https://www.ft.com/content/bdd61718-4b10-11e9-bbc9 -6917dce3dc62 (accessed 6 January 2021).

4 Anthony Pereira, "Paper cemeteries, informal barriers to Brazilian public security reform", *Revista da Ciência Policial Brasileira* 10, no. 1 (2019): 55–98.

5 Ibid., 60.

6 Mercedes Hinton, *The State on the Streets: Police and Politics in Argentina and Brazil* (Lynne Rienner Publishers, 2006), 101.

7 Clara Velasco, Felipe Grandin, Gabriela Caesar and Thiago Reis, "Nº de pessoas mortas pela polícia cresce no Brasil no 1º semestre em plena pandemia; assassinatos de policiais também sobem", *G1 Monitor da Violência*, 3 September 2020, https://g1.globo.com/monitor-da-violencia/noticia/2020/09/03/no-de-pessoas-mortas-pela-policia-cresce-no-brasilno-1o-semestre-em-plena-pandemia-assassinatos-de-policiais-tambem-so bem.ghtml (accessed 6 January 2021).

8 Dom Philips, "Police in Brazilian city aided revenge killings, report says", *Washington Post*, 7 March 2015, https://www.washingtonpost.com/world/the_americas/after-cop-turned-gangster-is-shot-revenge-killings-rip-bra

zilian-city-apart/2015/03/06/9d6e7a3e-c111-11e4-a188-8e4971d37a8d_s
tory.html (accessed 6 January 2021); Final Report of the Parliamentary
Commission of Inquiry into the operation of extermination groups and
militias in the State of Pará, Legislative Assembly of Pará State (Relatório
Final, Comissão Parlamentar de Inquérito para Apuração da Atuação
de Grupos de Extermínio e Milícias no Estado do Pará, Assembleia
Legislativa do Estado do Pará), 30 January 2015. https://alpara.com.br/
midias/midias/11_relatorio_final_da_comissao_parlamentar_de_inque
rito_para_apuracao_da_atuacao_de_grupos_de_exterminio_e_milicias_
no_estado_do_para-teste-envio.pdf (accessed 7 January 2021).

9   Author interview with Bruno Paes Manso, December 2020.

10   The population of Rio de Janeiro's centre and established suburbs
     declined between 1970 and 1990, but overall – including these newly
     settled areas to the north and west – the population increased from 4.3
     million to 5.8 million.

11   See Bruno Paes Manso, *A república das milícias: dos esquadrões de morte à era do
     Bolsonaro* (Todavia, 2020), Kindle edition, loc. 136.

12   Ibid., loc. 168.

13   Ibid., loc. 249.

14   Dom Philips, "'Lesser evil': how Brazil's militias wield terror to seize
     power from gangs", *The Guardian*, 18 July 2018, https://www.theguardian.
     com/world/2018/jul/12/brazil-militia-paramilitary-wield-terror-seize-po
     wer-from-drug-gangs (accessed 6 January 2021).

15   See Paes Manso, *A república das milícias*, loc. 957.

16   Ibid.

17   Ibid., loc. 312.

18   In Brazil, firemen or *bombeiros militares* constitute a police unit subject to
     the orders of elected state governors.

19   Marcos Sá Corrêa, "Agora é tolerância total: Cesar Maia diz por que
     prefere as milícias aos traficantes", *Piauí*, March 2007, https://piaui.
     folha.uol.com.br/materia/agora-e-tolerancia-total/ (accessed 6 January
     2021).

20   Malu Gaspar, "O pitbull de papai", *Piauí*, July 2019, https://piaui.folha.
     uol.com.br/materia/o-pit-bull-do-papai/ (accessed 6 January 2021).

21   Luigi Mazzo, "Os condenados e os condecorados", *Piauí*, 22 February
     2019, https://piaui.folha.uol.com.br/flavio-os-condenados-e-os-condec
     orados/ (accessed 6 January 2021).

22   Ibid.

23   See Paes Manso, *A república das milícias*, loc. 729.

24   Ibid., loc. 742.

25   Ibid., loc. 782–9.

26   Italo Nogueira and Cristina Camargo, "Flávio Bolsonaro é denunciado sob
     acusação de liderar organisazação criminosa da 'rachadinha'", *Folha de São*

Paulo, 4 November 2020, https://www1.folha.uol.com.br/poder/2020/11/ministerio-publico-denuncia-flavio-bolsonaro-por-organizacao-criminosa-peculato-lavagem-de-dinheiro-e-apropriacao-indebita.shtml (accessed 6 January 2021).

27 Robert Muggah et al., "Rio de Janeiro's militia on the rise (again)", *Open Democracy*, 22 May 2018, https://www.opendemocracy.net/en/democra ciaabierta/rio-de-janeiros-militia-on-rise-ag/ (accessed 6 January 2021).

28 José Nêumanne, "O poder político das milícias do Rio", *O Estado de São Paulo*, 19 October 2020, https://politica.estadao.com.br/blogs/neuman ne/o-poder-politico-das-milicias-do-rio/ (accessed 6 January 2021).

29 Author interview Bruno Paes Manso, 19 November 2020.

30 Author interview with Simone Sibilio, 25 November 2020.

31 Abreu, "A metástase".

32 See Centro de Estudos de Segurança e Cidadania, https://cesecseguranca. com.br/participacao/pesquisa-datafolha-forum-brasileiro-de-seguranca-publica-medo-de-milicia-supera-medo-de-traficante-nas-comunidades-e-na-zona-sul-do-rio/ (accessed 6 January 2021).

33 Author interview with Simone Sibilio, 25 November 2020.

34 Ibid.

35 The ministry of justice and public security is the parent agency of three smaller forces, the highways, national and federal police.

36 See Pereira, "Paper cemeteries", 60.

37 Ibid.; Júlia Leite Valente, "Polícia militar é um oximoro, a militarização da segurança pública no Brasil", *Revista do Laboratório de Estudos da Violência da UNESP*, December 2012, https://revistas.marilia.unesp.br/index. php/levs/article/view/2646 (accessed 6 January 2021).

38 Renata Mendonça, "Está na hora de mudar a estrutura da polícia bra-sileira?", *BBC News Brasil*, 11 February 2017, https://www.bbc.com/por tuguese/brasil-38895293, (accessed 6 January 2021).

39 See Macaulay, "Bancada da bala", loc. 982.

40 In a formal sense the lower house of the Brazilian congress brings together groups of deputies concerned with security matters in two bodies: the Parliamentary Front for Public Security, which in 2018 had 247 deputies, and the Permanent Commission of Public Security, which had 66. These groups provide a forum for politicians who have a range of views and who do necessarily agree that repression is the best tactic. Nor do mem-bers of these committees necessarily have military or police backgrounds. A more narrowly defined caucus would include those deputies who have a police or military background. In a recent study, Eveline Ribeiro dos Santos of the University of Brasília defines this as the "hard-core" bullet bench. See Eveline Ribeiro dos Santos, "A bancada da bala na cámara, quem são e que propõem esses deputados", MA thesis, Universidade Federal de Brasília, 2018. And to add a further twist, for the first time in

2018 seven army officers were elected to parliament, all for Bolsonaro's PSL. These officers have proposed forming a separate *bancada militar*. Although the Brazilian armed forces are often brought into domestic policing issues – and at least one general, Girão Monteiro, had been involved in running a state police force – they see themselves as separate from, and superior to, the military police and would prefer that the term 'militar' was used exclusively for the armed forces.

41 Ribeiro dos Santos, "A bancada da bala na cámara"; author interview with Eveline Santos, June 2020.

42 Renato Sérgio de Lima and Samira Bueno, "A tropa de choque de Bolsonaro", *Piauí*, 8 August 2020, https://piaui.folha.uol.com.br/tropa-de-choque-de-bolsonaro/ (accessed 6 January 2021).

Notes to Chapter 9

1 In Brazilian Portuguese, the term *evangélico* refers to all Protestants. The term evangelist – someone who spreads the gospel – could refer to either Catholics or Protestants, although in Brazil this category of Catholics is more generally referred to as 'charismatic'. I'm indebted to Amy Erika Smith for the distinction.

2 Datafolha predicted that among Catholics, Bolsonaro would win 29.94 million votes against 28.77 million for Haddad. Among evangelicals he would win 21.7 million votes against 9.75 million for the PT's candidate. See José Eustáquio Diniz Alves, "O voto evangélico garantiu a eleição de Jair Bolsonaro", *EcoDebate*, 31 October 2018, https://www.ecodebate.com.br/2018/10/31/o-voto-evangelico-garantiu-a-eleicao-de-jair-bolsonaro-artigo-de-jose-eustaquio-diniz-alves/ (accessed 15 December 2020).

3 Ibid.

4 The sheer number of churches in Brazil is also impressive, having risen from 97,239 in 2003 to 180,411 in 2014 and to an estimated 220,000 in 2020 (that compares with only 16,000 in the UK and 300,000 in US). See figures from "Imunidade de igrejas é usada para lavagem de dinheiro", *Consultor Jurídico*, 25 March 2014, https://www.conjur.com.br/2014-mar-25/imunidade-tributaria-igrejas-utilizada-lavagem-dinheiro (accessed 15 December 2020).

5 Lamia Oualalou, "Los evangélicos y el hermano Bolsonaro", *Nueva Sociedad* 280 (March–April 2019), https://nuso.org/articulo/los-evangelicos-y-el-hermano-bolsonaro/ (accessed 7 January 2021).

6 The founder, Manoel de Mello e Silva, left his native Pernambuco to work on construction sites in São Paulo, and after seeing a vision of Christ he began to preach, and rapidly recruited followers in the working-class suburbs of eastern São Paulo.

7 The philosophy developed in the nineteenth century by Allan Kardec, a French teacher and philosopher, is the best known spiritist doctrine in Brazil, even though it was formally prohibited by the Catholic hierarchy in 1917.

8 Author interview with Paul Freston, 18 March 2020.

9 See Edir Macedo and Nada A. Perder, *Mina história* (Unipro Editora, 2018); Gilberto Nascimento, *O Reino: a história de Edir Macedo e um radiografia da Igreja Universal* (Companhia das Letras, 2020).

10 Robert McAlister, a Canadian missionary whose broadcast sermons had initially excited Macedo's interest, was one of the first to bring the new message to Brazil. But two US theologians, Essek Williams Kenyon and Kenneth Hagin, had been pioneers of these ideas. They offered biblical justification for controversially arguing that financial and material well-being were the will of God, and that by contrast physical suffering, poverty and disease reflected an absence of faith. See Kate Bowler, *Blessed: A History of the American Prosperity Gospel* (Oxford University Press, 2013).

11 Edir Macedo and Margarida Oliva, *O diabo no reino de Deus*, 139, quoted in Odêmio Antonio Ferrari, *Bispo S/A: A Igreja Universal do Reino de Deus e o exercício do poder* (Editora Ave-Maria, 2012), Kindle edition, loc. 1561.

12 Ricardo Mariano, *O reino da prosperidade da Igreja Universal*, 253, quoted in Ferrari, *Bispo S/A*, loc. 2060.

13 Paul Freston, *A Igreja Universal do Reino de Deus, Nem anjos nem demônios*, 145, quoted in Ferrari, *Bispo S/A*, loc. 2568.

14 See Nascimento, *O Reino*, esp. chs 4 and 5, for a comprehensive recent history.

15 Author interview with Ramos, July 2019.

16 Ari Pedro Oro and Marcelo Tadvald, "Consideraciones sobre el campo evangêlico brasileño", *Nueva Sociedad* 280 (March–April 2019), https://nuso.org/media/articles/downloads/3.TC_Oro_280.pdf (accessed 7 January 2021).

17 Thanks to Michael Stott, Latin America editor at the *Financial Times*, for this detail. In a report written in December 2019, Stott describes the São Paulo church as a "Brazilian version [of the temple] with creature comforts King Solomon would not have recognised: air conditioning, cinema-style seating in padded chairs, giant screens, a sound system worthy of a rock concert and a giant underground car park." See Michael Stott, "Brazil's evangelical church preaches the Bolsonaro revolution", *Financial Times*, 16 December 2019, https://www.ft.com/content/e7a47196-1817-11ea-9ee4-11f260415385 (accessed 7 January 2021).

18 Alex Cuadros, *Brazillionaires* (Profile Books, 2016), 110.

19 Stott, "Brazil's evangelical church preaches the Bolsonaro revolution".

20 Brand Arenari, "Pentecostalism as religion of periphery: an analysis of Brazilian case", PhD thesis, Humboldt Universität zu Berlin, 2013.

21 Author interview with Paul Freston, 18 March 2020.

22 Cesar Romero Jacob, Dora Rodrigues Hees, Philippe Waniez and Violette Brustlein, "Eleições presidenciais de 2002 no Brasil: uma nova geografia eleitoral?", *ALCEU* 3, no. 6 (2003): 287–327.

23 See Paul Freston, "Pentecostalism and global politics: three questionable approaches", Institute of Culture, Religion and World Affairs, 3 March 2014.

24 Ibid.

25 Ibid.

26 Author interview with Paul Freston, 18 March 2020.

27 Author interview with Amy Erika Smith, 27 December 2020.

28 Amy Erika Smith, *Religion and Brazilian Democracy: Mobilising the People of God* (Cambridge University Press, 2019).

29 Javier Corrales, "Understanding the uneven spread of LGBT rights in Latin America and the Caribbean, 1999–2013", *Journal of Research in Gender Studies* 7, no. 52 (2017): 52–82, doi: 10.22381/JRGS7120172.

30 Maria das Dores Campos Machado, "Aborto e ativismo nas eleiçoes de 2010", *Revista Brasileira de Ciência Política* 7 (2012), http://dx.doi.org/10.1590/S0103-33522012000100003 (accessed 7 January 2021).

31 Ibid.

32 Nascimento, *O Reino*, 290–1.

33 Fernando Haddad, "Vivi na pele o que aprendi nos livros", *Piauí*, June 2017, https://piaui.folha.uol.com.br/materia/vivi-na-pele-o-que-aprendi-nos-livros/ (accessed 7 January 2020).

34 Marcella Ramos, "Pedofilia, estupro, incesto, dois boatos de difamação desmentidos por dia no segundo turno", *Piauí*, 28 October 2018, https://piaui.folha.uol.com.br/pedofilia-estupro-incesto-dois-boatos-de-difamacao-desmentidos-por-dia-no-2o-turno/ (accessed 15 February 2020).

35 Author interview, 3 July 2019.

36 Gay marriage was effectively legalised by a Supreme Court decision of 2013, although the right remains fragile.

Notes to Chapter 10

1 Author interview with Ramalho, 5 February 2020.

2 Author interview with Viera, January 2020.

3 See *O Estado de São Paulo*, 12 April 2018.

4 Susanna B. Hecht and Alexander Cockburn, *The Fate of the Forest* (University of Chicago Press, 2010), 122.

5 John Hemming, *Tree of Rivers: The Story of the Amazon* (Thames and Hudson, 2012), Kindle Edition, loc. 1365.

6 Quoted in Adriana Gomes Santos, "Garimpos e trababalhadores dos garimpos: o intricado jogo de interesses políticos e econômicos em Roraima", MA thesis, Universidad Federal de Uberlândia, 5, https://www.historia.uff.br/estadoepoder/7snep/docs/088.pdf (accessed 20 November 2020).

7 David Cleary, *Anatomy of the Amazon Gold Rush* (University of Iowa Press, 1990), 171.

8 Gordon MacMillan, *At the End of the Rainbow? Gold, Land and People in the Brazilian Amazon* (Columbia University Press, 1995), 37.

9 "Haunting black and white images of the Brazilian gold rush by Sebastião Salgado", *The Independent*, 19 September 2019, https://www.independent.co.uk/arts-entertainment/photography/haunting-black-white-photos-brazil-gold-sebastiao-salgado-a9110031.html (accessed 15 December 2020).

10 See Heloisa M. Starling and Lilia Moritz Schwarcz, *Brazil: A Biography* (Allen Lane, 2018), esp. ch. 4.

11 See also Getúlio de Souza Cruz, *Ambientalismo e indigenismo: Roraima com laboratório dos regimes internacionais* (Editora Leitura XXI, 2016).

12 Augusto Heleno, speech to Club Militar Rio de Janeiro, April 2008, quoted in Eugênia Lopes, Luciana Nunes Leal and Tânia Monteiro, "Lula cobra general por crítica à reserve Raposa Serra do Sol", *O Estado de São Paulo*, 17 April 2008.

Notes to Chapter 11

1 See Kris Bramwell, "Brazil fires prompt 'prayers' for Amazon rainforest", BBC News, 23 August 2019, https://www.bbc.co.uk/news/blogs-trending-49406519 (accessed 15 December 2020).

2 See Phoebe Weston, "Amazon rainforest fires: Jair Bolsonaro sends Brazilian army to put out huge blaze as G7 leaders hold emergency talks", *The Independent*, 24 August 2019, https://www.independent.co.uk/environment/amazon-rainforest-fires-latest-brazil-army-jair-bolsonaro-g7-a9077171.html (accessed 15 December 2020).

3 See Jonathan Watts, "Jair Bolsonaro claims NGOs behind Amazon forest fire surge – but provides no evidence", *The Guardian*, 21 August 2019, https://www.theguardian.com/world/2019/aug/21/jair-bolsonaro-accuses-ngos-setting-fire-amazon-rainforest (accessed 15 December 2020).

4 Thomas Lovejoy and Carlos Nobre, "Amazon tipping point: last chance for action", *Science Advances* 5, no. 12 (20 December 2019), https://advances.sciencemag.org/content/5/12/eaba2949 (accessed 7 January 2021).

5   See https://rainforests.mongabay.com/amazon/deforestation-rate.html for updated monthly numbers.

6   See "Under Brazil's far-right leader, Amazon protections slashed and forests fall", *New York Times*, 28 July 2019, https://www.nytimes.com/2019/07/28/world/americas/brazil-deforestation-amazon-bolsonaro.html (accessed 7 January 2021).

7   Bernardo Esteves, "A guerra contra o termômetro", *Piauí*, September 2019, https://piaui.folha.uol.com.br/materia/a-guerra-contra-o-termometro/ (accessed 7 January 2021).

8   Fabiano Maisonnave and Lalo de Almeida, "A segunda morte de Chico Mendes", *Folha de São Paulo*, 6 March 2020, https://temas.folha.uol.com.br/amazonia-sob-bolsonaro/a-segunda-morte-de-chico-mendes/sob-bolsonaro-ex-seringueiros-aceleram-desmatamento-e-a-troca-de-extrativismo-por-gado.shtml (accessed 7 January 2021).

9   Sergio Mergulis, *Causes of Deforestation of the Brazilian Amazon*, World Bank working paper no. 22 (World Bank, 2003), 9.

10   See Hemming, *Tree of Rivers*, loc. 5974.

11   Author interview with Roberto Mangabeira Unger, 23 July 2019.

12   Ricardo Abramovay, *Amazonia* (Outras Palavras, 2019), 20.

13   For a good account of the controversies surrounding Belo Monte, see Eliane Brum, *Brasil, construtor de ruínas: um olhar sobre o Brasil, de Lula a Bolsonaro* (Archipélago Editorial, 2019).

14   See Bernardo Esteves, "O meio ambiente como estorvo", *Piauí*, June 2019, https://piaui.folha.uol.com.br/materia/the-environment-as-an-obstacle/ (accessed 15 December 2020).

15   Ibid.

16   Jon Lee Anderson, "Blood gold in the Brazilian rain forest", *The New Yorker*, 4 November 2019, https://www.newyorker.com/magazine/2019/11/11/blood-gold-in-the-brazilian-rain-forest (accessed 7 January 2021).

17   See Daniel Camargos, "Fazendeiros e empresários organizaram 'dia do fogo', apontam investigações", *Folha de São Paulo*, 23 October 2019, https://www1.folha.uol.com.br/ambiente/2019/10/fazendeiros-e-empresarios-organizaram-dia-do-fogo-apontam-investigacoes.shtml (accessed 7 January 2021); Leandro Machado, "O que se sabe sobre o 'Dia do Fogo', momento-chave das queimadas na Amazônia", BBC Brasil, 19 August 2019, https://www.bbc.com/portuguese/brasil-49453037 (accessed 7 January 2021).

18   See Daniel Camargos and Dom Phillips, ""Dia do Fogo" foi invenção da imprensa', diz principal investigado por queimadas na Amazônia", *Repórter Brasil*, 25 October 2019, https://reporterbrasil.org.br/2019/10/dia-do-fogo-foi-invencao-da-imprensa-diz-principal-investigado-por-queimadas-na-amazonia/ (accessed 7 January 2021).

19 https://www.nytimes.com/2019/10/06/video/amazon-rainforest-fires-burning.html?searchResultPosition=1 (accessed 15 February 2021).

20 Esteves, "O meio ambiente como estorvo".

21 Ibid.

22 Ibid.

23 Ibid.

24 See Suely Araújo and Fabio Feldman, "Política ambiental, o que o orçamento mostra e promote", *Valor Econômico*, 15 January 2020, https://valor.globo.com/opiniao/coluna/politica-ambiental-o-que-o-orcamento-mostra-e-promete.ghtml (accessed 7 January 2020).

25 See Danielle Brant and Phillippe Watanabe, "Sob Bolsonaro, multas ambientais came 34% para menor nível em 24 anos", *Folha de São Paulo*, 9 March 2020, https://www1.folha.uol.com.br/ambiente/2020/03/sob-bolsonaro-multas-ambientais-caem-34-para-menor-nivel-em-24-anos.shtml (accessed 7 January 2021).

26 Esteves, "O meio ambiente como estorvo".

27 Ibid.

28 Dom Phillips, "Bolsonaro pick for Funai agency horrifies indigenous leaders", *The Guardian*, 21 July 2019, https://www.theguardian.com/world/2019/jul/21/bolsonaro-funai-indigenous-agency-xavier-da-silva (accessed 7 January 2021).

29 Author interview with Luis Ventura, Boa Vista, 28 January 2020.

30 See Ernesto Londoño and Letícia Casado, "As Bolsonaro keeps Amazon vows, Brazil's indigenous fear 'ethnocide'", *New York Times*, 19 April 2020, https://www.nytimes.com/2020/04/19/world/americas/bolsonaro-brazil-amazon-indigenous.html (accessed 7 January 2021).

31 Lovejoy and Nobre, "Amazon tipping point".

32 See Philip Stouffer, "Enigmatic bird declines in pristine Amazon rainforest", *American Ornithological Society*, 11 November 2020, https://americanornithology.org/enigmatic-bird-declines-in-pristine-amazon-rainforest/ (accessed 7 January 2021).

33 Author interview with Adriane Esquivel Muelbert, May 2020.

34 Lovejoy and Nobre, "Amazon tipping point".

Notes to Chapter 12

1 See Richard Lapper, "Bolsonaro took aim at China. Then reality struck", *Americas Quarterly*, 23 April 2019, https://www.americasquarterly.org/article/bolsonaro-took-aim-at-china-then-reality-struck/ (accessed 7 January 2021).

2 See Daniel Yergin, *The New Map: Energy, Climate, and the Clash of Nations* (Penguin Press, 2020).

3   For trade figures, see http://www.mdic.gov.br/index.php/comercio-exterior/estatisticas-de-comercio-exterior/balanca-comercial-brasileira-acumulado-do-ano (accessed 7 January 2021), and https://www.statista.com/statistics/1105976/brazil-trade-value-china/ (accessed 7 January 2021).

4   See Su-Lin Tan, "Brazil mining giant Vale agrees deal with China port to expand iron ore handling capacity", *South China Morning Post*, 13 October 2020, https://www.scmp.com/economy/global-economy/article/3105248/brazil-mining-giant-vale-agrees-deal-china-port-operator (accessed 7 January 2021).

5   See PWC survey at https://www.poder360.com.br/infograficos/os-investimentos-da-china-no-brasil-e-o-quanto-isso-andou-em-2019/ (accessed 7 January 2021).

6   Yergin, *The New Map*, 180–1.

7   Bruno Maçaes, *Belt and Road: A Chinese World Order* (Hurst, 2018).

8   Brenno Grillo, "Why is China investing in Brazilian oil, when no one else is?", *Brazil Reports*, 19 November 2019, https://brazilian.report/business/2019/11/19/china-investing-brazilian-oil-no-one-cnooc-cnodc/ (accessed 7 January 2021).

9   See Maçaes, *Belt and Road*, 79–80.

10 Interview with author, July 2019.

11 Author interview with Rubens Sawaya, January 2019.

12 Lapper, "Bolsonaro took aim at China".

13 Ibid.

14 "Brasil-China: por uma parceria estratégica global sustentável para o século XXI", http://www.cebri.org/portal/publicacoes/cebri-artigos/position-papers-2018 (accessed 15 February 2021).

15 Lapper, "Bolsonaro took aim at China".

Notes to Chapter 13

1   See Celso Rocha de Barros, "How Lava Jato died – and what comes next", *Americas Quarterly*, 15 October 2019, https://www.americasquarterly.org/article/how-lava-jato-died-and-what-comes-next/ (accessed 6 January 2021).

2   Robert Simon, "Bolsonaro's siege against law enforcement agencies", *Americas Quarterly*, 12 September 2019, https://www.americasquarterly.org/article/bolsonaros-siege-against-law-enforcement-agencies/ (accessed 6 January 2021). See also André Shalders, "Bolsonaro cria 'situação dramática' ao tentar proteger Flávio, diz ex-procurador da Lava Jato", *BBC Brasil*, 19 September 2019, https://www.bbc.com/portuguese/brasil-49562267 (accessed 6 January 2021).

3 "Federal police names Carlos Bolsonaro as organizer of fake news criminal scheme", *Folha de São Paulo*, 25 April, 2020, https://www1.folha.uol.com.br/internacional/en/brazil/2020/04/federal-police-names-carlos-bolsonaro-as-organizer-of-fake-news-criminal-scheme.shtml (accessed 6 January 2021).

4 Patricia Campos de Mello, "Operação contra fake news reforça suspeitas das eleições de 2018", *Folha de São Paulo*, 1 June 2020, https://www1.folha.uol.com.br/poder/2020/06/operacao-contra-fake-news-reforca-suspeitas-das-eleicoes-de-2018.shtml (accessed 6 January 2021).

5 Patricia Campos de Mello, "Brazil's troll army moves into the streets", *New York Times*, 4 August 2020, https://www.nytimes.com/2020/08/04/opinion/bolsonaro-office-of-hate-brazil.html (accessed 6 January 2021).

6 Tom Philips, "Brazil's star justice minister Sergio Moro resigns in blow to Jair Bolsonaro", *The Guardian*, 24 April 2020, https://www.theguardian.com/world/2020/apr/24/brazil-justice-minister-sergio-moro-resigns-jair-bolsonaro (accessed 6 January 2021).

7 Vera Rosa, "Uma reunião ministerial com destempero verbal, ofensas e pitos", *O Estado de São Paulo*, 23 May 2020, https://politica.estadao.com.br/noticias/geral,uma-reuniao-ministerial-com-destempero-verbal-ofensas-e-pitos,70003312050 (accessed 6 January 2021).

8 Ernesto Londoño, Letícia Casado and Manuela Andreoni, "'A perfect storm' in Brazil as troubles multiply for Bolsonaro", *New York Times*, 25 April 2020, https://www.nytimes.com/2020/04/25/world/americas/bolsonaro-moro-brazil.html (accessed 6 January 2021).

9 Martim Vasques da Cunha, "Tragédia ideológica: o bolsolavismo foi o hospedeiro perfeito para as tendências totalitárias de uma geração", *Piauí*, August 2020, https://piaui.folha.uol.com.br/materia/tragedia-ideologica/ (accessed 6 January 2021).

10 Ernesto Araújo, "Trump e o ocidente", *Cadernos de Política Exterior* 3, no. 6 (2017): 345–6. English translation, https://www.centerforsecuritypolicy.org/about-us/ (accessed 24 December 2020).

11 Tom Hennigan, "Mystical influence agitating Brazil's Bolsonaro administration", *Irish Times*, 30 April 2019, https://www.irishtimes.com/news/world/mystical-influence-agitating-brazil-s-bolsonaro-administration-1.3875385 (accessed 6 January 2021).

12 "Please don't let me be misunderstood: Jair Bolsonaro's contentious first year in office", *The Economist*, 4 January 2020, https://www.economist.com/the-americas/2020/01/04/jair-bolsonaros-contentious-first-year-in-office (accessed 6 January 2021).

13 General Walter Souza Braga Netto took over from Lorenzoni in 2019, and General Eduardo Pazuello became the third health minister in 2020.

14 Laís Lis, "Governo Bolsonaro mais que dobra número de militares em cargos civis, aponta TCU", *G1*, 17 July 2020, https://g1.globo.com/politica/noticia/2020/07/17/governo-bolsonaro-tem-6157-militares-em-cargos-civis-diz-tcu.ghtml (accessed 15 February 2021).

15 Winter, "Messiah complex".

16 Oliver Stuenkel, "The backlash against Brazil's politicised military", *Americas Quarterly*, 24 August 2020, https://www.americasquarterly.org/article/the-backlash-against-brazils-politicized-military/ (accessed 6 January 2021).

17 Brian Winter, "'It's complicated': inside Bolsonaro's relationship with Brazil's military", *Americas Quarterly*, 12 December 2019, https://www.americasquarterly.org/article/its-complicated-inside-bolsonaros-relationship-with-brazils-military/ (accessed 6 January 2021).

18 Fabio Victor, "O vice a cavalo: Hamilton Mourão e o lugar dos militares no governo Bolsonaro", *Piauí*, December 2018, https://piaui.folha.uol.com.br/materia/o-vice-cavalo/ (accessed 6 January 2021).

19 Oyama, *Tormenta*, 38.

20 Victor, "O vice a cavalo".

21 Ibid.

22 Oyama, *Tormenta*, 20–1.

23 Ibid., 148–9.

24 Hélio Schwartsman, "O presidente das pequenas coisas", *Folha de São Paulo*, 30 April 2019, quoted in Oyama, *Tormenta*, 139.

25 Oyama, *Tormenta*, 151.

26 Jenny Gonzales, "Brazil minister advises using COVID-19 to distract from Amazon deregulation", *Mongabay*, 26 May 2020, https://news.mongabay.com/2020/05/brazil-minister-advises-using-covid-19-to-distract-from-amazon-deregulation/ (accessed 6 January 2021).

27 Oyama, *Tormenta*, 93.

28 Winter, "Messiah complex".

29 Ibid. The pension reform saved Brazil about R$800bn over a ten-year period.

30 Winter, "Messiah complex".

31 See Luiz Henrique Mandetta, *Um paciente chamado Brasil* (Objetiva, 2020).

32 Ibid., 143.

33 Monica Gugliano, "O dia em que Bolsonaro decidiu mandar tropas para o Supremo", *Piauí*, August 2020, https://piaui.folha.uol.com.br/materia/vou-intervir/ (accessed 6 January 2021).

34 Brian Harris and Andrés Schipani, "Bolsonaro and the generals: will the military defend Brazil's democracy?", *Financial Times*, 11 August 2020, https://www.ft.com/content/86f361a0-c78c-4683-8da1-b5e337c98365 (accessed 6 January 2021).

35 Simon Romero, Letícia Casado and Manuela Andreoni, "Threat of
    military action rattles Brazil as virus deaths surge", *New York Times*, 10
    June 2020, https://www.nytimes.com/2020/06/10/world/americas/bo
    lsonaro-coup-coronavirus-brazil.html (accessed 6 January 2021).

Notes to Chapter 14

1 Edoardo Ghirotto, José Benedito Da Silva and João Pedroso de Campos,
    "Auxílio emergencial: o risco da bonança artificial", *Veja*, 9 September
    2020, https://veja.abril.com.br/economia/auxilio-emergencial-o-risco-
    da-bonanca-artificial/ (accessed 16 January 2021).

2 The payment rose to R$1,200 for women with children, but fell to a flat
    R$300 in the last two months of the year. The payment was made auto-
    matically to beneficiaries of the Bolsa Familia and the so-called Cadastro
    Unico scheme.

3 During 2020 several separate teams of researchers pored over the impact
    of the emergency grant. For example, a study by researchers at the
    Pernambuco Federal University looked at the impact on different states and
    municipalities: Ecio de Farias Costa and Marcelo Acioly dos Santos Freire,
    "Estudo de avaliação do programa de auxílio emergencial: um análise
    sobre focalização e eficácia a nível municipal", https://forum.outerspace.
    com.br/index.php?threads/estudo-de-avalia%C3%87%C3%830-do-pro
    grama-de-aux%C3%8Dlio-emergencial-uma-an%C3%81lise-sobre-foca
    liza%C3%87%C3%830-e-efic%C3%81cia-a-n%C3%8Dvel-municipal.56
    2701/ (accessed 15 February 2021). Research by the Centre of Microfinance
    and Financial Inclusion of the FGV looked at the impact on different
    categories of workers: Lauro Gonzalez and Bruno Barreira, "Efeitos do
    auxílio emergencial sobre a renda", FGV EASP Centro de Estudos de
    Microfinanças e Inclusão Financiera, https://eaesp.fgv.br/producao-
    intelectual/efeitos-auxilio-emergencial-sobre-renda (accessed 15 February
    2021). Finally, Marcelo Neri of the Centre of Social Policy at the FGV
    led an investigation of the broader effect of the COVID-19 pandemic
    on different economic classes, https://cps.fgv.br/pesquisas/covid-classes-
    economicas-e-o-caminho-do-meio (accessed 15 February 2021).

4 Thomas Traumann, "Paulo Guedes' biggest dilemma", *Americas Quarterly*,
    19 November 2020, https://www.americasquarterly.org/article/paulo-
    guedes-biggest-dilemma/ (accessed 16 January 2021).

5 Datafolha, 8–10 December 2020, http://media.folha.uol.com.br/data
    folha/2020/12/14/ad8a599af4864554583c395d7dde7aedagp.pdf (accessed
    22 December 2020).

6 José Roberto de Toledo, "Um trilhão na grelha: a nova popularidade de
    Bolsonaro e os 'pobres coitados'", *Piauí*, September 2020, https://piaui.

folha.uol.com.br/materia/um-trilhao-na-grelha/ (accessed 22 December 2020).

7   To confuse matters even more, the names of these parties had changed at regular intervals. The Progressive Party was earlier known as the Brazilian Progressive Party, the Republicanos were earlier known as the Brazilian Republican Party.

8   Agência Estado news agency, "Kassab: PSD não será 'nem esquerda, direita ou centro'", *O Estado de São Paulo*, 29 March 2011, https://politica. estadao.com.br/noticias/geral,kassab-psd-nao-sera-nem-esquerda-direita-ou-centro,698756 (accessed 16 January 2021).

9   Fernando de Barros E. Silva, "O Centrão e a distopia nacional", *Piauí*, December 2020, https://piaui.folha.uol.com.br/materia/o-centrao-e-distopia-nacional/ (accessed 16 January 2021).

10 "Centrão começou a assumir vagas negociadas; presidente Jair Bolsonaro tenta se blindar com apoio do grupo", *O Estado do São Paulo*, 8 May 2020, https://politica.estadao.com.br/noticias/geral,relembre-as-investigacoes-que-envolvem-lideres-do-centrao-com-quem-bolsonaro-negocia, 70003296967 (accessed 16 January 2021).

11 Author interview with Beatriz Rey, 13 January 2021.

12 Vinicius Valfré, "Em dois anos, Bolsonaro deixa no papel 12 grandes eixos do seu governo prometidos na campanha", *O Estado de São Paulo*, 21 December 2020, https://politica.estadao.com.br/noticias/geral,em-dois-anos-bolsonaro-deixa-no-papel-12-grandes-eixos-do-seu-governo-prometidos-na-campanha,70003559031 (accessed 16 January 2021).

13 Edoardo Ghirotto, Eduardo Gonçalves and Juliana Castro, "O avanço do retrocesso", *Veja*, 13 January 2021, https://veja.abril.com.br/brasil/na-pandemia-o-governo-gasta-energia-tentando-impor-agenda-conservadora/ (accessed 2 February 2021).

14 "Relembre as investigações que envolvem lideres do Centrão com quem bolsonaro negocia", *O Estado de São Paulo*, 8 May 2020, https://politica. estadao.com.br/noticias/geral,relembre-as-investigacoes-que-envolvem-lideres-do-centrao-com-quem-bolsonaro-negocia,70003296967 (accessed 16 January 2021).

15 Editorial comment, *O Estado de São Paulo*, 2 February 2021, https://politica.estadao.com.br/noticias/geral,governo-tratora-para-eleger-aliados-de-bolsonaro-no-congresso,70003602296 (accessed 3 February 2021).

16 See https://www.bcb.gov.br/en/statistics (accessed 2 February 2021).

17 Michael Stott, "Brazil's borrowing binge gives investors the jitters", *Financial Times*, 8 December 2020, https://www.ft.com/content/dfc8ba5c-0ef9-483a-ab76-4d821ccf0031 (accessed 16 January 2021).

18 José Roberto Mendonça de Barros, "Politica ambiental e entrave ao crescimento", *O Estado de São Paulo*, 3 January 2021, https://economia.

estadao.com.br/noticias/geral,poitica-ambiental-e-entrave-ao-crescime nto,70003568905 (accessed 16 January 2021).

19 See Celso Ming, "O Brasil não está quebrado. Está sem rumo", *O Estado de São Paulo*, 6 January 2021, https://economia.estadao.com.br/noticias/geral,o-brasil-nao-esta-quebrado-esta-sem-rumo,70003572738 (accessed 16 January 2021).

20 Celso Ming, "A desistência da Ford", *O Estado de São Paulo*, 13 January 2021, https://economia.estadao.com.br/noticias/geral,a-desistencia-da-ford,70003580307 (accessed 16 January 2021).

21 According to a National Chamber of Commerce survey, the total number of factories fell from 384,700 to 348,100 between 2015 and 2020. Quoted in Daniela Amorim, Mariana Durão and Márcia De Chiara, "Por dia, pelo menos 17 fábricas fecharam as portas nos últimos cinco anos", *O Estado de São Paulo*, 17 January 2021, https://economia.estadao.com.br/noticias/geral,por-dia-pelo-menos-17-fabricas-fecharam-as-por tas-nos-ultimos-cinco-anos,70003583832 (accessed 2 February 2021).

22 Poll by Instituto Travessia, *Valor Econômico*, 8 January 2021, https://valor.globo.com/eu-e/noticia/2021/01/08/desemprego-e-precariedade-da-saude-serao-os-fantasmas-da-nova-decada.ghtml (accessed 16 January 2021).

23 See IMF report on commodity prices, https://www.imf.org/en/Res earch/commodity-prices27.2 (accessed 21 January 2021).

24 "'Trump é meu ídolo', diz Bolsonaro diante de comparação feita por jornalista", *Istoé*, 1 August 2019, https://istoe.com.br/trump-e-meu-idolo-diz-bolsonaro-diante-de-comparacao-feita-por-jornalista/ (accessed 16 January 2021).

25 Brian Winter, "Bolsonaro goes all in on Trump, isolation may await", *Americas Quarterly*, 12 January 2021, https://www.americasquarterly.org/article/bolsonaro-goes-all-in-on-trump-isolation-may-await/ (accessed 16 January 2021).

26 Oliver Stuenkel, "Política antiglobalista de Bolsonaro tem um preço", *O Estado de São Paulo*, 3 January 2021, https://economia.estadao.com.br/noticias/geral,politica-antiglobalista-de-bolsonaro-tem-um-preco,70 003568982 (accessed 16 January 2021).

27 Mendonça de Barros, "Politica ambiental e entrave ao crescimento".

28 Larissa Wachholz and Lígia Dutra, "A agenda ambiental da China e a agropecuária brasileira", *Valor Econômico*, 18 January 2021, https://valor.globo.com/opiniao/coluna/a-agenda-ambiental-da-china-e-a-agropec uaria-brasileira.ghtml (accessed 2 February 2021).

29 Stuenkel, "Política antiglobalista de Bolsonaro tem um preço".

30 Anthony Boadle, "New Brazil coronavirus variant found in nearly half of Amazon city cases", *Reuters*, 22 January 2021, https://www.reuters.com/article/instant-article/idUSL1N2JX12T (accessed 2 February 2021).

31 See Joel Zinberg, "Trump isn't the one politicizing science", *Wall Street Journal*, 14 December 2020, https://www.wsj.com/articles/trump-isnt-the-one-politicizing-science-11607969209 (accessed 16 January 2021).

32 See Michael S. Saag, "Misguided use of hydroxychloroquine for COVID-19: the infusion of politics into science", *JAMA Journal of the American Medical Association (JAMA Network)*, 9 November 2020, https://jamanet work.com/journals/jama/fullarticle/2772921 (accessed 16 January 2021).

33 See Mandetta, *Um paciente chamado Brasil*, 144–5.

34 Gabriel Stargardter and Lisandra Paraguassu, "Bolsonaro bets 'miraculous cure' for Covid 19 can save Brazil and his life", *Reuters*, 8 July 2020, https://www.reuters.com/article/us-health-coronavirus-brazil-hydrox ychlo-idUSKBN249396 (accessed 16 January 2021); Estella Ektorp, "Death threats after a trial on chloroquine for Covid 19", *The Lancet*, June 2020, https://www.thelancet.com/journals/laninf/article/PIIS1473-30 99(20)30383-2/fulltext (accessed 16 January 2021); Claudio Angelo, "Contra a besta-fera: a luta dos cientistas brasileiros para combater o vírus é dura – vai de propaganda enganosa a ameaça de mort", *Piauí*, July 2020, https://piaui.folha.uol.com.br/materia/contra-besta-fera/ (accessed 2 April 2021).

35 Paulo Sampaio, "Para médica Nise Yamaguchi, comunidade científica conspira contra a vida", *UOL*, 19 July 2020, https://noticias.uol.com. br/colunas/paulo-sampaio/2020/07/19/para-medica-nise-yamaguchi-comunidade-cientifica-conspira-contra-a-vida.htm (accessed 16 January 2021).

36 Ibid.

37 Ibid.

38 Simone Preissler Iglesias and Samy Adghirni, "Brazil's evangelicals take over while Bolsonaro's allies jump ship", *Bloomberg*, 5 June 2020, https://www.bloomberg.com/news/articles/2020-06-05/evangelicals-take-over-while-bolsonaro-s-allies-jump-ship (accessed 16 January 2021).

39 Edoardo Ghirotto, Gabriel Mascarenhas, Laryssa Borges and Nonato Viegas, "Ele está entre nós", *Veja*, 27 January 2021, https://veja.abril.com. br/politica/inicio-da-vacinacao-muda-jogo-politico-e-aumenta-pressao-sobre-bolsonaro/ (accessed 2 February 2021).

40 Ibid.

41 Ibid.

42 https://interactives.lowyinstitute.org/features/covid-performance/#ran kings (accessed 22 March 2021).

43 "Na íntegra: o que diz a dura carta de banqueiros e economistas com críticas a Bolsonaro e propostas para pandemia", BBC News Brazil, 22 March 2021, https://www.bbc.com/portuguese/brasil-56485687 (accessed 2 April 2021).

44 André Shalders, "Lira dá 'sinal amarelo' ao governo por erros na pandemia e diz que 'remédio legislativo' pode ser 'fatal'", *O Estado de São Paulo*, 24 March 2021, https://politica.estadao.com.br/blogs/fausto-macedo/lira-da-sinal-amarelo-ao-governo-por-erros-na-pandemia-e-diz-que-remedio-legislativo-pode-ser-fatal/ (accessed 2 April 2021).

45 Fausto Pinato, deputy for the Progressive Party, quoted in Felipe Frazão and André Shalders, "Centrão e mercado dão ultimato a Bolsonaro", *O Estado de São Paulo*, 28 March 2021, https://politica.estadao.com.br/noticias/geral,centrao-e-mercado-dao-ultimato-a-bolsonaro,70003662819 (accessed 2 April 2021).

INDEX

CPSIA information can be obtained
at www.ICGtesting.com
Printed in the USA
LVHW092009140921
697832LV00009B/454/J